The Holocaust and Other Genocides

A project of the
Tennessee Holocaust Commission, Inc.,
in association with
the Zimmerman Foundation,
Vanderbilt University,
and the Robert Penn Warren
Center for the Humanities,
Vanderbilt University

The Holocaust and Other Genocides

History, Representation, Ethics

Edited by
Helmut Walser Smith

In association with
William James Booth
Penelope H. Brooks
Joel Dark
Paul B. Fleming
Ernest Freudenthal
Jay Geller
Sue Chaney Gilmore
Teresa A. Goddu
Peter Haas
Sonja Maria Hedgepeth
David Allan Patterson
Gary A. Phillips
Margaret Vandiver
Meike G. Werner

Vanderbilt University Press
NASHVILLE

© 2002 Tennessee Holocaust Commission, Inc.
Published by Vanderbilt University Press
All rights reserved
First edition 2002
Fourth printing 2006

This book is printed on acid-free paper.
Manufactured in the United States of America

Library of Congress Cataloging-in-Publication Data

The Holocaust and other genocides : history, representation, ethics /
edited by Helmut Walser Smith ... [et al.].— 1st ed.
    p. cm.
Includes bibliographical references and index.
    ISBN 0-8265-1402–2 (cloth : alk. paper)
    ISBN 0-8265-1403-0 (pbk. : alk. paper)
    1. Holocaust, Jewish (1939–1945)—Study and teaching. 2. Holocaust, Jew-
ish (1939–1945)—Influence. 3. Genocide—Study and teaching. 4. Atrocities—
Europe—20th century. 5. Genocide—Rwanda. 6. Ethnic relations—Study and
teaching. 7. Armenian massacres, 1915–1923—Influence. I. Smith, Helmut
Walser, 1962–
    D804.33 .H65 2002
    940.53'18—dc21

                                                                2002001705

For Bev Asbury
University Chaplain, Emeritus
who for many years taught students and faculty
at Vanderbilt about the hard work of openness

Contents

Figures

Acknowledgments

This work is the result of the labors and support of many people. The initial inspiration came from Beverly A. Asbury, who, as Vanderbilt University Chaplain from 1967 to 1996, was the principal force behind the study of the Holocaust at Vanderbilt and a founding spirit of the Tennessee Holocaust Commission. The vision and generosity of Raymond Zimmerman, who encouraged a larger and more significant project than first planned, made our work financially possible. He was the initial benefactor and his support allowed us to approach the project in ambitious and even unorthodox ways. From its inception, the Tennessee Holocaust Commission also supported the project with a generous grant and a great deal of encouragement and hard work. Finally, the project could not have worked were it not for the engagement of Mona Frederick of the Robert Penn Warren Center for the Humanities at Vanderbilt University. The Center served as a congenial place to meet and Mona, with the help of Paul Burch and Sherry Willis, invested a great deal of time, energy, and thought into this book. We often think of books as being written, but they are also made. Without Mona, this book would never have come together, and this is true not in a vague sense but in the very real sense that without her intervention toward the end, the diverse efforts of many people might not have culminated in a finished work.

This book is also the result of a genuinely cooperative effort among its authors. The contributors come from universities across the state of Tennessee and from high schools in Nashville. We met every two weeks for an academic year to discuss how to teach the Holocaust and how to put together a work that would be of help to professors and teachers across a range of disciplines and at different levels of instruction. I chaired these talks with Peter Haas, formerly of Vanderbilt, now the Abba Hillel Silver Professor of Judaic Studies and Director of the Samuel Rosenthal Center for Judaic Studies at Case Western Reserve University in Cleveland. The talks were frank and open, insightful and contentious, and I believe that everyone learned a great deal from them. During these deliberations, we were also aided by the wise counsel of several visitors to our forum, including Michael Berenbaum, the President of the Survivors of the Shoah Visual History Foundation and former Director of the United States Holocaust Memorial Museum, and James E. Young, Professor of English and Judaic Studies at the University of Massachusetts, Amherst. We were also blessed with the inspiring presence, for it can only be called that, of John K. Roth, the Russell K. Pitzer Professor of Philosophy at Claremont McKenna College in California. On many occasions, John came to Nashville to advise us on the progress of the work, its strengths and its shortcomings, and to lend his measured but keen insight.

A special feature of the cooperation that went into the making of this book involves the teamwork between university professors and high school teachers. During the academic year, two remarkable teachers, Paul Fleming of Hume Fogg High School and Sue Chaney Gilmore of Hillsboro High School, not only participated in the discussions and helped compose the curriculum but also taught the university professors a good deal about what it is to convey the meaning of the Holocaust to young people. In the summer that followed, they also co-directed a teacher workshop in which teachers from the Nashville area discussed the curriculum, worked out lesson plans, corrected mistakes, told us what worked and what to cast away, and encouraged us, indeed inspired us, to revise and reshape the book. They too have had a significant hand in the making of this book, and it is a great pleasure to thank each of them: Carmen Anderson of Hillsboro High School, Robin Jubela of Wharton Middle School, Nancy Kemp of Centennial High School in Franklin, Lilian Lawrence-Crabtree of Hunter's Lane High School, Griff Watson of McGavock High School, and Andrea Joy York of Martin Luther King High School.

It is also a pleasure to thank Felicia Anchor and Ruth Tanner of the Tennessee Holocaust Commission for their support, for their work, and for their advice. The Tennessee Holocaust Commission has run wonderful programs with high school teachers and we hope that this curriculum will aid them in their further work. Pam Rothstein, a historian and friend, read the manuscript at an early stage and offered detailed criticism. Paul Elledge, then Interim Director of Vanderbilt University Press, was encouraging when we first broached the idea that the book might be published by Vanderbilt, and Michael Ames, who has since become Director of the Press, has worked tirelessly to make this a reality. Dariel Mayer, the editing and production manager, and Debby Stuart Smith, the copyeditor, have also put a great deal of care and attention into this book, significantly improving it.

Preface

> Of all the memories that I lack, perhaps the one that I would most like to have is of my mother combing my hair. . . . I do not speak the language my parents spoke, I do not share in any of the memories they might have had; something which was theirs, which made them who they were, their history, their culture, their hope, was not passed on to me. . . . I write because we lived together, shadow among their shadows, body next to their bodies; I write because they left an indelible mark on me, of which the written word is the trace.

The author of these lines is the French writer Georges Perec. His mother, a Jew, was deported to Auschwitz in 1943 and murdered there. From 1933 to 1945, Nazi Germany killed some six million Jews: in concentration camps, in ghettos, and by mobile death squads. Infants, children, women, and men were destroyed systematically and methodically because they were Jews. The purpose of this criminal policy was not just to kill as many individuals as possible but to erase from the face of the earth Jewish history, culture, and faith. That is what genocide is. It is not the number of dead that distinguishes genocide from other mass crimes but the goal of extinguishing by violence a people and its way of life. Perec's observations express in a very intimate and human way the personal and social loss that the Holocaust left as a "shadow" over our world.

All genocides attack fundamental human values and, for this reason, force us to remember and to reflect. In this curriculum, we start with the Holocaust because it constitutes a paradigm of genocide in modern society. Germany, an advanced nation, attempted to eradicate a people, the Jews, completely and utterly, so that they would no longer exist on this earth.

According to the United Nations Convention on the Prevention and Punishment of the Crime of Genocide, genocide entails the attempt to "destroy, in whole or in part, a national, ethnic, racial or religious group." The Holocaust was not the only genocide, nor the first or the last. The attempt of the Ottoman Turks to eradicate the Armenians preceded it and the genocide in Rwanda followed. Yet, as the historian Yehuda Bauer argues, the Holocaust constituted the most extreme form of genocide. It was extreme, and to date singular, but not because of the numbers of Jews killed or because of the suffering involved. Rather, the Holocaust was a genocide unrivaled for its purely racist motivation, for its global reach, and for its totality. As the Holocaust scholar Steven T. Katz has written: "Never before has a state set out, as a matter of international principle and actualized policy, to annihilate physically every man, woman, and child belonging to a specific people. . . . Only in the case of Jewry under the Third Reich was such all-inclusive non-compromising, unmitigated murder intended."

Studying the Holocaust nevertheless also teaches us lessons about other genocides. We start from the assumption that, to cite Gerard Prunier, author of *The Rwanda Crisis*: "Genocides are a modern phenomenon . . . and they are likely to become more frequent in the future." Between the Holocaust in Europe and the genocides that have marked the post-Holocaust world (in Cambodia, Rwanda, and Bosnia and Kosovo), there are parallels: national and racial ideologies that deny human diversity; political campaigns that target, identify, marginalize, and expel minority groups; frighteningly efficient bureaucracies with no sense of remorse; brutal perpetrators and indifferent killers; and bystanders and rescuers. It is our conviction that the study of the Holocaust—how it happened, how it is represented, and how it has changed our moral and religious world—can be the starting point for a fuller understanding of the world we live in, a world in which genocide has, to our great misfortune, become part of who we are.

This curriculum is meant as an introduction and as a resource. There are four parts, which examine (1) the history of the Holocaust, (2) representations of the Holocaust, (3) other genocides, and (4) the ethical and religious dilemmas bequeathed to us by the fact of genocide in the modern world. Parts I–III have three or more chapters. Each chapter includes a narrative that is supplemented with "documents" (primary texts or discussions of literary or artistic works), as well as questions for discussion, "links" to other readings in the curriculum, and suggestions for further reading. Some chapters also include a glossary and a timeline. Part IV is unique. It raises ethical questions associated with the Holocaust and other genocides and suggests ways to answer them.

The links that follow the questions in each chapter are very important to the overall conception of the curriculum. Each link is identified by part, chapter, and document number and can readily be located from the Contents. For example, a chapter on passive bystanders during the Holocaust might be linked to the poem "You Onlookers" in Part II, "Representations,"

Chapter 6, "Literature and the Holocaust," or to a similar document about passivity during the Armenian genocide or to an essay in Part IV, "Ethics" addressing the question "How Does Good Happen?" In this way, we hope that teachers and students might think about the Holocaust from multiple perspectives and through different media. We also hope that they will reflect on the lessons of the Holocaust for the study of other genocides.

We have tried to encourage interactive learning. For example, in Chapter 7, "Monuments and Memorials," Document 7.2 is an examination of the memorial at Treblinka, the death camp where 850,000 Jews were killed. The memorial (seen in Figure 7.2) consists of granite shards that resemble broken, imperfectly edged tombstones. Teachers and students might discuss the ideas behind these shards; but they might also consider designing a memorial themselves. Throughout the curriculum, we have included suggestions for making learning about the Holocaust and other genocides as interactive as possible.

The focus on texts and on interactive learning also reflects our sense that with respect to the Holocaust and other genocides, the questions evoked are as important as the answers given. But good questions often follow from a consideration of detail in a text. One might consider a railway schedule for January 1943 (Document 3.8) that details a transport carrying Jews from Berlin to their death in Auschwitz. The transport must be scheduled; it must pass by many train stations. Because the schedule is not secret, many stationmasters know that the train carries a full cargo of Jews to a place called Auschwitz. Then, on this one sheet of paper, they see that the train must be turned around and, now empty, return. The document raises questions about what people knew, about what they did, about complicity and about secrecy. It also suggests that the people involved were sometimes very ordinary people, the man at the train station, and that they said nothing. Why?

In this curriculum, we offer a wide array of materials, which teachers and students can use as they choose and according to the amount of time they devote to the Holocaust and other genocides. We are well aware that some instructors may be able to devote only one classroom session to the Holocaust and other genocides, while other instructors may spend a week, even a semester, discussing the issues raised by modern genocide. Teachers may also teach this material from different disciplinary perspectives. Thus, a unit on the Holocaust might be differently taught in English, history, civics, or religious studies.

On the whole, then, the curriculum is not an attempt to pass on a pre-formed body of knowledge. Rather, we intend to provide material and guidance so that teachers and students of the Holocaust and modern genocide can use it as a starting point for reflecting on central, if deeply disturbing, events of our time. The material, we hope, will both raise questions about people's capacity for inhumanity and deepen an appreciation for their capacity for compassion. It may also raise questions of a more personal nature: concerning one's own capacity to resist, or one's own ability to see violence when it occurs. For some people, the Holocaust and the continuing legacy of genocide necessarily undermines all-too-easily held assumptions: that progress brings an end to human savagery, for example, or that culture self-evidently blunts a civilization's capacity for evil. For others, the Holocaust and other genocides continue to pose profound questions about education and its purposes, about morality, and about God. In the opening scene of Elie Wiesel's *Night*, Moshe the Beadle prays that God will give him "the strength to ask Him the right questions." It is in the spirit of trying to find the right questions that we have worked through this material.

A teacher's curriculum guide, written by Paul Fleming, a social studies teacher from Hume-Fogg Magnet High School in Davidson County, is available from the Tennessee Holocaust Commission, 2417 West End Ave., Nashville, TN 37240. It contains guidelines for teaching about genocide as well as a variety of interdisciplinary approaches tied directly to the text of this book.

Contributors

The writing of *The Holocaust and Other Genocides* was a cooperative effort of university professors and high school teachers from the state of Tennessee who met twice a month at Vanderbilt University in the 1999–2000 academic year. The cooperation was initially made possible by generous grants from the Raymond Zimmerman Foundation and the Tennessee Holocaust Commission. This cooperation has also been supported by Vanderbilt University and by the Robert Penn Warren Center for the Humanities at Vanderbilt.

The following individuals edited parts and wrote specific contributions.

William James Booth, Professor of Political Science, Vanderbilt University, author of "What Is the Relationship Between Ethics and Remembrance?"

Penelope H. Brooks, Professor of Psychology, Peabody College at Vanderbilt University, author of "Photographs."

Joel Dark, Assistant Professor of History, Tennessee State University, main editor of "Other Genocides" and author of "The Armenian Genocide."

Paul B. Fleming, Teacher, Hume Fogg High School, contributor, in particular, of questions for discussion for "History of the Holocaust."

Ernest Freudenthal, Associate Professor of Engineering, Vanderbilt University, contributor, in particular, of translations in "History of the Holocaust."

Jay Geller, Senior Lecturer of Modern Jewish Culture, Vanderbilt University, author of "Language and the Holocaust" and "Film."

Sue Chaney Gilmore, Teacher, Hillsboro High School, author of "Rwanda."

Teresa A. Goddu, Associate Professor of English, Vanderbilt University, author of the introductory text for "Representations of the Holocaust in the Arts" and of "Monuments and Memorials."

Peter Haas, Abba Hillel Silver Professor, Judaic Studies, and Director, Samuel Rosenthal Center for Judaic Studies, Case Western Reserve University, author of "What Are the Limits of Forgiveness and Reconciliation?" and "How Have Christians Responded to the Holocaust?" and, with Gary Phillips, the introductory texts for "Ethics" and "Ethical Questioning."

David Patterson, Bornblum Chair of Excellence in Judaic Studies and Director of the Bornblum Judaic Studies program, University of Memphis, author of "Is Genocide More Than Mass Murder?" and "How Does Good Happen?"

Gary Phillips, Professor of Religion and Chair, Religion Department, University of the South, main editor of "Ethics" and author of "Is Prejudice a Prelude to Annihilation?" "What Is a Choiceless Choice and the Extent of Moral Blame?" and, with Peter Haas, the introductory texts for "Ethics" and "Ethical Questioning."

Helmut Walser Smith, Associate Professor of History, Vanderbilt University, general editor of the work, main editor and author of "History of the Holocaust."

Margaret Vandiver, Assistant Professor of Criminology and Criminal Justice, University of Memphis, author of "Bosnia and Kosovo."

Meike G. Werner, Assistant Professor of German, Vanderbilt University, author of "Literature and the Holocaust."

The Holocaust and Other Genocides

Part I
History of the Holocaust

The Holocaust refers to Nazi Germany's attempt to eradicate the Jews of Europe. The attempt nearly succeeded. In the course of World War II, Nazi Germany killed nearly six million Jews. The Jews were not casualties of war, however, but victims of modern genocide. The endpoint of racism, genocide refers to the deliberate effort to exterminate an ethnic or racial group. In the Holocaust, the number of killings mounted with astounding swiftness. "In mid-March 1942," the historian Christopher Browning writes in his book *Ordinary Men,* "some 75 to 80 percent of all victims of the Holocaust were still alive, while 20 to 25 percent had perished. A mere eleven months later, in mid-February 1943, the percentages were exactly the reverse. At the core of the Holocaust was a short, intense wave of mass murder."

Germans killed Jews in myriad ways. Some Jews died in hastily constructed, densely crowded, disease-ridden ghettos. Many more were killed systematically by mobile killing units of the German SS. These units rounded up Jewish men, women, and children, forced them to dig their own graves, and shot them. In this way, the Germans murdered more than two million Jews. The Germans murdered a still larger number of Jews in killing centers, factories of death that included Chelmno, Belzec, Sobibor, Majdanek, Treblinka, and Auschwitz. The history of the Holocaust is about this killing: who killed, how, and why. But it is also about the antecedents to the killing, the habits of hate that allowed the Holocaust to happen in the first place.

We present this history in four chapters. Chapter 1 concerns the genesis of racist hatred. Chapter 2 addresses the "racist state" that paved the way to the Holocaust and the Germans who participated, watched, or looked the other way. Chapter 3 examines the killing process itself, and Chapter 4 examines resistance and rescue. Throughout we try to show how the Holocaust came about, but we also raise questions about those who were involved—the degree of their complicity, the range of their motivations, the shadows of their moral universe—and about what could have been done to prevent the Holocaust.

1
From Religious Prejudice to Racism

At the root of the Holocaust lies a long-standing animosity of Christians toward Jews. Based at first on religious differences, this animosity increasingly assumed secular hues and eventually was transformed by the tarbrush of modern racism. Both continuity and change mark this history. In the modern period, many of the images of old religious prejudice resurfaced in remarkably similar guise. But modern racism also broke with fundamental assumptions, arguing that Jews constituted a people apart, not a separate religion, and that the two groups, Germans and Jews, now defined as two races, should not coexist. Some took modern racism a step further and argued that, as a race and as a people, the Jews themselves should no longer exist.

Medieval prejudice against Jews centered on the religious beliefs that Jews were blind to the truth of Jesus and that the Jews had killed Christ. In the New Testament the missionizing Paul (Acts 13–15) attempts to convince the Jews of the truth of the resurrection of Christ. The specific idea of Jewish blindness comes from Acts 13:8–11. Paul meets a Jewish sorcerer named Elymas and says to him: "Will you never stop perverting the right ways of the Lord? Now the hand of the Lord is against you. You are going to be blind, and for a time you will be unable to see the light of the sun." Scholars place Paul's attempt to missionize the Jews in the year 59. At the time there was no notion that the Jews killed Christ, only that they did not believe in his resurrection. The idea of Jews as Christ-killers derives from the Gospel of John, written at the end of the first century, a time of changing fortunes for the Christians in the Roman Empire, when it had become clear that the Jews would not convert. It is instructive to compare John's rendition of the passion with those of Matthew, Mark, and Luke, composed earlier. John writes about "the Jews," Matthew, for example, about "the crowd." In the fourth century, Augustine reiterated the charge that the Jews killed Christ but argued that the continuing presence of the Jews in a miserable, humbled state bore truth to the victory of Christianity. He therefore argued against destroying them.

Because of the paucity of sources, it is difficult to ascertain the attitudes of Christians toward Jews in the succeeding centuries. From the period of Pope Gregory I, in the eighth century, we know that the Church prohibited Jews from keeping Christian slaves, servants, and wet nurses, and that there were ordinances forbidding Christians to dine with Jews and to visit Jewish physicians. From the period of Charlemagne, in the ninth century, we know that Jews lived under separate laws "for aliens" and depended completely on the graces and the protection of their immediate sovereign. Still, and despite discrimination, there is strong evidence to suggest that the first thousand years of Christianity witnessed very little violence against Jews.

The especially vexing problems began in the eleventh century, when Christians increasingly focused on the suffering and the martyrdom (as opposed to the glory) of Christ. During this time, Christians placed transubstantiation at the center of the liturgy, believing more fervently than ever before that the Eucharistic wafer, or Host, and the wine were the actual (as opposed to the symbolic) body and blood of Christ. In this context, the idea that "the Jews" had tortured Christ assumed greater immediacy.

Ideas initially religious became increasingly colored by superstition. By the thirteenth century, some Christians believed that Jews stole the Host (now conceived of as the actual body of Christ), desecrating and torturing it (Figure 1.1a). Others believed that Jews ritually murdered Christian children (symbolically standing for Christ) and used their blood in the baking of the matzo during Passover. Chimeras of the medieval imagination then mixed with beliefs in magic (that Jews, in alliance with the devil, possessed special powers) and with more ordinary stereotypes. Because Jews, unlike Christians, were allowed to lend money with interest, for example, all Jews were seen as usurious. The image of Jews in the Christian imagination was reinforced by special dress codes and later by ordinances requiring Jews to wear a yellow badge (Figure 1.1b).

Violence against Jews also increased. During the First Crusade, Christians on their way to the Holy Land to combat the infidels stopped to massacre Jews along the route, "for here in our midst dwell the archenemies and murderers of our redeemer." In the twelfth and thirteenth centuries massacres often accompanied accusations of Host desecration and ritual murder. Further violence resulted from popular wrath against Jews as moneylenders, and, in the fourteenth century, from the fictitious assertion that Jews had poisoned the wells, thus causing the Black Death. Where violence did not suffice, expulsion followed. In the medieval period, England and France expelled the Jews in the thirteenth century. Many German cities expelled the Jews in the thirteenth and fourteenth centuries. And in 1492, Spain expelled the Jews as well.

The Reformation of the sixteenth century promised to undermine the vast buttresses of superstition, including legends about Jews, that had artificially supported Christian faith in the medieval period. Martin Luther in his early writings counted the ill treatment of Jews among the failures of medieval Catholicism. "The Jews had been dealt with as though they were dogs, not humans," the father of the Reformation wrote in a pamphlet published in 1523. But when he saw that the Jews would not convert to his "purer" Christianity, his tone changed utterly. His *The Jews and Their Lies,* published in 1543, illustrates this changed tone (Document 1.2). Brusque and inflammatory, the pamphlet had an extremely deleterious effect on Christian attitudes toward Jews in post-Reformation Europe.

After 1800, racism rather than religious prejudice increasingly informed anti-Jewish sentiment. In 1879 Wilhelm Marr popularized the word *anti-Semitism* to describe the prejudice based on the alleged racial characteristics of the Jews. In the Christian tradition, Jews could convert. But the anti-Semites like Marr denied that Jews could be anything other than Jewish. They argued that Jews could never become true Germans because nationality is defined by blood and the Jews belonged to a different race and not merely a different religion.

The anti-Semites hoped to undo any progress that had been achieved toward the emancipation of the Jews, and they hoped to curtail what they saw as harmful Jewish influence on the German nation. To this end, the anti-Semites circulated a petition in 1881 that called for a special Jewish census, limits on Jewish immigration, and the preservation of the "Christian character" of schools and of all positions of state authority. With its mixture of Christian and racist language, the petition garnered 265,000 signatures and represented a watershed in the history of racial anti-Semitism. It proved that there was widespread support for the concept that Jews were outside the nation, that indeed they were an alien race. The first explicitly anti-Semitic political parties flourished in certain regions of Germany in the 1890s. Nevertheless, at the height of their popularity before World War I, these parties failed to win 4 percent of the vote in a national election. Even though they remained on the fringe of politics, they nevertheless had a deleterious effect on public discourse, making it more and more acceptable to denigrate Jews. The anti-Semitic political parties were also home to ruthless, viscerally racist, politicians. Adolf Hitler, who would emerge at the head of the Nazi Party, was a politician of this kind. In his earliest political writing, dated September 16, 1919, he emphasizes that Jews are a race, not a religious community (Document 1.3). He also argues that older forms of violence against Jews, such as pogroms, no longer suffice. The final aim of a modern anti-Semitic policy, he insists, "must be the uncompromising removal of the Jews altogether." Five years later, Hitler would elaborate his anti-Semitic position in greater detail in his book *Mein Kampf* (My Struggle), which he wrote while imprisoned for his part in the abortive "Beer Hall Putsch" in Munich in 1923. Here, and in subsequent speeches, he would speak more explicitly of annihilation.

The great historian of the Holocaust Raul Hilberg has summarized the shift from religiously based anti-Judaism to the policies of Nazi Germany, a modern racist state, as follows: "Since the fourth century after Christ there have been three anti-Jewish policies: conversion, expulsion, and annihilation. The second appeared as an alternative to the first, and the third emerged as an alternative to the second."

Document 1.1. Images of Jews in the Medieval Period

Figure 1.1a. The Stealing of the Host in Passau, 1470.

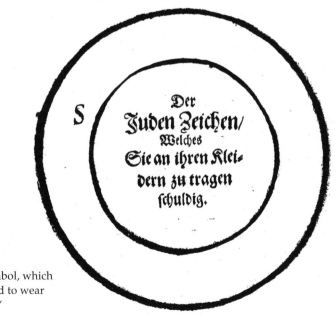

Der
Juden Zeichen/
Welches
Sie an ihren Klei-
dern zu tragen
schuldig.

Figure 1.1b.
"The Jewish symbol, which Jews are required to wear on their clothes."

Document 1.2. The Jews and Their Lies by Martin Luther, 1543

Learn from this, dear Christian, what you are doing if you permit the blind Jews to mislead you. Then the saying will truly apply, "When a blind man leads a blind man, both will fall into the pit" [cf. Luke 6:39]. You cannot learn anything from them except how to misunderstand the divine commandments. . . .

Therefore be on your guard against the Jews, knowing that wherever they have their synagogues, nothing is found but a den of devils in which sheer self-glory, conceit, lies, blasphemy, and defaming of God and men are practiced most maliciously. . . .

Moreover, they are nothing but thieves and robbers who daily eat no morsel and wear no thread of clothing that they have not stolen and pilfered from us by means of their accursed usury. Thus they live from day to day, together with wife and child, by theft and robbery, as arch-thieves and robbers, in the most impenitent security.

Over and above that we let them get rich on our sweat and blood, while we remain poor and they suck the marrow from our bones. . . .

What shall we Christians do with this rejected and condemned people, the Jews? . . .

First to set fire to their synagogues or schools and to bury and cover with dirt whatever will not burn, so that no man will ever again see a stone or cinder of them. This is to be done in honor of our Lord and of Christendom, so that God might see that we are Christians, and do not condone or knowingly tolerate such public lying, cursing, and blaspheming of his Son and of his Christians. . . .

Second, I advise that their houses also be razed and destroyed. For they pursue in them the same aims as in their synagogues. Instead they might be lodged under a roof or in a barn, like the gypsies. This will bring home to them that they are not masters in our country, as they boast, but that they are living in exile and in captivity, as they incessantly wail and lament about us before God.

Third, I advise that all their prayer books and Talmudic writings, in which such idolatry, lies, cursing and blasphemy are taught, be taken from them. . . .

Fourth, I advise that their rabbis be forbidden to teach henceforth on pain of loss of life and limb. . . .

Fifth, I advise that safe-conduct on the highways be abolished completely for the Jews. For they have no business in the countryside, since they are not lords, officials, tradesmen, or the like. . . .

Sixth, I advise that usury be prohibited to them, and that all cash and treasure of silver and gold be taken from them and put aside for safe-keeping. . . .

Seventh, I commend putting a flail, an ax, a hoe, a spade, a distaff, or a spindle into the hands of young, strong Jews and Jewesses and letting them earn their bread in the sweat of their brow, as was imposed on the children of Adam. . . .

Source: *Luther's Works*, vol. 47, edited by Franklin Sherman, The Christian in Society, vol. 4 (Philadelphia: Fortress Press, 1971), 268–93.

Document 1.3. Political Statement by Adolf Hitler, September 16, 1919

Anti-Semitism as a political movement must not be, cannot be, determined by emotional criteria, but only through the recognition of facts. The facts are as follows: First, the Jews are definitely a race and not a religious community. The Jew himself never calls himself a Jewish German, a Jewish Pole, a Jewish American, but only a German, a Polish, an American Jew. From the foreign nations in whose midst he lives the Jew has adopted little more than their language. A German who is compelled to use French in France, Italian in Italy, Chinese in China, does not thereby become a Frenchman, an Italian, or a Chinese; similarly a Jew who happens to live among us and is thereby compelled to use the German language cannot be called a German. . . .

Through a thousand years of inbreeding, often practiced within a very narrow circle, the Jew has in general preserved his race and character much more rigorously than many of the peoples among whom he lives. And as a result, there is living amongst us a non-German, foreign race, unwilling and unable to sacrifice its racial characteristics, to deny its own feeling, thinking and striving, and which none the less possess all the political rights that we ourselves have. . . .

Anti-Semitism stemming from purely emotive reasons will always find its expression in the form of pogroms. But anti-Semitism based on reason must lead to the systematic legal combating and removal of the rights of the Jew, which he alone of the foreigners living among us possesses (legislation to make them aliens). Its final aim, however, must be the uncompromising removal of the Jews altogether.

Source: *Nazism 1919–1945: A Documentary Reader*, vol. 1, *The Rise to Power 1919–1934*, edited by J. Noakes and G. Pridham (Exeter: University of Exeter Press, 1983).

Questions

Document 1.1. Images of Jews in the Medieval Period

1. How do the lines from Rudyard Kipling "All the people like us are We,/ And everyone else is They" relate to these two pictures?
2. How could medieval Christians have come to believe that Jews torture the Host and drain the blood of Christians?
3. What was the effect of forcing Jews to wear special dress and special markings, such as the yellow badge?

LINKS

Document 1.2. The Jews and Their Lies by Martin Luther, 1543

1. How does Luther use the Christian religion to justify his opinion of Jews?
2. What words or phrases are most persuasive in his arguments?
3. Do you see precedents for later atrocities?

LINKS

Document 1.3. Political Statement by Adolf Hitler, September 16, 1919

1. What is race? What is the difference between race and religion?
2. Why does Hitler declare "the Jews are definitely a race and not a religious community?" How does this "fact" help justify his opinions about Jews?

LINKS

Further Reading

Meyer, Michael A. *German-Jewish History in Modern Times.* 4 vols. New York: Columbia University Press, 1996–98.

Niewyk, Donald, and Francis Nicosia. *The Columbia Guide to the Holocaust.* New York: Columbia University Press, 2000.

Vital, David. *A People Apart: The Jews in Europe, 1789–1939.* New York: Oxford University Press, 1999.

2
The Creation of a Racist Society

Adolf Hitler and the National Socialists seized power on January 30, 1933, placing a ruthless racist at the head of a modern national state. Within a short period, Hitler eradicated the opposition and consolidated power in his own hands. But Nazi Germany was more than just a simple dictatorship; it was a totalitarian society defined both by a repressive regime of terror and by the appeal of a "national community." Thus, schools, churches, and civic organizations no longer served their own ends but instead served those of a community defined by race. For the non-Jewish Germans in this community, the pull of being an insider must have been attractive. Yet this was a community built on the exclusion of others— "those alien to the race." Jews constituted the most conspicuous group deemed "alien to the race." But there were others: Communists, Socialists, people with mental illness, homosexuals, and Roma and Sinti ("Gypsies"). In Nazi Germany, sustaining a sense of "we" among the Germans depended on the repression, the marginalization, and ultimately the extermination of "others."

In April 1933, the Nazi Party organized a nationwide boycott of Jewish stores. Typically Hitler's Brownshirts, or Storm Troopers, displayed signs saying, "Don't buy from the Jews" (Figure 2.1a) and taunted those who bought from Jewish stores nevertheless. The boycott proved only a partial success. Many people crossed the lines, and the general reaction of the wider population was, in the words of one historian, "markedly cool."

Slowly, however, segregation deepened. Clubs, hotels, restaurants, movie theaters, youth organizations, even whole communities closed their doors to Jews (Figures 2.1b, c). As public contacts were severed, private contacts unraveled as well. Non-Jews increasingly avoided Jews they knew, pretending they had never been acquainted. For Jews, who had long thought of themselves as an integral part of this society, the deepening division was disheartening and demoralizing. "The problem," as the German-Jewish philosopher Hannah Arendt writes, "was not what our enemies did, but what our friends did."

The "racist state" was also built on a foundation of spurious laws, the most famous of which included the Nuremberg Laws (Document 2.2). Promulgated in September 1935, the Nuremberg Laws stated the determinants of German citizenship, proscribed sexual relations and forbade marriages between Jews and non-Jews, and defined the category "Jew." Before the enactment of the Nuremberg Laws, Jews counted as German citizens in the same measure as did Protestants and Catholics. Since the Nazi seizure of power, there had been a series of discriminatory measures directed against the Jews, but the new laws were considered special measures. They deprived Jews of the full protection accorded to citizens and juridically enshrined a racial, as opposed to a religious, definition of Jews in Germany. Previously, it did not make legal sense to speak of Germans and Jews as separate categories, since Jews, legally and in terms of their own identity, were Germans. The Nuremberg Laws also forbade sexual contact between Jews and non-Jews and prohibited interfaith (redefined as interracial) marriage. In the years before World War I, Imperial Germany had set a precedent for the intervention of a racist state in the private lives of citizens when it outlawed and annulled marriages between whites and blacks in the colonies. Other countries, and the states of the American South, had such legislation as well. In Nazi Germany, following passage of the Nuremberg Laws, the penalty for extramarital intercourse between Jews and non-Jews, henceforth called race defilement (*Rassenschande*), was severe: up to fifteen years in prison. Moreover, a disproportionate number of anonymous denunciations to the secret police concerned such relations. The third section of the Nuremberg Laws addresses the problem of defining who is Jewish in a society where many Jews lived in interfaith marriages, and some had converted to Christianity. The law artificially constructed a racial category where previously there had only been a religious category and introduced the racist term *Mischling* to mean a person of mixed blood. In reality, such a person was the son or daughter of interfaith parents. According to the racist definitions in the laws, there were nearly five hundred thousand Jews in Germany, and two hundred thousand *Mischlinge*.

More and more racist laws were passed in months following the promulgation of the Nuremberg Laws. On October 18, 1935, the government passed the Law for the Protection of the Hereditary Health of the German People. This law, requiring "alien races" and "less valuable" groups to register with the government, was supplemented by a decree that prohibited Germans from engaging in sexual relations with or marrying people of "alien blood." The Ministry of the Interior defined such people as "Gypsies, Negroes, and their bastards." In 1935, the National Socialist government also intensified the persecution of homosexuals and gave wide powers to the police to arrest anyone who even glanced at another person of the same sex in an "enticing" way. Not for the first or for the last time (witness the American South in the "Jim Crow" years, South Africa during apartheid, the continuing force of legal discrimination against gays), the immense power of a modern government fueled and fortified racist prejudice as well as the general prejudice against people defined as different.

Roma and Sinti ("Gypsies") especially were targets of the prejudice against those who were different. "Racial experts" and bureaucrats employed by the Nazi state defined Roma and Sinti according to spurious racial criteria and classified them as "criminal" and "asocial." In a circular originally dated December 8, 1939, Heinrich Himmler, the head of the SS, used this "scientific knowledge" to lay the groundwork for state policies that would ultimately lead to the killing of, according to one recent estimate, 150,000 Gypsies in Nazi-occupied Europe (Document 2.3). Similar policies also led the Nazis to define the people with mental or physical disabilities in racial terms and, through a program euphemistically called "euthanasia," to kill more than 70,000 people with disabilities in Germany and thousands more in Nazi occupied Europe.

Ordinary citizens first watched then participated in the increasing violence against others. Crystal Night—or Kristallnacht, the "night of broken glass"—is the name given to a government-sponsored pogrom against Jews that began late in the night of November 9, 1938. In the course of the riot, Hitler's Storm Troopers demolished Jewish storefronts, tore down and tossed out the wares inside, ransacked Jewish homes, and set synagogues on fire throughout Germany. Aided by ordinary citizens, the Storm Troopers taunted and assaulted Jews in their hometowns, and, in the fray, killed over a hundred German Jews.

The violence began when a young Polish Jew named Herschel Grynszpan assassinated Ernst vom Rath, a German diplomat in Paris. Grynszpan had been driven to despair by the expulsion from Germany of Polish Jews, his mother and sister among them. Adolf Hitler and the leaders of Nazi Germany retaliated immediately. They instructed district leaders to set fire to the synagogues ("where there is no danger of fire in neighboring buildings") and to wreak havoc (but not loot) Jewish businesses. The next morning, the Nazis forced the Jews to clean up the glass and debris that littered the streets. They also arrested thousands of Jewish men, whom they marched through the streets before sending them to concentration camps in Dachau, Buchenwald, and Sachsenhausen.

The German government attempted to portray the riot as a "spontaneous" response of the German people to the murder of Ernst vom Rath. In fact, the pogrom was highly organized, and the reactions of the non-Jewish German traversed the spectrum from enthusiastic support to shame and dismay (Document 2.4), from unmotivated malice to conspicuous kindness. Most of the population did not support the violence. But whether this lack of support derived from genuine fellow feeling, from distress at the lack of orderliness, or from worry about the impact on Germany's international image remains unclear. Historians have documented a few cases of active solidarity, of Christians helping their Jewish neighbors. Mainly, however, there was indifference to the plight of the Jews and, significantly, no public demonstrations opposed the violence.

Crystal Night was only a prelude. It was followed by a battery of discriminatory measures that by fall 1941 included curfews, designated shopping hours, bans from public transportation and from many public spaces, forced labor, and confinement to "Jewish houses." Between Crystal Night and the outbreak of World War II, Germany passed more than two hundred anti-Semitic laws and ordinances. When the war began, the pace only quickened.

In September 1941, a new ordinance required Jews over the age of six to wear a yellow Star of David, recalling a medieval form of demarcation and segregation. This measure also constituted an important further step in the identification of victims slated for future deportation. The first major deportations began in the following month, October 1941. By this time, the Jewish community in Germany had dwindled from 500,000 people in 1933 to 163,696. Of the Jews left in Germany, a disproportionate number were women and more than two-thirds were over forty-five years of age. Of the German Jews deported, 90 percent died.

Although it is difficult to discern exactly what non-Jewish Germans thought about these measures, it is possible to reconstruct the popular mood through periodic opinion reports prepared by district governors, a number of which have survived for the state of Bavaria. The reports point to two of the most prevalent reactions of the German population to the ordinance requiring the Star of David: indifference and an insistence on ironing out further inconsistencies (Document 2.5). It should also be noted that most reports pass over the ordinance without mention. It simply did not concern the local population, one may surmise.

The German population also reacted with indifference to the deportations. Here too there are few reports, few instances of disturbances. There are some reports of support, but they are scattered. Yet the deportations occurred in daylight. Nazi officials informed the Jews that they were to be resettled and would be required to work. They were ordered to gather at assembly points (synagogues, government office buildings, and even slaughterhouses) and from there they were taken by vans to the train stations. Sometimes families were split apart. Holding onto last threads of hope, some Jews believed they were being deported merely for resettlement. Resigned, many others feared the worst. Among German Jews, as the reports make clear, there was a wave of suicides.

Document 2.1. Signs of Racism, Symbols of Segregation

Figure 2.1a. Boycott of Jewish stores, April 1933.
Courtesy of Bildarchiv Preussischer Kulturbesitz.

Figure 2.1b. Signs of a segregated society: "Only for Jews." Institute of Contemporary History and Wiener Library Limited, courtesy of United States Holocaust Memorial Museum.

Figure 2.1c. Signs of exclusion: "Jews are not wanted here." Courtesy of Yad Vashem Film and Photo Archive.

Document 2.2. Excerpts from the Texts of the Nuremberg Laws

Reich Citizenship Law, September 15, 1935

The Reichstag has unanimously enacted the following law, which is promulgated herewith:

§ 1

1) A subject of the State is a person who enjoys the protection of the German Reich and who in consequence has specific obligations towards it.
2) The status of subject of the State is acquired in accordance with the provisions of the Reich and State Citizenship Law.

§ 2

1) A Reich citizen is a subject of the State who is of German or related blood, who proves by his conduct that he is willing and fit faithfully to serve the German people and Reich.
2) Reich citizenship is acquired through the granting of a Reich Citizenship Certificate.
3) The Reich citizen is the sole bearer of full political rights in accordance with the Law.

§ 3

The Reich Minister of the Interior, in coordination with the Deputy of the Führer, will issue the Legal and Administrative orders required to implement and complete this Law.

Nuremberg, September 15, 1935
At the Reich Party Congress of Freedom

The Führer and Reich Chancellor,
Adolf Hitler
The Reich Minister of the Interior
Frick

Source: *Reichsgesetzblatt*, vol. 1 (1935), 1146; electronic files, Documents of the Holocaust, pt. 1, Germany and Austria, document 32, at yadvashem.org (retrieved November 2001).

**Nuremberg Law for the Protection of German Blood
and German Honor, September 15, 1935**

Moved by the understanding that purity of the German Blood is the essential condition for the continued existence of the German people, and inspired by the inflexible determination to ensure the existence of the German Nation for all time, the Reichstag has unanimously adopted the following Law, which is promulgated herewith:

§ 1

1) Marriages between Jews and subjects of the state of German or related blood are forbidden. Marriages nevertheless concluded are invalid, even if concluded abroad to circumvent this law.

2) Annulment proceedings can be initiated only by the State Prosecutor.

§ 2

Extramarital intercourse between Jews and subjects of the state of German or related blood is forbidden.

§ 3

Jews may not employ in their households female subjects of the state of German or related blood who are under 45 years old.

§ 4

1) Jews are forbidden to fly the Reich or National flag or to display the Reich colors.

2) They are, on the other hand, permitted to display the Jewish colors. The exercise of this right is protected by the State.

§ 5

1) Any person who violates the prohibition under §1 will be punished by a prison sentence with hard labor.

2) A male who violates the prohibition under § 2 will be punished with a prison sentence with or without hard labor.

3) Any person violating the provisions under § 3 or 4 will be punished with a prison sentence of up to one year and a fine, or with one or the other of these penalties.

§ 6

The Reich Minister of the Interior, in coordination with the Deputy of the Führer and the Reich Minister of Justice, will issue the Legal and Administrative regulations required to implement and complete this Law.

§ 7

The Law takes effect on the day following promulgations except for § 3, which goes into force on January 1, 1936.

Nuremberg, September 15, 1935
at the Reich Party Congress of Freedom

The Führer and Reich Chancellor
Adolf Hitler
The Reich Minister of the Interior
Frick
The Reich Minister of Justice
Dr. Guertner
The Deputy of the Führer
R. Hoess

Source: *Reichsgesetzblatt,* vol. 1 (1935), 1146–47; electronic files, Documents of the Holocaust, pt. 1, Germany and Austria, document 33, at yadvashem.org (retrieved November 2001).

First Regulation to the Reich Citizenship Law,
November 14, 1935

§ 4

1) A Jew cannot be a Reich citizen. He has no voting rights in political matters; he cannot occupy a public office.
2) Jewish officials will retire as of December 31, 1935. . . .

§ 5

1) A Jew is a person descended from at least three grandparents who are full Jews by race. . . .
2) A *Mischling* who is a subject of the state is also considered a Jew if he is descended from two full Jewish grandparents
   a) who was a member of the Jewish Religious Community at the time of the promulgation of this Law, or was admitted to it subsequently;
   b) who was married to a Jew at the time of the promulgation of this Law, or subsequently married to a Jew;
   c) who was born from a marriage with a Jew in accordance with paragraph 1, contracted subsequently to the promulgation of the law for the Protection of German Blood and German Honor of September 15, 1935;
   d) who was born as the result of extramarital intercourse with a Jew in accordance with Paragraph 1, and was born illegitimately after July 31, 1936.

Source: *Reichsgesetzblatt*, vol. 1 (1935), 1333, electronic files, Documents of the Holocaust, pt. 1, Germany and Austria, document 34, at yadvashem.org (retrieved November 2001).

Document 2.3. Combating the Gypsy Nuisance by Heinrich Himmler, December 8, 1938

Experience gained in combating the Gypsy nuisance, and knowledge derived from race-biological research, have shown that the proper method of attacking the Gypsy problem seems to be to treat it as a matter of race. Experience shows that part-Gypsies play the greatest role in Gypsy criminality. On the other hand, it has been shown that efforts to make the Gypsies settle have been unsuccessful, especially in the case of pure Gypsies, on account of their strong compulsion to wander. It has therefore become necessary to distinguish between pure and part-Gypsies in the final solution of the Gypsy question.

To this end, it is necessary to establish the racial affinity of every Gypsy living in Germany and of every vagrant living a Gypsy-like existence.

I therefore decree that all settled and non-settled Gypsies, and also all vagrants living a Gypsy-like existence, are to be registered with the Reich Criminal Police Office-Reich Central Office for Combating the Gypsy Nuisance.

The police authorities will report (via the responsible Criminal Police offices and local offices) to the Reich Criminal Police Office-Reich Central Office for Combating the Gypsy Nuisance all persons who by virtue of their looks and appearance, customs or habits, are to be regarded as Gypsies or part-Gypsies.

Because a person considered to be a Gypsy or part-Gypsy, or a person living like a Gypsy, as a rule confirms the suspicion that marriage (in accordance with clause 6 of the first decree on the implementation of the Law for the Protection of German Blood and Honor ... or on the basis of stipulations in the law on Fitness to Marry must not be contracted, in all cases the public registry officials must demand a testimony of fitness to marry from those who make such an application [to be married].

Treatment of the Gypsy question is part of the National Socialist task of national regeneration. A solution can only be achieved if the philosophical perspectives of National Socialism are observed. Although the principle that the German nation respects the national identity of alien peoples is also assumed in combating the Gypsy nuisance, nonetheless the aim of measures taken by the State to defend the homogeneity of the German nation must be the physical separation of Gypsydom from the German nation, the prevention of miscegenation, and finally, the regulation of the way of life of pure and part-Gypsies. The necessary legal foundation can only be created through a Gypsy Law which prevents further intermingling of blood, and which regulates all the most pressing questions which go together with the existence of Gypsies in the living space of the German nation.

Source: Michael Burleigh and Wolfgang Wippermann, *The Racial State: Germany, 1933–1945* (New York: Cambridge University Press, 1991), 120–21. Reprinted with permission of Cambridge University Press.

Document 2.4. Report on Crystal Night from Berlin

At half past nine I ride to the office. The bus conductor looks at me as if he had something important to say; but then he just shakes his head, and looks away guiltily. My fellow passengers don't look up at all. Everyone's expression seems somehow to be asking forgiveness. The Kurfurstendamm is a sea of broken glass. At the corner of the Fasanenstrasse people are gathering—a mute mass looking in dismay at the synagogue, whose dome is hidden in clouds of smoke.

"A damn shame!" a man beside me whispers.

I look at him lovingly. This, it occurs to me, is really the time to call your neighbor "brother." But I don't do it. One never does; one just thinks it. And if you really do pluck up courage for a running start, in the end you just ask, "Pardon me, but could you tell me the time?" And then you're instantly ashamed of being such a coward.

Yet we all feel that we are brothers as we sit here in the bus, ready to die of shame. Brothers in shame; comrades in humiliation. But if everyone is ashamed, who smashed those windows? It wasn't you, it wasn't I. Then who is X, the great unknown?

Source: Ruth Andreas-Friedrich, *Berlin Underground, 1938–1945*, translated by Barrows Mussey (New York: Henry Holt, 1947), 19.

Document 2.5. Public Reactions to the Yellow Star and Deportations

From the Monthly Report of the District Governor of Ober and Mittelfranken, October 7, 1941

The identification with yellow stars of the Jews took place without incident, also the appearance of the marked Jews in public did not lead to any disturbances. On the other hand there were anonymous and also open accusations on the part of the German population against supposed Jews, those Jews who according to regulations are exempt from wearing the yellow star.

From the Monthly Report of the District Governor of Schwaben, October 8, 1941

According to the report of the mayor of Augsburg, the identification of the Jews was very much approved by all German citizens. However, the question of shopping facilities for the Jews still requires a solution, since not every businessman is willing to tolerate the marked Jews in his place of business as this may be a cause of disturbance.

From the Monthly Report of the District Governor of Ober and Mittelfranken, December 7, 1941

In the Jew evacuation action of 29 Nov., a special train with 1001 Jews and nine children departed from Nuremberg to Riga. Three Jewesses committed suicide, presumably because of fear of the impending evacuation. . . . During the night from the 15th to the 16th of November a gallows was erected in front of the city hall in Windsbach (County Ansbach), in protest against the only Jewish person still present in the County, the spouse of the watchmaker Reuter. The gallows had a sign "For the Jewess."

From the Situation Report of the President of the District Court, Nuremberg, January 5, 1942

The appropriation of Jewish realty property continues steadily. In Nuremberg, already four-fifths of the real property signed over to the former deputy Gauleiter Holz has been appropriated. As about 500 Jews were evacuated in December 1941, the number of remaining Jews in the area has been reduced substantially. Further deportations of Jews are planned during the next few months. However, the shortage of apartments in Nuremberg will not be improved much by this.

Source: Martin Broszat, Elke Fröhlich, Falk Wiesemann, eds., *Bayern in der NS-Zeit* (Munich: R. Oldenbourg, 1977), 1:483–84. Reprinted with permission of Oldenbourg Verlag.

Questions

_____

Document 2.1. Signs of Racism, Symbols of Segregation

1. Imagine that someone is walking along this sidewalk and sees the men with the sign that says, "Don't buy from the Jews." What are the possible responses? What motivates different responses?
2. Do you see parallels between the segregation that occurred in Nazi Germany and segregation in the United States? How were the experiences of segregation similar? How were they different? Does this kind of segregation exist today?
3. List some of the characteristics of a community that would put up a sign saying, "Jews are not wanted here"? How is this community the same as and how is it different from your own community?

LINKS

_____

Document 2.2. Excerpts from the Texts of the Nuremberg Laws

1. "Moved by the understanding that purity of the German Blood is the essential condition for the continued existence of the German people" (from the Law for the Protection of German Blood and German Honor). Do these words make sense to you? If they do not, why do you think such ideas became so powerful and widespread in Nazi Germany?
2. Reread the Nuremberg Laws and think about what citizenship means to you. If tomorrow your U.S. citizenship were taken away, how would your attitude and outlook about your country and yourself change?
3. The Nazis attempt to justify "racial laws" that are based on the religious identification and heritage of Jews. What potential problems does the use of the religious identification raise for enforcing racial laws?

LINKS

Document 2. 3. Combating the Gypsy Nuisance by Heinrich Himmler, December 8, 1938

1. What words and concepts in this document do we normally associate with the Holocaust against the Jews?
2. What are the similarities, and what are the differences, between Himmler's circular and the ideas behind the Nuremberg Laws?
3. Using the Nuremberg Laws and Himmler's circular, outline the basic features of a racist state.

LINKS

Document 2.4. Report on Crystal Night from Berlin

1. Why do you think the majority of the German people did not respond vigorously against the violence of Crystal Night?
2. Can you think of a time when you had thoughts like those of the author of the document "Report on Crystal Night from Berlin"? Can you think of a time when you should have intervened but did not? What kept you from doing what you thought was right?

LINKS

Document 2.5. Public Reactions to the Yellow Star and Deportations

1. How does the following quotation from Albert Einstein relate to these documents: "The world is too dangerous to live in—not because of the people who do evil, but because of the people who sit and let it happen"?
2. According to the historian Ian Kershaw, "The road to Auschwitz was built by hate, but paved by indifference." Explain.

LINKS

Further Reading

Burleigh, Michael, and Wolfgang Wippermann. *The Racial State: Germany, 1933–1945*. New York: Cambridge University Press, 1991.

Friedländer, Saul. *Nazi Germany and the Jews*. Vol. 1, *The Years of Persecution, 1933–1939*. New York: HarperPerennial, 1997.

Kaplan, Marion A. *Between Dignity and Despair: Jewish Life in Nazi Germany*. New York: Oxford University Press, 1999.

3
The Killing Process

The killing process brings us to central issues in the study of the Holocaust: who killed, who participated, and how and why? The answers are not easy, especially to the question why, and our language often subtly prefigures our responses. Should we talk of Germans as killers or should we use the more neutral term *perpetrators?* Should we write of the machinery of destruction, which drew people sometimes against their will into its murderous cogs and levers, or should we write of the hatred that motivated individual people not just to kill but to kill in cruel ways? Historians do not agree on these issues, partly for reasons of analytical temperament, partly because the killing process was itself diverse. It involved sadists as well as ordinary men, Nazi ideologues as well as blind, unthinking, unfeeling careerists. Some pulled triggers, others conducted cruel medical experiments, and still others gratuitously murdered children. There were also people who simply pushed pen and paper and rendered bureaucratically efficient the daily traffic of death.

In approaching these problems, one hopes to avoid what the historian Inga Clendinnen calls the "Gorgon effect": "the sickening of the imagination and curiosity and the draining of the will which afflicts so many of us when we try to look squarely at the persons and processes implicated in the Holocaust." The purpose is to go beyond simply facing the killing process with horror and to try to understand if not the whole then aspects of it. To follow Clendinnen: "The understanding I seek comes from framing sufficiently precise questions to be able to see exactly what is before us, whether persons or processes. It is both cumulative, and never complete."

For historians, a central interpretive issue has been the degree to which Adolf Hitler intervened in decision making and at what level. The evidence points to what one historian calls "government by announcement." Hitler announced his intentions and subordinates worked out the precise details.

An important such announcement could be heard in a now-famous speech delivered eight months before the outbreak of World War II, in which Hitler prophesied that a coming war would bring about the "annihilation of the

Jewish race in Europe." The speech strongly suggests that Hitler had envisioned the annihilation of the Jews even before the war, though concrete plans for annihilation were neither commissioned nor forthcoming until 1941. From other documents, historians can infer that Hitler's prophecy was taken very seriously, both by himself and by other Nazi leaders. In a document drafted by Reinhard Heydrich, head of the Security Service (SD), and signed by Hermann Göring, who was still officially responsible for Jewish affairs, Göring issued the following order in the context of the euphoria surrounding the initial German victories after the German Army attacked the Soviet Union on June 22, 1941:

> In completion of the task which was entrusted to you in the Edict dated January 24, 1939, of solving the Jewish question by means of emigration or evacuation in the most convenient way possible, given the present conditions, I herewith charge you with making all necessary preparations with regard to organizational, practical and financial aspects for an overall solution [*Gesamtlösung*] of the Jewish question in the German sphere of influence in Europe.

The timing of the order is important. Mobile killing units had already begun to murder thousands of Jews in the Soviet Union. Historians therefore speculate that Hitler considered this the opportune time to commence what he called "the annihilation of the Jewish race of Europe." The order also documents the beginnings of a qualitatively new phase in the unfolding of the Holocaust: a call for an overall plan. "I further charge you," Göring wrote to Heydrich, "with submitting to me promptly an overall plan of the preliminary organizational, practical and financial measures for the execution of the intended final solution (*Endlösung*) of the Jewish question." The language of the document implies that until this point no such "overall plan" existed but that Nazi leaders understood that such a "solution" was "intended."

Historians reason that in the course of the next six months, an "overall plan" was in fact worked out, and that its contents were conveyed to high-ranking Nazi leaders at the Wannsee Conference of January 20, 1942 (Document 3.1). It is important to note, however, that at the Wannsee Conference, the leaders of Nazi Germany did not decide upon the "final solution," as is sometimes assumed. In Nazi Germany, decisions were not ordinarily made in conferences. Moreover, the destruction of European Jewry was already under way. Systematic murder of Jews in the Soviet Union had begun in June 1941, and by the end of the year, approximately 500,000 Jews had been killed by mobile killing units, the *Einsatzgruppen.* Starting on December 8, 1941, Germans had also begun to use gas vans to kill Jews in Chelmno, Poland. The Wannsee Conference was, instead, a meeting of influential Nazi leaders in which Heydrich announced that he was principally responsible for coordinating efforts to exterminate the Jews of Europe. The document is important also because it shows the degree to which the killing process still rested on the spurious racial distinctions of the Nuremberg Laws and because it demonstrates Nazi resolve to wipe out all the Jews of Europe. Finally, the document, heavily edited by Heydrich, is not an accurate protocol of the discussion. Nevertheless, one can discern the eagerness of other German bureaucrats to forge ahead to solve "the Jewish question" as quickly as possible.

The destruction of European Jewry happened in stages. Raul Hilberg identifies these stages as definition by decree, concentration, mobile killing operations, deportations, and killing center operations.

Immediately after the German invasion of Poland in September 1939, Nazi leaders devised plans to concentrate the Jews of Poland in walled ghettos, though the measures were to be temporary, pending further deportation. The first major ghetto was established in Lodz in April 1940, and by September 1941 it housed 144,000 Jews in an area of 1.6 square miles. The largest ghetto was in Warsaw, where nearly half a million Jewish men, women, and children were pressed into a few city blocks. Roughly 3.5 square miles in size, the Warsaw ghetto constituted a human prison of immense density and privation. In less than two years, eighty-three thousand people died in the Warsaw ghetto, many of them of starvation, others of diseases, most typically typhus (Documents 3.2, 3.3). Those who survived were subsequently sent to their death in Treblinka. In an effort to resist the deportations, Jews in the Warsaw ghetto rose up against the German forces. The uprising (which we consider in more detail in Chapter 4) lasted nearly a month, from April 19 to May 16, 1943. But the Jews had few weapons and the Germans reduced the ghetto to rubble.

Similar rates of mortality occurred in Lodz and in other ghettos of occupied Poland, and, as in Warsaw, those who did not succumb were sent to death camps. The Jews (and the Roma and Sinti—"Gypsies") of Lodz were initially sent to Chelmno, where they were killed in gas vans. Yet in one important respect, the story of Lodz was different.

In Lodz, the chair of the Jewish council, which the Nazis had set up in order to administer the ghetto, was a man named Chaim Rumkowski. He believed that if he made the Jews of the Lodz ghetto indispensable to the Nazi war machine, he could save them from deportation to certain death. It was a desperate gamble, a choiceless choice. As a strategy for survival, it ensured that the Lodz ghetto would be turned into a forced labor camp, and that, consequently, children and older people and sick people would be sacrificed. This is the subject of Rumkowski's now-famous address on September 4, 1942 (Document 3.4). The Nazis demanded a quota of 20,000 people, which Rumkowski bargained down from 24,000. In his position as the head of the Jewish council, Rumkowski asked parents to give up their children and to turn over the elderly. In the days before, the Nazis, aided by the Jewish ghetto police, had already taken many of the sick from their hospital beds. Rumkowski's appeal would now unleash a great panic, as mothers and fathers desperately tried to hide their children, and others frantically tried to get jobs for those people, especially the elderly, who were not yet employed. When many of the children and the elderly and the sick had been sent off, major deportations from the Lodz ghetto to the killing center in Chelmno suddenly ceased. From September 1942 to May 1944, the ghetto became a production center for the Nazis, with the Jews of the ghetto working long hours on meager rations. As a gamble born of despair, it seemed to work. By spring 1944, Lodz was the only major ghetto still in existence, its people still alive. There were now 75,000 Jews in the ghetto. They had seen their children taken away. And they had endured terrible privation. But then, with the Soviet forces bearing down and the German army in retreat, deportations began anew. In June and July 1944, 3,000 Jews were deported to Chelmno. In August, the rest were deported either to work camps or to Auschwitz. It is estimated that altogether 60,000 Jews died in the Lodz ghetto, and that 130,000 Jews from the ghetto were killed in the camps. Yet 10,000 people survived, more, some researchers claim, than from any other ghetto of Nazi-occupied eastern Europe.

The concentration in ghettos was a temporary stage; it was followed by mobile killing operations, the first wave of mass murder. There were four units totaling three thousand men, though because of a high rate of rotation the number of men who participated in the killings is significantly higher. Reinhard Heydrich, as head of the SD, created the mobile killing units and men from his office made up most of the higher-level leadership. College-educated, typically in their thirties, the men who led the battalions came from all walks of life, but typically they were professional men, with a disproportionate number of lawyers among them. They did not necessarily choose active duty murdering Jews, yet they became efficient killers. Below the level of leadership, the members of the mobile killing units were drawn principally from the SS and from various police agencies. Their task was to follow the German Army into Soviet territory, to descend upon cities, towns, and villages with Jewish populations, and kill every Jewish man, woman, and child.

The Jäger report (Document 3.5), offers a detailed description of the "work" of Einsatzkommando 3, a company-sized (150 men) detachment of Einsatzgruppe A, the largest mobile killing unit. Between July 4 and December 1, 1941, this detachment rained in on seventy-one different Jewish communities, in some instances returning more than once. In all, the Jäger report has 112 entries for "actions"—the euphemism for mass killings. The vast majority of those killed were Jews, but Russians, Poles, Communists, Gypsies and the "mentally sick" are also mentioned. The detachments rounded up their victims, forced them to march to a place outside the community, and shot them, often in front of mass graves. In this period, the detachments worked behind the lines of the German Army and never faced regular Soviet troops in a military confrontation. Behind the lines the Einsatzkommando 3 had killed 137,346 people by December 1941. In the "first sweep" from June 1941, when the first mass killings occurred, to April 1942, the mobile killing units murdered approximately 750,000 people, almost all of whom were Jews.

As the murders carried out by the mobile killing units were widespread and continual, there were many witnesses. In particular, German civilians and members of the German Army often watched the murders. The testimony of Hermann Graebe, the chief engineer of a constructing firm, concerns the massacre of the Jews of Dubno, a provincial city in the Ukraine on October 5, 1942 (Document 3.6). The killings were part of the "second sweep" of 1942–43, in which mobile killing units murdered 1.5 million Jews. Historians estimate the total number of Jews killed by mobile killing units to be 2.2 million.

Besides eradicating human lives, the mobile killing units erased a vast and complex Jewish culture. Jews had settled in eastern Europe in the early Middle Ages and had built vibrant communities called shtetl (the Yiddish diminutive of *Shtot,* the word for town). Evoked in the paintings of Marc Chagall, the shtetl were Jewish hometowns. Poor, often with crooked earthen streets, they were places where neighbors knew each other and where Jewish families had been in close contact for hundreds of years, one generation after the next. In many of the shtetl, Jews also lived side-by-side with Christians, whether Polish, Ukrainian, Russian, Lithuanian, or German. In these close quarters, there was a great deal of interaction, with each learning something of the other's language and custom. But there was also separation. Interfaith marriages, for example, were extremely uncommon. The Jews of the shtetl were deeply religious and marked out the days and the years by the rituals of the Jewish calendar. They were also deeply committed to learning. And the shtetels were centers of craftsmanship and trade. This too is what was lost. As the poet Antoni Slonimski wrote in his "Elegy for the Jewish Villages."

> Gone now are those little towns where the shoemaker was a poet
> The watchmaker a philosopher, the barber a troubadour.
> Gone now are those little towns where the wind joined
> Biblical songs with Polish tunes and Slavic rue,
> Where old Jews in orchards in the shade of cherry trees
> Lamented for the holy walls of Jerusalem.

The Jäger report demonstrates the chillingly violent efficiency of the Germans, especially in the way town after town, shtetl after shtetl, the exact numbers of people killed were tallied. Yet there is evidence that the numbers are not as exact as they seem and that many are based on conjecture that sometimes underestimated the number of Jews killed. Yaffa Eliach, in her book *There Once Was a World: A Nine-Hundred-Year Chronicle of the Shtetl of Eishyshok,* has reconstructed how one of these massacres took place in the shtetl in which she was born (Document 3.7). In the Jäger report, the shtetl is called by its German name, and the entry reads as follows:

27.9.41 Eysisky   989 Jews, 1,636 Jewesses, 821 Jewish children   3,446

Yet the date of the entry is not correct, as the massacre took place over two days. On September 25 the men were killed, on September 26 the women and children. On September 27, there were drinking parties in Eisyshok, with Germans, Lithuanians, and Poles celebrating. Moreover, Jews from the surrounding villages were also killed, and the total number was closer to five thousand. The reports also do not describe the other atrocities that happened in these days. As one escaped witness wrote: "I saw my beautiful cousin raped and raped until death must have been the only thing she longed for."

But for the Nazis, even this was not enough. With the help of collaborators of different nationalities, Germans rounded up the Jews in towns and villages across Europe and forced them to deportation centers in the cities. Jews were then packed into trains, almost always cattle cars, and sent on an arduous journey to the killing centers: Chelmno, Treblinka, Belzec, Sobibor, Majdanek, and Auschwitz. Very few survived the killing centers.

Adolf Eichmann, a ruthless "desk murderer," was the principal organizer of this death traffic. But it also required a considerable degree of cooperation among many people and many institutions, including the Transport Ministry, one of the largest government bureaucracies in Germany, and the German Railway Authority (Document 3.8). For the Jews, the journey was harrowing. Within the trains, overcrowding, heat, and thirst so debilitated the passengers that many were already dead upon arrival. By summer 1942, the fate of deported Jews became increasingly apparent, and resistance (including hiding, armed revolt, and suicide) increasingly common. When children were taken away from the ghetto in Lodz in summer 1944, they screamed, "we don't want to die."

When discussing the killing centers, historians insist on a distinction between concentration camps and extermination camps. In concentration camps, people were illegally detained, usually under inhumane conditions. In Germany, prominent concentration camps included Dachau, north of Munich, Buchenwald, near Weimar, and Sachsenhausen, just north of Berlin. In these camps, as well as in a vast system of concentration camps across Europe, hundreds of thousands of people (including political prisoners, homosexuals, Gypsies, and Jews) were either killed or died of illness and disease associated with camp life. Extermination camps, by contrast, were death camps, pure and simple. Their sole function was to kill. There were six extermination camps: Chelmno, Belzec, Sobibor, Treblinka, Auschwitz, and Majdanek. Auschwitz and Majdanek also served as concentration camps and as labor camps. All of the extermination camps were located in former Polish territory.

The Nazis constructed the first extermination camp at Chelmno, a small town northwest of Lodz. Here they used poison gas, carbon monoxide, for the first time. They forced Jews in groups of fifty to seventy into a van fitted so that the exhaust pipe ran back into the hermetically sealed compartment where the passengers were crowded. When the van drove off the Jews inside perished. At Chelmno, an estimated 300,000 Jews died. Only a few survived.

The extermination camps of Belzec, Sobibor and Treblinka were set up as part of Operation Reinhard, a program named after the recently assassinated Reinhard Heydrich and designed to exterminate the Jews of southern Poland. In these camps, Jews were killed in sealed gas chambers that were filled with carbon monoxide generated by stationary engines. As in Chelmno, there were few survivors. Historians estimate that at Belzec 600,000 Jews died, and only one person, Rudolf Reder, survived. At Sobibor, 250,000 Jews were killed. Over 100 survived, mainly because of a partly successful escape. At Treblinka nearly 800,000 Jews, including most of the Jews from the Warsaw ghetto, were killed.

Auschwitz and Majdanek were mixed camps. At Majdanek, 235,000 people were killed; at Auschwitz, a massive factory of death, around 1.1 million were killed. In Auschwitz, a selection occurred upon arrival. Some people were selected for work. Most, however, were transported directly to the gas chambers, where they were poisoned by Zyklon B (crystalline hydrogen cyanide) and their bodies subsequently burned in crematoria. Historians estimate that at least 1 million Jews died in Auschwitz, along with roughly 75,000 Poles, 21,000 Roma (Gypsies), and 15,000 Soviet prisoners of war.

The introduction of death camps marked a shift from the use of mobile killers and stationary victims (deemed "inefficient") to stationary killers and mobile victims. The nearly 800,000 Jews killed in Treblinka were murdered by fewer than 150 camp personnel (Document 3.9).

Document 3.1. Protocol of the Wannsee Conference, January 20, 1942

Reich Secret Document

30 Copies

Protocol of Conference

I. The following took part in the conference on the final solution [*Endlösung*] of the Jewish question held on January 20, 1942, in Berlin, Am Grossen Wannsee No. 56–58: Gauleiter Dr. Meyer and Reich Office Director Dr. Leibbrandt, Reich Ministry for the Occupied Eastern Territories

Secretary of State Dr. Stuckart, Reich Ministry of the Interior
Secretary of State Neumann, Plenipotentiary for the Four-Year Plan
Secretary of State Dr. Freisler, Reich Minister of Justice
Secretary of State Dr. Buehler, Office of the Governor General
Undersecretary of State Dr. Luther, Foreign Ministry
SS Oberführer Klopfer, Party Chancellery
Ministerial Director Kritzinger, Reich Chancellery
SS Gruppenführer Hofmann, Race and Settlement Main Office
SS Gruppenführer Mueller, Reich Security Main Office
SS Obersturmbannführer Eichmann, Reich Security Main Office
SS Oberführer Dr. Schoengarth, Commander of the Security Police and the
     SD in the Government-General, Security Police and the SD
SS Sturmbannführer Dr. Lange, Commander of the Security Police and the
     SD in the Generalbezirk Latvia as representative of the Commander of
     the Security Police and the SD for the Reichskommissariat for the Ostland,
     Security Police and the SD

II. The meeting opened with the announcement by the Chief of the Security Police and the SD, SS Obergruppenführer Heydrich, of his appointment by the Reich Marshal [Hermann Göring] as Plenipotentiary for the Preparation of the Final Solution of the European Jewish question. He noted that this Conference had been called in order to obtain clarity on questions of principle. The Reich Marshal's request for a draft plan concerning the organizational, practical and economic aspects of the final solution of the European Jewish question required prior joint consideration by all central agencies directly involved in these questions, with a view to maintaining parallel policy lines.

Responsibility for the handling of the final solution of the Jewish question, he said, would lie centrally with the Reichsführer SS and the Chief of the German Police (Chief of the Security Police and the SD), without regard to geographic boundaries.

The Chief of the Security Police and the SD then gave a brief review of the struggle conducted up to now against this foe. The most important elements are:

a) Forcing the Jews out of the various areas of life (*Lebensgebiete*) of the German people.
b) Forcing the Jews out of the living space (*Lebensraum*) of the German people.

In pursuit of these aims, the accelerated emigration of the Jews from the area of the Reich, as the only possible provisional solution, was pressed forward and carried out according to plan.

On instructions by the Reich Marshal, a Reich Central Office for Jewish Emigration was set up in January 1939, and its direction entrusted to the Chief of the Security Police and the SD. Its tasks were, in particular:

a) To take all measures for the *preparation* of increased emigration of the Jews;
b) To *direct* the flow of emigration;
c) To speed up emigration in *individual* cases.

The aim of this task was to cleanse the German living space of Jews in a legal manner.

The disadvantages engendered by such forced pressing of emigration were clear to all the authorities. But in the absence of other possible solutions, they had to be accepted for the time being.

In the period that followed, the handling of emigration was not a German problem alone, but one with which the authorities of the countries of destination or immigration also had to deal. Financial difficulties—such as increases ordered by the various foreign governments in the sums of money that immigrants were required to have and in landing fees—as well as lack of berths on ships and continually tightening restrictions or bans on immigration, hampered emigration efforts very greatly. Despite these difficulties a total of approximately 537,000 Jews were caused to emigrate between the [Nazi] assumption of power and up to October 31, 1941.

These consisted of the following:

> From January 30, 1933: from the *Altreich* [Germany before 1938] approx.
> 360,000
> From March 15, 1938: from the *Ostmark* [Austria] approx. 147,000
> From March 15, 1939: from the Protectorate of Bohemia and Moravia
> approx. 30,000

The financing of the emigration was carried out by the Jews or Jewish political organizations themselves. To prevent the remaining behind of proletarianized Jews, the principle was observed that wealthy Jews must finance the emigration of the Jews without means; to this end, a special assessment or emigration levy, in accordance with wealth owned, was imposed, the proceeds being used to meet the financial obligations of the emigration of destitute Jews.

In addition to the funds raised in German marks, foreign currency was needed for the monies which emigrants were required to show on arrival abroad and for landing fees. To conserve the German holdings of foreign currency, Jewish financial institutions abroad were persuaded by Jewish organizations in this country to make themselves responsible for finding the required sums in foreign currency. A total of about $9,500,000 was provided by these foreign Jews as gifts up to October 30, 1941.

In the meantime, in view of the dangers of emigration in war-time, and the possibilities in the East, the Reichsführer SS and Chief of the German Police has forbidden the emigration of Jews.

III. Emigration has now been replaced by evacuation of the Jews to the East, as a further possible solution, with the appropriate prior authorization by the Führer.

However, this operation should be regarded only as a provisional option; but it is already supplying practical experience of great significance in view of the coming final solution of the Jewish question.

In the course of this final solution of the European Jewish question approximately 11 million Jews may be taken into consideration, distributed over the individual countries as follows:

Country	Number
A. Altreich	131,800
Ostmark	43,700
Eastern Territories [districts of western	420,000
Poland annexed to the Reich]	420,000
Government-General	284,000
Bialystok	400,000
Protectorate of Bohemia and Moravia	74,200
Estonia—free of Jews	
Latvia	3,500
Lithuania	34,000
Belgium	43,000
Denmark	5,600
France: Occupied territory	165,000
France: Unoccupied territory	700,000
Greece	69,600
Netherlands	160,800
Norway	1,300
B. Bulgaria	48,000
England	330,000
Finland	2,300
Ireland	4,000
Italy, including Sardinia	58,000
Albania	200
Croatia	40,000
Portugal	3,000
Rumania, including Bessarabia	342,000
Sweden	8,000
Switzerland	18,000
Serbia	10,000
Slovakia	88,000
Spain	6,000
Turkey (in Europe)	55,500
Hungary	742,800
U.S.S.R	5,000,000
Ukraine	2,994,684
Byelorussia, without Bialystok	446,484
Total:	over 11,000,000

As far as the figures for Jews of the various foreign countries are concerned, the numbers given include only Jews by religion (*Glaubensjuden*), since the definition of Jews according to racial principles is in part still lacking there. Owing to the prevailing attitudes and concepts, the handling of this problem in the individual countries will encounter certain difficulties, especially in Hungary and Rumania. For instance, in Rumania the Jew can still obtain, for money, documents officially certifying that he holds foreign citizenship.

The influence of the Jews in all spheres of life in the U.S.S.R. is well known. There are about 5 million Jews in European Russia, and barely another 250,000 in Asiatic Russia.

The distribution of Jews according to occupation in the European area of the U.S.S.R. was roughly as follows:

Agriculture 9.1%
Urban workers 14.8%
Trade 20.0%
State employees 23.4%
Professions—medicine, press, theater, etc. 32.7%

Under appropriate direction the Jews are to be utilized for work in the East in an expedient manner in the course of the final solution. In large (labor) columns, with the sexes separated, Jews capable of work will be moved into these areas as they build roads, during which a large proportion will no doubt drop out through natural reduction. The remnant that eventually remains will require suitable treatment; because it will without doubt represent the most [physically] resistant part, it consists of a natural selection that could, on its release, become the germ-cell of a new Jewish revival. (Witness the experience of history.)

Europe is to be combed through from West to East in the course of the practical implementation of the final solution. The area of the Reich, including the Protectorate of Bohemia and Moravia, will have to be handled in advance, if only because of the housing problem and other socio-political needs.

The evacuated Jews will first be taken, group by group, to so-called transit ghettos, in order to be transported further east from there.

An important precondition, SS Obergruppenführer Heydrich noted further, for the carrying out of the evacuation in general is the precise determination of the groups of persons involved. It is intended not to evacuate Jews over 65 years old, but to place them in an old-age ghetto—Theresienstadt is being considered.

In addition to these age groups—about 30% of the 280,000 Jews who were present in the Altreich and the Ostmark on October 31, 1941, were over 65 years old—Jews with severe war injuries and Jews with war decorations (Iron Cross, First Class) will be admitted to the Jewish old-age ghetto. This suitable solution will eliminate at one blow the many applications for exceptions.

The start of the individual major evacuation Aktionen will depend largely on military developments. With regard to the handling of the final solution in the European areas occupied by us and under our influence, it was proposed that the officials dealing with this subject in the Foreign Ministry should confer with the appropriate experts in the Security Police and the SD.

In Slovakia and Croatia the matter is no longer too difficult, as the most essential, central problems in this respect have already been brought to a solution there. In Rumania the government has in the meantime also appointed a Plenipotentiary for Jewish Affairs. In order to settle the problem in Hungary, it will be necessary in the near future to impose an adviser for Jewish questions on the Hungarian Government.

With regard to setting in motion preparations for the settling of the problem in Italy, SS Obergruppenführer Heydrich considers liaison with the Police Chief in these matters would be in place. In occupied and unoccupied France the rounding-up of the Jews for evacuation will, in all probability, be carried out without great difficulties.

On this point, Undersecretary of State Luther stated that far-reaching treatment of this problem would meet with difficulties in some countries, such as the Nordic States, and that it was therefore advisable to postpone action in these countries for the present. In view of the small number of Jews involved there, the postponement will in any case not occasion any significant curtailment. On the other hand, the Foreign Ministry foresees no great difficulties for the southeast and west of Europe.

SS Gruppenführer Hofmann intends to send a specialist from the Main Office for Race and Settlement to Hungary for general orientation when the subject is taken in hand there by the Chief of the Security Police and the SD. It was decided that this specialist from the Race and Settlement Main Office, who is not to take an active part, will temporarily be designated officially as Assistant to the Police Attaché.

IV. In the implementation of the plan for the final solution, the Nuremberg Laws are to form the basis, as it were; a precondition for the total clearing up of the problem will also require solutions for the question of mixed marriages and *Mischlinge.*

The Chief of the Security Police and the SD then discussed the following points, theoretically for the time being, in connection with a letter from the Chief of the Reich Chancellery:

1. Treatment of first-degree *Mischlinge*

   First-degree *Mischlinge* are in the same position as Jews with respect to the final solution of the Jewish question. The following will be exempt from this treatment:

   a) First-degree *Mischlinge* married to persons of German blood, from whose marriages there are children (second-degree *Mischlinge*). Such second-degree *Mischlinge* are essentially in the same position as Germans.

   b) First-degree *Mischlinge* for whom up to now exceptions were granted in some (vital) area by the highest authorities of the Party and the State. Each individual case must be re-examined, and it is not excluded that the new decision will again be in favor of the *Mischlinge*. The grounds for granting an exception must always, as a matter of principle, be the deserts of the *Mischling* himself (not the merits of the parent or spouse of German blood.)

   The first-degree *Mischling* exempted from evacuation will be sterilized in order to obviate progeny and to settle the *Mischling* problem for good. Sterilization is voluntary, but it is the condition for remaining in the Reich. The sterilized *Mischling* is subsequently free of all restrictive regulations to which he was previously subject.

2. Treatment of second-degree *Mischlinge*

   Second-degree *Mischlinge* are on principle classed with persons of German blood, with the exception of the following cases, in which the second-degree *Mischlinge* are considered equivalent to Jews:

   a) Descent of the second-degree *Mischling* from a bastard marriage (both spouses being *Mischlinge*).

   b) Racially especially unfavorable appearance of the second-degree *Mischling*, which will class him with the Jews on external grounds alone.

   c) Especially bad police and political rating of the second-degree *Mischling*, indicating that he feels and behaves as a Jew.

Even in these cases exceptions are not to be made if the second-degree *Mischling* is married to a person of German blood.

3. Marriages between full Jews and persons of German blood
   Here it must be decided from case to case whether the Jewish spouse should be evacuated or whether he or she should be sent to an old-age ghetto in consideration of the effect of the measure on the German relatives of the mixed couple.

4. Marriages between first-degree *Mischlinge* and persons of German blood
   a) Without children
      If there are no children of the marriage, the first-degree *Mischling* is evacuated or sent to an old-age ghetto. (The same treatment as in marriages between full Jews and persons of German blood, [see] para. 3.)
   b) With children
      If there are children of the marriage (second-degree *Mischlinge*), they will be evacuated or sent to a ghetto, together with the first-degree *Mischlinge,* if they are considered equivalent to Jews. Where such children are considered equivalent to persons of German blood (the rule), they and also the first-degree Mischling are to be exempted from evacuation.

5. Marriages between first-degree *Mischlinge* and first-degree *Mischlinge* or Jews
   In such marriages all parties (including children) are treated as Jews and therefore evacuated or sent to an old-age ghetto.

6. Marriages between first-degree *Mischlinge* and second-degree *Mischlinge*
   Both partners to the marriage, regardless of whether or not there are children, are evacuated or sent to an old-age ghetto, since children of such marriages commonly are seen to have a stronger admixture of Jewish blood than the second-degree Jewish *Mischlinge.*
   SS Gruppenführer Hofmann is of the opinion that extensive use must be made of sterilization, as the *Mischling,* given the choice of evacuation or sterilization, would prefer to accept sterilization.

Secretary of State Dr. Stuckart noted that in this form the practical aspects of the possible solutions proposed above for the settling of the of mixed marriages and *Mischlinge* would entail endless administrative work. In order to take the biological realities into account, at any rate, Secretary of State Dr. Stuckart proposed a move in the direction of compulsory sterilization.

To simplify the problem of the *Mischlinge* further possibilities should be considered, with the aim that the Legislator should rule something like: "These marriages are dissolved."

As to the question of the effect of the evacuation of the Jews on the economy, Secretary of State Neumann stated that Jews employed in essential war industries could not be evacuated for the present, as long as no replacements were available.

SS Obergruppenführer Heydrich pointed out that those Jews would not be evacuated in any case, in accordance with the directives approved by him for the implementation of the current evacuation Aktion.

Secretary of State Dr. Buehler put on record that the Government-General would welcome it if the final solution of this problem *was begun in the Government-General,* as, on the one hand, the question of transport there played no major role and considerations of labor supply would not hinder the course of this Aktion. Jews must be removed as fast as possible from the Government-General, because it was there in particular that the Jew as carrier of epidemics spelled a great danger, and, at the same time, he caused constant disorder in the economic structure of the country by his continuous black-market dealings. Furthermore, of the approximately 2 million Jews under consideration, the majority were in any case *unfit for work.*

Secretary of State Dr. Buehler further states that the solution of the Jewish question in the Government-General was primarily the responsibility of the Chief of the Security Police and the SD and that his work would have the support of the authorities of the Government-General. He had only one request: that the Jewish question in this area be solved as quickly as possible.

In conclusion, there was a discussion of the various possible forms which the solution might take, and here both Gauleiter Dr. Meyer and Secretary of State Dr. Buehler were of the opinion that certain preparatory work for the final solution should be carried out locally in the area concerned, but that, in doing so, alarm among the population must be avoided.

The conference concluded with the request of the Chief of the Security Police and the SD to the participants at the conference to give him the necessary support in carrying out the tasks of the [final] solution.

Source: Electronic files, Documents of the Holocaust, pt. 2, Poland, document 117, at yadvashem.org (retrieved November 2001).

Document 3.2. Images of the Warsaw Ghetto

Figure 3.2a. Warsaw ghetto: Jewish child dying on the sidewalk. Steidel Verlag, Goettingen, courtesy of Gunther Schwarberg.

Figure 3.2b. Warsaw ghetto: Victims of starvation. Steidel Verlag, Goettingen, courtesy of Gunther Schwarberg.

Document 3.3. Excerpt from the Warsaw Ghetto Diary of Avraham Levin, Friday, June 5, 1942

One of the most surprising side-effects of this war is the clinging to life, the almost total absence of suicides. People die in great numbers of starvation, the typhus epidemic or dysentery, they are tortured and murdered by the Germans in great numbers, but they do not escape from life by their own desire. On the contrary, they are tied to life by all their senses, they want to live at any price and to survive the war. The tensions of this historic world conflict are so great that all wish to see the outcome of the gigantic struggle and the new regime in the world, the small and the great, old men and boys. The old have just one wish: the privilege of seeing the end and surviving Hitler.

I know a Jew who is all old age. He is certainly about 80. Last winter a great tragedy befell the old man. He had an only son who was about 52. The son died of typhus. He has no other children. And the son died. He did not marry a second time and lived with his son. A few days ago I visited the old man. When I left—his mind is still entirely clear—he burst out crying and said: "I want to see the end of the war, even if I live only another half an hour!"

Why should the old man wish so much to stay alive? There it is: even he wants to live, "if only half an hour" after the last shot is fired. This is the burning desire of all the Jews.

Source: A. Levin, *Mi-Pinkaso shel ha-More mi-Yehudiya* (From the notebook of the teacher from Yehudiya) (Beit Lohameiha-Geta'ot, 1969), 70, electronic files, Documents of the Holocaust, pt. 2, Poland, document 89, at yadvashem.org (retrieved November 2001).

Document 3.4. Chaim Rumkowski's Address on the Deportation of the Children from the Lodz Ghetto, September 4, 1942

The ghetto has been struck a hard blow. They demand what is most dear to it—children and old people. I was not privileged to have a child of my own and therefore devoted my best years to children. I lived and breathed together with children. I never imagined that my own hands would be forced to make this sacrifice on the altar. In my old age I am forced to stretch out my hands and to beg: "Brothers and sisters, give them to me!—Fathers and mothers, give me your children . . ." (Bitter weeping shakes the assembled public). . . . Yesterday, in the course of the day, I was given the order to send away more than 20,000 Jews from the ghetto, and if I did not—"we will do it ourselves." The question arose: "Should we have accepted this and carried it out ourselves, or left it to others?" But as we were guided not by the thought: "how many will be lost?" but "how many can be saved?" we arrived at the conclusion—those closest to me at work, that is, and myself— that however difficult it was going to be, we must take upon ourselves the carrying out of this decree. I must carry out this difficult and bloody operation, I must cut off limbs in order to save the body! I must take away children, and if I do not, others too will be taken, God forbid . . . (terrible wailing).

I cannot give you comfort today. Nor did I come to calm you today, but to reveal all your pain and all your sorrow. I have come like a robber, to take from you what is dearest to your heart. I tried everything I knew to get the bitter sentence canceled. When it could not be canceled, I tried to lessen the sentence. Only yesterday I ordered the registration of nine-year-old children. I wanted to save at least one year—children from nine to ten. But they would not yield. I succeeded in one thing—to save the children over ten. Let that be our consolation in our great sorrow.

There are many people in this ghetto who suffer from tuberculosis, whose days or perhaps weeks are numbered. I do not know, perhaps this is a satanic plan, and perhaps not, but I cannot stop myself from proposing it: "Give me these sick people, and perhaps it will be possible to save the healthy in their place." I know how precious each one of the sick is in his home, and particularly among Jews. But at a time of such decrees one must weigh up and measure who should be saved, who can be saved and who may be saved.

Common sense requires us to know that those must be saved who can be saved and who have a chance of being saved and not those whom there is no chance to save in any case.

Source: Isaiah Trunk, *Lodzsher Geto* (Lodz Ghetto) (New York, 1962), 311–12, electronic files, Documents of the Holocaust, pt. 2, Poland, document 129, at yadvashem.org (retrieved November 2001).

Document 3.5. The Jäger Report

The Commander of
the Security Police and
the SD
Einsatzkommando 3   Kauen [Kaunas], 1 December 1941

Secret Reich Business!

5 copies
4th copy

Complete list of executions carried out in the EK 3 Area
up to 1 December 1941.

Security police duties in Lithuania taken over by Einsatzkommando 3 on 2 July 1941.

(The Wilna [Vilnius] area was taken over by EK 3 on 9 Aug. 1941, the Schaulen area on 2 Oct. 1941. Up until these dates EK 9 operated in Wilna and EK 2 in Schaulen.)

On my instructions and orders the following executions were conducted by Lithuanian partisans:

| 4.7.41 | Kauen–Fort VII – 416 Jews, 47 Jewesses | 463 |
| 6.7.41 | Kauen–Fort VII – Jews | 2,514 |

Following the formation of a raiding squad under the command of SS-Obersturmführer Hamann and 8–10 reliable men from the Einsatzkommando the following actions were conducted in cooperation with Lithuanian partisans:

7.7.41	Mariampole	Jews	32
8.7.41	Mariampole	14 Jews, 5 Comm. officials	19
8.7.41	Girkalinei	Comm. officials	6
9.7.41	Wendziogala	32 Jews, 2 Jewesses, 1 Lithuanian (f.), 2 Lithuanian Comm., 1 Russian Comm.	38
9.7.41	Kauen–Fort VII –	21 Jews, 3 Jewesses	24
14.7.41	Mariampole	21 Jews, 1 Russ., 9 Lith. Comm.	31
17.7.41	Babtei	8 Comm. officials (inc. 6 Jews)	8
18.7.41	Mariampole	39 Jews, 14 Jewesses	53
19.7.41	Kauen–Fort VII –	17 Jews, 2 Jewesses, 4 Lith. Comm., 2 Comm. Lithuanians (f.), 1 German Comm.	26

21.7.41	Panevezys	59 Jews, 11 Jewesses, 1 Lithuanian (f.),	
		1 Pole, 22 Lith. Comm., 9 Russ. Comm.	103
22.7.41	Panevezys	1 Jew	1
23.7.41	Kedainiai	83 Jews, 12 Jewesses, 14 Russ. Comm.,	
		15 Lith. Comm., 1 Russ. O-Politruk	125
25.7.41	Mariampole	90 Jews, 13 Jewesses	103
28.7.41	Panevezys	234 Jews, 15 Jewesses, 19 Russ. Comm.,	
		20 Lith. Communists	288
		Total carried forward	3,384

		Sheet 2	
		Total carried over:	3,384
29.7.41	Rasainiai	254 Jews, 3 Lith. Communists	257
30.7.41	Agriogala	27 Jews, 11 Lith. Communists	38
31.7.41	Utena	235 Jews, 16 Jewesses, 4 Lith.	
		Comm., 1 robber/murderer	256
11/31.7.41	Wendziogala	13 Jews, 2 murderers	15
August:			
1.8.41	Ukmerge	254 Jews, 42 Jewesses, 1 Pol.	
		Comm., 2 Lith. NKVD	
		agents, 1 mayor of Jonava	
		who gave order to set fire to Jonava	300
2.8.41	Kauen–Fort VII –	170 Jews, 1 US Jew, 1 US Jewess,	
		33 Jewesses, 4 Lith. Communists	209
4.8.41	Panevezys	362 Jews, 41 Jewesses, 5 Russ. Comm.,	
		14 Lith. Communists	422
5.8.41	Rasainiai	213 Jews, 66 Jewesses	279
7.8.41	Uteba	483 Jews, 87 Jewesses, 1 Lithuanian	
		(robber of corpses of German	
		soldiers)	571
8.8.41	Ukmerge	620 Jews, 82 Jewesses	702
9.8.41	Kauen–Fort IV–	484 Jews, 50 Jewesses	534
11.8.41	Panevezys	450 Jews, 48 Jewesses, 1 Lith. 1 Russ. C.	500
13.8.41	Alytus	617 Jews, 100 Jewesses, 1 criminal	719
14.8.41	Jonava	497 Jews, 55 Jewesses	552
15 and	Rokiskis	3,200 Jews, Jewesses, and J. Children,	
16.8.41		5 Lith. Comm., 1 Pole, 1 partisan	3,207

9 to 16.8.41	Rassainiai	294 Jewesses, 4 Jewish children	298
27.6 to 4.8.41	Rokiskis	493 Jews, 432 Russians, 56 Lithuanians (all active communists)	981
18.8.41	Kauen–Fort IV –	689 Jews, 402 Jewesses, 1 Pole (f.), 711 Jewish intellectuals from Ghetto in reprisal for sabotage action	1,812
19.8.41	Ukmerge	298 Jews, 255 Jewesses, 1 Politruk, 88 Jewish children, 1 Russ. Communist	645
22.8.41	Dünaburg	3 Russ. Comm., 5 Latvians, incl. 1 murderer, 1 Russ Guardsman, 3 Poles, 3 gypsies (m.), 1 gypsy (f.), 1 gypsy child, 1 Jew, 1 Jewess, 1 Armenian (m.), 2 Politruks (prison inspection in Dünanburg	21
		Total carried forward	16,152

Sheet 3
Total carried over: 16,152

22.8.41	Aglona	Mentally sick: 269 men, 227 women, 48 children	544
23.8.41	Panevezys	1,312 Jews, 4,602 Jewesses, 1,609 Jewish children	7,523
18 to 22.8.41	Kreis Rasainiai	466 Jews, 440 Jewesses, 1,020 Jewish children	1,926
25 and 26.8.41	Obeliai	112 Jews, 627 Jewesses, 421 Jewish children	1.160
25 and 26.8.41	Seduva	230 Jews, 275 Jewesses, 159 Jewish children	664
26.8.41	Zarasai	767 Jews, 1,113 Jewesses, 1 Lith. Comm., 687 Jewish children, Russ. Communist (f.)	2,569
28.8.41	Pasvalys	402 Jews, 738 Jewesses, 209 Jewish children	1,349
26.8.41	Kaisiadorys	All Jews, Jewesses and Jewish children	1,911
27.8.41	Prienai	All Jews, Jewesses and Jewish children	1,078
27.8.41	Dagda and Kraslawa	212 Jews, 4 Russ. POWs	216

27.8.41	Joniskia	47 Jews, 165 Jewesses, 143 Jewish children	355
28.8.41	Wilkia	76 Jews, 192 Jewesses, 134 Jewish children	402
28.8.41	Kedainiai	710 Jews, 767 Jewesses, 599 Jewish children	2,076
29.8.41	Rumsiskis and Ziezmariai	20 Jews, 567 Jewesses, 197 Jewish children	784
29.8.41	Utena and Moletai	582 Jews, 1,731 Jewesses, 1,469 Jewish children	3,782
13 to 31.8.41	Alytus and environs	233 Jews	233

September:

| 1.9.41 | Mariampole | 1,763 Jews, 1,812 Jewesses, 1,404 Jewish children, 109 mentally sick, 1 German subject (f.), married to a Jew, 1 Russian (f.) | 5,090 |

| | | Total carried forward | 47,814 |

Sheet 4

| | | Total carried over: | 47,814 |

28.8 to 2.9.41	Darsuniskis	10 Jews, 69 Jewesses, 20 Jewish children	99
	Carliava	73 Jews, 113 Jewesses, 61 Jewish children	247
	Jonava	112 Jews, 1,200 Jewesses, 244 Jewish children	1,556
	Petrasiunai	30 Jews, 72 Jewesses, 23 Jewish children	125
	Jesuas	26 Jews, 72 Jewesses, 46 Jewish children	144
	Ariogala	207 Jews, 260 Jewesses, 195 Jewish children	662
	Jasvainai	86 Jews, 110 Jewesses, 86 Jewish children	282
	Babtei	20 Jews, 41 Jewesses, 22 Jewish children	83
	Wenziogala	42 Jews, 113 Jewesses, 97 Jewish children	252
	Krakes	448 Jews, 476 Jewesses, 97 Jewish children	1,125
4.9.41	Pravenischkis	247 Jews, 6 Jewesses	253
	Cekiske	22 Jews, 64 Jewesses, 60 Jewish children	146
	Seredsius	6 Jews, 61 Jewesses, 126 Jewish children	193
	Velinona	2 Jews, 71 Jewesses, 86 Jewish children	159
	Zapiskis	47 Jews, 118 Jewesses, 13 Jewish children	178

5.9.41	Ukmerge	1,123 Jews, 1,849 Jewesses, 1,737 Jewish children	4,709
25.8 to 6.9.41	Mopping up in Rasainiai	16 Jews, 412 Jewesses, 415 Jewish children	843
	in Georgenburg	all Jews, all Jewesses, all Jewish children	412
9.9.41	Alytus	287 Jews, 640 Jewesses, 352 Jewish children	1,279
9.9.41	Butrimonys	67 Jews, 370 Jewesses, 303 Jewish children	740
10.9.41	Merkine	223 Jews, 640 Jewesses, 276 Jewish children	854
10.9.41	Varena	541 Jews, 141 Jewesses, 149 Jewish children	831
11.9.41	Leipalingis	60 Jews, 70 Jewesses, 25 Jewish children	155
11.9.41	Seirijai	229 Jews, 384 Jewesses, 340 Jewish children	953
12.9.41	Simnas	68 Jews, 197 Jewesses, 149 Jewish children	414
11 and 12.9.41	Uzusalis	Reprisal against inhabitants who fed Russ.partisans; some in possession of weapons	43
26.9.41	Kauen–F.IV	412 Jews, 615 Jewesses, 581 Jewish children (sick and suspected epidemic cases)	1,608
		Total carried forward	66,159

		Sheet 5	
		Total carried over:	66,159
October:			
2.10.41	Zagare	633 Jews, 1,107 Jewesses, 496 Jewish chil. (as these Jews were being led away a mutiny arose, which was however immediately put down; 150 Jews were shot immediately; 7 partisans wounded)	2,236
4.10.41	Kauen–F.IX –	315 Jews, 712 Jewesses, 818 Jewish children (Reprisal after German police officer shot in ghetto)	1,845

29.10.41	Kauen–F.IX –	2,007 Jews, 2,920 Jewesses, 4,273 Jewish children (mopping up ghetto of superfluous Jews)	9,200

November:

3.11.41	Lazdijai	485 Jews, 511 Jewesses, 539 Jewish children	1,535
15.11.41	Wilkowiski	36 Jews, 48 Jewesses, 31 Jewish children	115
25.11.41	Kauen–F.IX –	1,159 Jews, 1,600 Jewesses, 175 Jewish children (resettlers from Berlin, Munich and Frankfurt am Main)	2,934
29.11.41	Kauen–F.IX –	693 Jews, 1,155 Jewesses, 152 Jewish children (resettlers from Vienna and Breslau)	2,000
29.11.41	Kauen–F.IX	17 Jews, 1 Jewess, for contravention of ghetto law, 1 Reichs German who converted to the Jewish faith and attended rabbinical school, then 15 terrorists from the Kalinin group	34

EK 3 detachment in Dünanberg in the period 13.7–21.8.41:		9,012 Jews, Jewesses and Jewish children, 573 active Communists	9,585

EK 3 detachment in Wilna:			
12.8 to 1.9.41	City of Wilna	425 Jews, 19 Jewesses, 8 Communists (m.), 9 Communists (f.)	461
2.9.41	City of Wilna	864 Jews, 2,019 Jewesses, 817 Jewish children (Sonderaktion because German soldiers shot at by Jews)	3,700
		Total carried forward	99,084

Sheet 6

		Total carried over:	99,084
12.9.41	City of Wilna	993 Jews, 1,670 Jewesses, 771 Jewish children	3,334
17.9.41	City of Wilna	337 Jews, 687 Jewesses, 247 Jewish children and 4 Lith. Communists	1,271

20.9.41	Nemencing	128 Jews, 176 Jewesses, 99 Jewish children	403
22.9.41	Novo-Wilejka	468 Jews, 495 Jewesses, 196 Jewish children	1,159
24.9.41	Riesa	512 Jews, 744 Jewesses, 511 Jewish children	1,767
25.9.41	Jahiunai	215 Jews, 229 Jewesses, 131 Jewish children	575
27.9.41	Eysisky	989 Jews, 1,636 Jewesses, 821 Jewish children	3,446
30.9.41	Trakai	366 Jews, 483 Jewesses, 597 Jewish children	1,446
4.10.41	City of Wilna	432 Jews, 1,115 Jewesses, 436 Jewish children	1,983
6.10.41	Semiliski	213 Jews, 359 Jewesses, 390 Jewish children	962
9.10.41	Svenciany	1,169 Jews, 1,840 Jewesses, 17 Jewish children	3,726
16.10.41	City of Wilna	382 Jews, 507 Jewesses, 257 Jewish children	1,146
21.10.41	City of Wilna	718 Jews, 1,063 Jewesses, 586 Jewish children	2,367
25.10.41	City of Wilna	— Jews, 1,776 Jewesses, 812 Jewish children	2,578
27.10.41	City of Wilna	946 Jews, 184 Jewesses, 73 Jewish children	1,203
30.10.41	City of Wilna	382 Jews, 789 Jewesses, 362 Jewish children	1,553
6.11.41	City of Wilna	340 Jews, 749 Jewesses, 252 Jewish children	1,341
19.11.41	City of Wilna	76 Jews, 77 Jewesses, 18 Jewish children	171
19.11.41	City of Wilna	6 POWs, 8 Poles	14
20.11.41	City of Wilna	3 POWs	3
25.11.41	City of Wilna	9 Jews, 46 Jewesses, 8 Jewish children, 1 Pole for possession of arms and other military equipment	64

EK 3 detachment
in Minsk from
28.9–17.10.41:

Pleschnitza	620 Jews, 1,285 Jewesses,	
Bischolin	1,126 Jewish children and 19 Comm.	
Scak		
Bober		
Uzda		3,050
		133,346

Prior to EK 3 taking over security police duties, Jews liquidated by pogroms and executions (including partisans)	4,000
Total	137,346

Sheet 7

Today I can confirm that our objective, to solve the Jewish problem for Lithuania, has been achieved by EK 3. In Lithuania there are no more Jews, apart from Jewish workers and their families. . . The distance from the assembly point to the graves was on average 4 to 5 km.

Sheet 8 . . .

I consider the Jewish action more or less terminated as far as Einsatz-kommando 3 is concerned. Those working Jews and Jewesses still available are needed urgently and I can envisage that after the winter this workforce will be required even more urgently. I am of the view that the sterilization programme of the male worker Jews should be started immediately so that reproduction is prevented. If despite sterilization a Jewess becomes pregnant she will be liquidated. . . .

(signed) Jäger
SS-Standartenführer

Source: Reprinted with permission of The Free Press, a Division of Simon & Schuster, Inc. Ernst Klee, Willi Dressen, and Volker Riess, eds., from *"The Good Old Days": The Holocaust as Seen by Its Perpetrators and Bystanders,* translated by Deborah Burnstone. © 1988 by S. Fischer Verlag, Gmblt. Translation © 1993 by Deborah Burnstone.

Document 3.6. Testimony of Hermann Graebe, November 10, 1945

Accompanied by Moennikes, I then went to the work area. I saw great mounds of earth about 30 meters long and 2 high. Several trucks were parked nearby. Armed Ukrainian militia were making people get out, under the surveillance of SS soldiers. The same militia men were responsible for guard duty and driving the trucks. The people in the trucks wore the regulation yellow pieces of cloth that identified them as Jews on the front and back of their clothing.

Moennikes and I went straight toward the ditches without being stopped. When we neared the mound, I heard a series of rifle shots close by. The people from the trucks—men, women and children—were forced to undress under the supervision of an SS soldier with a whip in his hand. They were obliged to put their effects in certain spots: shoes, clothing, and underwear separately. I saw a pile of shoes, about 800–1,000 pairs, great heaps of underwear and clothing. Without weeping or crying out, these people undressed and stood together in family groups, embracing each other and saying goodbye while waiting for a sign from the SS soldier, who stood on the edge of the ditch, and also held a whip in his hand, too. During the fifteen minutes I stayed there, I did not hear a single complaint, or plea for mercy. I watched a family of about eight: a man and woman about fifty years old, surrounded by their children of about one, eight, and ten, and two big girls about twenty and twenty-four. An old lady, her hair completely white, held the baby in her arms, rocking it, and singing it a song. The infant was crying aloud with delight. The parents watched the groups with tears in their eyes. The father held the ten-year-old boy by the hand, speaking softly to him: the child struggled to hold back his tears. Then the father pointed a finger to the sky, and, stroking the child's head, seemed to be explaining something. At this moment, the SS man near the ditch called something to his comrade. The latter counted off some twenty people and ordered them behind the mound. The family of which I have just spoken was in the group. I still remember the young girl, slender and dark, who, passing near me, pointed at herself, saying, "Twenty-three." I walked around the mound and faced a frightful common grave. Tightly packed corpses were heaped so close together that only the heads showed. Most were wounded in the head and the blood flowed over their shoulders. Some still moved. Others raised their hands and turned their heads to show that they were still alive. The ditch was two-thirds full. I estimate that it held a thousand bodies. I turned my eyes toward the man who had carried out the execution. He was an SS man; he was seated, legs swinging, on the narrow edge of the ditch; an automatic rifle rested on his knees and he was smoking a cigarette. The people, completely naked, climbed down a few steps cut in the clay wall and stopped at the spot indicated by the SS man. Facing the dead and wounded, they spoke softly to them. Then I heard a series of rifle shots. I looked in the ditch and saw their bodies contorting, their heads, already inert, sinking on the corpses beneath. The blood flowed from the nape of their necks. I was astonished not to be ordered away, but I noticed two or three uniformed postmen nearby. A new batch of victims approached the place. They climbed down into the ditch, lined up in front of the previous victims, and were shot.

Source: *Trial of the Major War Criminals Before the International Military Tribunal* (Nuremberg: The Tribunal, 1948), vol. 31, *Documents and Other Material in Evidence,* 446–48 (2992–PS).

Document 3.7. Excerpts from *There Once Was a World* by Yaffa Eliach

Eishyshock (the Yiddish name for Ejszyszki, as it is known in Polish, and Eisiskes in Lithuanian) had been home not just to my family and to several thousand other Jews just before the Holocaust, but home to generation upon generation of Jews, going back to the eleventh century. In fact, Eishyshock is the site of one of the oldest Jewish settlements in that part of the world. My paternal ancestors had been among the first five Jewish families to settle there in that long-ago time, and their descendants had lived on its soil for all the centuries since then, under all the various governments that had fought for control of it: Lithuanian, Polish, German, Russian, and Soviet. But now, in the post-Holocaust era, it was for the first time in all those hundreds of years a town without Jews.

Nine hundred years of Jewish history in Eishyshok had been wiped out. In Eishyshok, as elsewhere in Poland and Lithuania, nearly a millennium of vibrant Jewish life had been reduced to stark images of victimization and death. . . .

In this shtetl as in so man others, the Jews lived and thrived in the midst of pagan, Muslim, and Christian neighbors, managing to be both of that world and apart from it for many centuries. By maintaining a strict adherence to their own customs, they created a Jewish homeland thousands of miles from the original homeland, a kind of Jerusalem of the spirit. Napoleon himself is said to have called nearby Vilna the Jerusalem of Lithuania on account of the strong ethnic identity of its Jewish population. Perhaps at no time since the destruction of the Second Temple in Jerusalem in 70 C.E., and at no other place in the Diaspora, had there been more successfully autonomous and intact set of Jewish institutions than those preserved in the shtetlekh of Eastern Europe.

Every stage of life in the shtetl—birth, circumcision, bar mitzvah, marriage, divorce, death and burial—was observed according to ancient law and tradition. So complete was the immersion in pre-Diaspora Jewish culture that the children of Eishyshok perceived the very topography of their surroundings as being a replica of the ancient land of Israel. In their lively imaginations, the local Kantil stream was the Jordan River, the plaza that was home to the synagogue and the two houses of study was Mount Moriah, the sacred ground of the Temple in Jerusalem.

But even though Eishyshok was a place whose very heart and soul were dedicated to religion—with a bit of superstition thrown in the mix—its people, like Lithuanian shtetl-dwellers in general, were so intellectually rigorous and questioning that other Jews expressed doubts about their piety. Hence the popular Yiddish expression "Litvak zelem-kop," an almost untranslatable phrase meaning, literally, "Lithuanian cross-head." It conveys the notion that every Lithuanian Jew has a little Christian cross inside his head. (It also conveys, in even more untranslatable fashion, the extreme stubbornness of Lithuanian Jews, who are known for never yielding to another opinion.)

If they were sometimes stubborn and unyielding, they were also openhearted. Eishyshok's Jews supported the yeshivah in their midst with a generosity so extraordinary that they were frequently invoked as models of devotion to Torah-learning.

But these generous people were also such aggressive traders that they were known as albe levones—half moons—because they would even try to buy the dark side of the moon. In short, Eishyshkians were complicated, contradictory, multifaceted, and fascinating, true representatives of the family of man in all its complexity and beauty.

Source: Yaffa Eliach. *There Once Was a World: A Nine-Hundred-Year Chronicle of the Shtetl of Eishyshok* (Boston: Little, Brown, 1998), 3, 6–7. By permission of Little, Brown, and Company, Inc.

Document 3.8. German Railway Schedule, January 16, 1943

[Note: The following document is an excerpt from a schedule for "special trains." In the language of the German Railway Authority, the term *special trains* merely designated trains that did not run according to the usual schedule. These trains, however, were carrying Jews to Auschwitz and Treblinka, as the destination, as well as the designation, reveals. Da (*Durchgangszüge für Aussiedler*) refers to through trains for people, typically Jews, being deported from Germany and western Europe. Thus, for example, Da 13 is a "special train" of Jews leaving Berlin Moabit at 17:20 P.M. on January 29 and arriving in Auschwitz the next morning at 10:48 A.M. Da 15 is the same train a week later. Other designations of importance to this train schedule include Vd (ethnic Germans), Rm (Romanians), Po (Poles), Pj (Polish Jews), Lp (empty passenger trains). The composition of the trains can be read from column 2. Psn, Op, and Dre are district train centers (Posen, Oppeln, Dresden); B and C refer to second and third class, respectively. Thus 1 B means one second-class car; 15 C means fifteen third-class cars. G refers to freight cars (*Güterwagen*). Train number 107, for example, is from the district of Dresden; it has twenty-one third-class cars and a freight car; it is bringing two thousand people from Theresienstadt to Auschwitz; the train is then emptied, and it returns to Theresienstadt as an empty passenger train.

The stationmasters to whom this telegram was sent understood the designations and therefore required no special clarification. Note the number of German train stations informed about the schedule. Note also that this document does not contain even the lowest level of security clearance.]

German Railroad
General Operations Management East
PW 113 Bfsv
Telegraphic letter
III
To the RBD [Railroad Managements]
Berlin, Breslau, Dreden, Erfurt, Frankfurt, Halle(s),
Karlsruhe, Koenigsberg (Pr), Linz, Mainz, Oppeln
East Frankfurt (M), Posen, Vienna,, General Management of the
East RR ni Cracow, Reichsprotectorate, RR. Group in Prague
GVD Warsaw, RVD Minsk, GBL Munich, GBL West Essen
each 3 x

Regarding: Special train for deportees during the time from 20 January to 28 February 1943. We will send a compilation of the specials trains agreed upon on 15 January 1943 in Berlin for deportees (Vd, Rm, Po, Pj and Da) during the period 20 January to 28 February 1943, and a rotation schedule for servicing these trains and the wagons to be used. The formation of trains is to be reported throughout the rotation and to be observed. After each trip the wagons are to be thoroughly cleaned, if need be disinfected, and after the end of the program to be made ready for future utilization.

Signed D. Jacobi
ROI

GBL East Berlin
PW 113 Bf sv of 16 January, 1943
Train Schedule

For the repeated utilization of freight trains for special trains [sdz] transporting deportees (Vd, Rm, Po, Pj, Da) in the period of 20.1 to 18.2.1943

1	2	3	4	5	6	7
Number	Train	Date	Train	From	To	No. of passengers
121	Psn 21 C	5/6.2.	Pj 107	Bialystok 9.00	Auschwitz 7.57	2000
		7/8.2.	Lp 108	Auschwitz	Bialystok	
		9.2.	Pj 127	Bialystok 9.00	Treblinka 12.10	2000
		9.2.	Lp 128	Treblinka 21.18	Bialystok 1.30	
		11.2.	Pj 131	Bialystok 9.00	Treblinka 12.10	2000
		11.2.	Lp 132	Treblinka 21.18	Bialystok 1.3	
		13.2.	Pj 135	Bialystok 9.00	Treblinka 12.10	2000
		13.2.	Lp 136	Treblinka 21.18	Bialystok 1.30	

1 Number	2 Train	3 Date	4 Train	5 From	6 To	7 No. of passengers
122	Psn 21 C	6/7.2.	Pj 109	Bialystok 9.00	Auschwitz 12.10	2000
		8/9.2.	Lp 110	Auschwitz	Bialystok	
		10.2.	Pj 129	Bialystok 9.00	Treblinka 12.10	2000
		10.2.	Lp 130	Treblinka 21.18	Bialystok 1.30	
		12.2.	Pj 133	Bialystok 9.00	Treblinka 12.10	2000
		12.2.	Lp 134	Treblinka 21.18	Grodno	
		14.2.	Pj 163	Grodno 5.40	Treblinka 12.10	2000
		14.2.	Lp 164	Treblinka	Scherfenwiese	
123	Psn 21 C	7/8.2.	Pj 111	Bialystok	Auschwitz	
		8.2	Lp 112	Auschwitz	Myslowitz	
126	Gedob 1 BC 16 C	25/26.1.	Po 61	Zamocz 8.20	Berlin Whgen 17.30	1000
		29/30.1.	Da 13	Berlin Mob 17.20	Auschwitz 10.48	1000
		31.1./1.2.	Lp 14	Auschwitz	Zamocz	
		3.2	Po 65	Zamocz	Auschwitz	1000
		4.2.	Lp 66	Auschwitz	Myslowitz	
127	Gedob 1 BC 16 C	29/30.1.	Po 63	Zamocz 8.20	Berlin Whgen 17.30	1000
		2/3.2	Da 15	Berlin Mob 17.20	Auschwitz 10.48	1000
		4/5.2.	Lp 16	Auschwitz	Litzmannstadt	
128	Dre 21 C 1 G	20/21.1	Da 101	Theresienstadt	Auschwitz	2000
		21/22.1	Lp 102	Auschwitz	Theresienstadt	
		23/24.1.	Da 103	Th	Au	2000
		24/25.1.	Lp 104	Au	Th	
		26/27.1.	Da 105	Th	Au	2000
		27/28.1.	Lp 106	Au	Th	
		29/30.1.	Da 107	Th	Au	2000
		30.31.1.	Lp 108	Au	Th	
		1.2	Da 109	Th	Au	2000
		2.2	Lp 110	Auschwitz	Myslowitz	

Source: Bundesarchiv-Außenstelle Ludwigsburg (BarchLB), Sig. UdSSR, Bd. 108, Bl.323–25 (film 2, Bild-Nr. 27818–278207). Reprinted with permission of the Bundesarchiv.

Document 3.9. Abraham Kszepicki on Treblinka

The square where we sat was guarded on all sides. By a telephone pole were two notice boards. I read the announcements on them printed in large letters: "Jews of Warsaw, Attention. . . ." These were instructions for people arriving at a labor camp; they were told to deposit their clothes for disinfecting and were promised that money and valuable would be returned. . . . An SS man arrived and selected ten young men out of our group; he didn't want older men. A while later another SS man demanded sixty men; I was among that group. They marched us two by two through the square we had traversed when we left the freight cars, then to the right, to a larger square, where we were confronted by a staggering sight: a huge number of corpses, lying one next to the other. I estimate there were 20,000 corpses there . . . most of whom had suffocated in the freight cars. Their mouths remained open, as if they were gasping for another breath of air. . . . Hundreds of meters away, a scoop-shovel dug large quantities of earth from the ditches. We saw a lot of Jews busy carrying the bodies to these huge ditches, row upon row. A group of laborers were pouring chlorine on the corpses. . . . I should mention that those buried at this square were not gas-chamber victims, but rather the bodies removed from the transports and those who had been shot at Treblinka. . . . Often we heard pistols shooting and bullets whistling. We didn't hear the screams of those shot; the Germans fired at the nape of the neck and the victim never moaned. . . .

The German who brought us to work had the impression that one of the youths in our group was working sloppily. He took his rifle from his shoulder, and before the youth knew what was happening, he was no longer alive. A few minutes later the same thing happened with another Jew, shot by a Ukrainian, who took a packet of money from the man he shot. . . . Within a short time, only ten men remained in our group. . . . At night another transport arrived at the camp. We ran toward the cars. I was shocked. All the cars were filled only with the dead—asphyxiated. They were lying on top of one another in layers, up to the ceiling of the freight car. The sight was so awful, it is difficult to describe. I asked where the transport had come from; it turned out from Miedzyrec. . . . There was nowhere to place the corpses. Near the railroad tracks were large piles of clothing, and under these were still unburied bodies. We laid the bodies in layers, near the railway. Occasionally, moans could be heard from under the piles of clothes as people recovered consciousness and asked in a weak voice for water. There was nothing we could do to help; we were dying of thirst ourselves. . . . Those still alive were moved to the side, nearer to the clothes. It was dark, and the Germans didn't notice. Among those living I found a baby, a year or a year and a half old, who had woken up and was crying loudly. I left him by the side. In the morning he was dead.

Source: Yitzhak Arad, *Belzec, Sobibor, Treblinka: The Operation Reinhard Death Camps* (Bloomington: Indiana University Press, 1987), 85–86.

Questions

Document 3.1. Protocol of the Wannsee Conference, January 20, 1942

1. The high-ranking Nazi officers attending the Wannsee Conference were all highly educated men calmly discussing "the final solution to the Jewish question." What does it mean to be an "educated" person? What specific characteristics does this kind of person have?
2. The document states, country by country, the number of Jews to be included in the "final solution of the European Jewish question." Why does the list include the 200 Jews of Albania? What does this reveal about Nazi ideology? How do these documents reflect the Nazis passion for efficiency, secrecy, and deception during the killing process?
3. The Nazis used the following euphemisms to refer to the killing of Jews in the death camps: *evacuation, the Final Solution, liquidated, made free of Jews, resettlement, special actions, treated appropriately.* Why?

Document 3.2. Images of the Warsaw Ghetto

1. How do these photographs reflect the human dimension of the Nazi's decision to make the ghettos temporary through the techniques of severe overcrowding and deliberate starvation?
2. Do these photographs of individuals move you more than other kinds of document? Why?

Document 3.3. Excerpt from the Warsaw Ghetto Diary of Avraham Levin, Friday, June 5, 1942

1. Is survival in extreme conditions, as described in Levin's diary, an act of resistance? In the Warsaw ghetto many Jews broke the "law" by writing poetry, newspapers, and plays. Are these examples acts of resistance even though they are not violent?
2. How would you define *resistance*?

LINKS

Document 3.4. Chaim Rumkowski's Address on the Deportation of the Children from the Lodz Ghetto, September 4, 1942

1. What questions come to mind when you read Rumkowski's address? What does this address tell us about the choices facing the Jews in Europe?
2. The literary critic Geoffrey Hartman has written of the Lodz ghetto: "The tragedy here is that there is no tragedy." What does he mean? Consider that in tragedy the hero makes choices that have momentous consequences (but he or she, at least, has choices).

LINKS

Document 3.5. The Jäger Report

1. In Lithuania very few Jews were deported to death camps because the mobile killing units murdered over 95 percent of the Jewish population by the end of 1941. What does this say about the ideology of the Germans and their collaborators?
2. Describe the moral universe of the man who wrote this report.
3. Using the Internet, go to www.jewishgen.org and click on ShtetlSeeker. This is a Web-based version of the book *Where Once We Walked: A Guide to the Jewish Communities Destroyed in the Holocaust,* edited by Gary Mokotoff and Sallyann Amdur Sack (Teaneck, N.J.: Avotaynu, 1991). Type in the names of some of the towns listed in the Jäger report. Using the Internet and other sources, what can you find out about these towns?

LINKS

Document 3.6. Testimony of Hermann Graebe, November 10, 1945

1. How does this eyewitness testimony personalize the number of number of Jews killed by town?
2. Which part of this account is most powerful to you?

LINKS

Document 3.7. Excerpts from *There Once Was a World* by Yaffa Eliach

1. The community of Eishyshok is listed on sheet 6 of Document 3.5, the Jäger report, by its German name, Eysisky. It is also the subject of one of the most moving exhibits of the Holocaust Memorial Museum in Washington, D.C. The exhibit is called "The Tower of Life" and includes sixteen hundred photographs from Eishyshok, many of which appear in *There Once Was a World*. Compare the account in Document 3.7, and if possible the photographic images in "The Tower of Life," with the one laconic entry on sheet 6 of the Jäger report.
2. How is Eishyshok like your town or neighborhood? How is it different?

LINKS

Document 3.8. German Railway Schedule, January 16, 1943

1. What does this train schedule tell us about how many people were actively involved in carrying out the Holocaust?
2. Are the individuals who worked for the German Railway Authority innocent bystanders or guilty accomplices to murder? Why?

LINKS

Document 3.9. Abraham Kszepicki on Treblinka

1. How was the killing done at Treblinka different from what preceded it?
   What does this difference suggest about the differences between the
   Holocaust and other genocides?

Further Reading

Arad, Yitzhak. *Belzec, Sobibor, Treblinka: The Operation Reinhard Death Camps.*
    Bloomington: Indiana University Press, 1987.
Browning, Christopher. *Ordinary Men: Reserve Police Battalion 101 and the Final
    Solution in Poland.* New York: HarperCollins, 1992.
Clendinnen, Inge. *Reading the Holocaust.* New York: Cambridge University
    Press, 1999.
Eliach, Yaffa. *There Once Was a World: A Nine-Hundred-Year Chronicle of the Shtetl
    of Eishyshok.* Boston: Little, Brown, 1998.
Gutman, Yisrael, and Michael Berenbaum, eds. *Anatomy of the Auschwitz Death
    Camp.* Bloomington: Indiana University Press, 1994.
Hilberg, Raul. *The Destruction of the European Jews.* Student edition. New York:
    Holmes & Meier, 1985.
The Holocaust Chronicle: A History in Words and Pictures. Lincolnwood, Ill.:
    Publications International, 2000. Available online at:
    holocaustchronicle.org.
United States Holocaust Memorial Museum. *Historical Atlas of the Holocaust.*
    New York: Macmillan, 1995.

4
Resistance and Rescue

Initially, the Nazi war machine bore down on Jewish communities through out eastern Europe with speed and overwhelming force. For most Jews there was no easy way to flee. Moreover, several factors militated against escape. At first, most Jews did not know their fate. Once they did, it was often too late. One must remember in this context that mass killings of a people in industrial killing centers had never happened before. Yes, there had been pogroms, massacres, and, in Armenia, even genocide. But never with this degree of ruthlessness and efficiency. For the Jews of Europe, and for those sympathetic to their plight, seeing what was before them demanded that they imagine the unimaginable. It was easier, however, to cling to other possibilities. Furthermore, the Nazis provisioned the last hopes of the Jews of Europe by the constant use of euphemism and deceit, telling them, for example, that they were being sent to work camps.

The Jews also were isolated. Especially in eastern Europe, they lived among hostile populations. When Jews hid in holes dug in the woods of Poland, Polish peasants often revealed their hiding places to the German occupiers. When they asked to hide in barns, they were sometimes turned in. But not always. Despite the threat of severe penalties, including death at the hands of the occupiers, some Poles helped Jews, either by keeping quiet or by taking them into their homes and barns (often for fees). According to one estimate, a little more than 1 percent of the Jews of Poland survived in hiding. In places farther east, the situation seemed equally desperate, especially for Jews who had not escaped to the Soviet Union at the beginning of the war. The peoples of Lithuania, Latvia, and the Ukraine were even less willing to hide Jews than were the people of Poland.

Paradoxically, the cohesiveness of Jewish families and communities often undermined attempts to escape and to offer resistance. Husbands were unwilling to flee if this meant leaving their wives and children behind. Sons and daughters would not abandon their elderly parents. Elie Wiesel, in his powerful memoir *Night*, writes that in Auschwitz his only thought was to hold onto his father. He was not alone in this determination. Resistance, moreover, was often met with severe reprisal, not only against the resister but also against his or her family and in some instances the whole community.

Still, there was resistance. In many ghettos, Jews desperately attempted to smuggle in arms and to resist with force. Twenty-four ghettos in western and central Poland had an underground of armed resistance; in northeastern Poland, armed resistance was more widespread still. In addition, in some ghettos, notably Minsk, many of the young men and women were able to escape and to join armed Jewish partisans in the forests. It is estimated that there were twenty thousand to thirty thousand armed Jewish partisans fighting in the woods, hampering German operations. The largest group, the so-called Bielski partisans (named after their leader, Tuvia Bielski), counted hundreds of families among its members.

Both within ghetto walls and outside of the ghettos, armed Jewish partisans engaged Nazi troops in battle. For the Jews, these battles were as heroic as they were doomed from the start. They were also fraught with dilemmas. Would armed resistance, which had only the slightest chance of success, not invite still harsher measures against the multitude of Jews still alive? "Were we entitled to offer people up in flames?" Abba Kovner, a resister in the Vilna ghetto, asked himself, even as the ghetto was about to be liquidated.

The most famous uprising occurred in the Warsaw ghetto. It started April 19, 1943, when the Jews of the ghetto refused to show up for deportation. Instead the roughly 750 men and women resolved to fight the Nazis. Many of them had revolvers and a few had rifles and a store of Molotov cocktails. But that was not enough. They faced numerically superior German troops equipped with heavy artillery and tanks. Under the command of General Jürgen Stroop, the German units reduced the ghetto to rubble, killing many of the people in hiding and many of the Jewish resisters in bunkers. Still, as Mordecai Anielewicz, the commander of the Warsaw ghetto revolt, wrote in his last letter, dated April 23, 1943: "Jewish armed resistance and revenge are facts. I have been a witness to the magnificent, heroic fighting of Jewish men in battle."

Revolts also occurred in the concentration camps and in the death camps, most notably in Sobibor, Treblinka and Auschwitz. In Sobibor, a revolt led by a Jewish Soviet officer nearly succeeded, and sixty people (of six hundred) escaped. In Treblinka a rebellion broke out involving hundreds of prisoners; historians estimate that seventy escaped. In Auschwitz, Jewish women, who engaged in myriad acts of resistance, had smuggled explosives to the "Sonderkommando," the inmates who worked in the crematoria (Document 4.1). The Jewish resisters hoped that the Sonderkommando would blow up the furnaces and thus halt the killings. In October 1944, members of the Sonderkommando did, in fact, destroy a crematorium and attempt a break. Most were captured and killed, a few got away; the killing did not abate and one crematorium was burned.

Jewish resistance, though heroic, could never have delivered the Jews from the clutches of threatened annihilation. For that, the Jews depended on those around them and on the military might of the countries fighting the Germans. But here they encountered staggering indifference, sometimes even hostility.

The story is particularly dismaying with respect to the Allies, and especially Great Britain and the United States. Members of the government of each of these countries knew early on that the Germans were committing atrocities. In August 1941, the British government intercepted codes from the German Order Police describing mass executions following the invasion of the Soviet Union. The British continued to intercept these codes throughout the war and shared them, though selectively, with the U.S. government. By March 1942 there were already reports documenting the privation and extraordinarily high death rate of the Jews in the Warsaw ghetto. And in June the Office of Strategic Services of the U.S. government received a detailed report on the situation in Warsaw, beginning with the statement: "Germany is no longer persecuting the Jews; it is systematically exterminating them." In early August the State Department learned of systematic killing in the extermination camps. That fall, the details only became more concrete, the information more exact. Meanwhile, the killing went on at a furious pace. On December 17, 1942, the Allied governments publicly condemned the murders and stated that those responsible "shall not escape retribution."

But they could have done much more. Part of the problem was the paucity of public awareness of the Holocaust. The American press was loath to publish reports that were not fully substantiated, and when they did run stories of the systematic killing of Jews they seldom put the articles on the front page. Thus, for example, on June 30, 1942, the *Nashville Tennessean* printed an Associated Press article on page 12 of the morning edition with the headline "1,000,000 Jews Said Killed by Germans" (Document 4.2). It is the most detailed article that this newspaper devoted to the killing of the Jews during the war. In its neglect, the *Nashville Tennessean* was not exceptional. Even the *New York Times* placed news of the Holocaust on the front page on only a few occasions. Americans could also read about the Holocaust in news magazines such as the *New Republic, Nation, Christian Century,* and even *Time* and *Newsweek*. Yet for various reasons, questions of credibility foremost among them, U.S. newspapers and news magazines avoided featuring the Holocaust as a central news item. One must ask why more journalists did not pursue the story, and why more readers did not demand clarification. Here the U.S. State Department only made matters worse. Starting in January 1943, it began to actively withhold information from the public.

A still larger problem was with the British Foreign Office, which, under the leadership of Anthony Eden, undermined almost any initiative to save the Jews of Europe. In summer 1943, for example, Eden had ruled out as "fantastically impossible" a proposal to publicly request that Hitler allow the Jews to leave Europe. He also undermined any attempt to intervene on behalf of the seventy thousand Jews of Bulgaria, arguing that there were not enough ships to transport them and, if the offer were made to Bulgaria, the Jews will want the Allies to make similar offers for the Jews of Poland. There were other proposals. One was to exchange German prisoners of war for five thousand Jewish children from Poland. The British rejected it. The Jews were not British nationals, Foreign Office officials argued. Another possibility was to exchange sixty thousand Jews in Rumania for private money to be deposited by Jewish organizations. The U.S. State Department dragged its heels, but after eight months of deliberation, provisionally acceded to the idea. But the British did not. The policy of the Western Allies was to concentrate on the military struggle, and to eschew any measures, including rescue, that might conceivably divert resources from the successful prosecution of the war.

The best chance to save Jewish lives involved the deportation of the Jews of Hungary. On January 22, 1944, President Franklin D. Roosevelt had established the War Refugee Board, thus centralizing efforts to save the victims. When a new government was installed in Hungary in March 1944, deportations to the killing centers in Poland began. Here was a chance to do something. By now, moreover, the U.S. and British governments could no longer be in doubt about the nature of the killing process. They had received detailed memoranda stating the capacity of the crematoria and the prodigious numbers of people murdered every day in the gas chambers of Auschwitz. In this context, and with the German Army in desperate retreat, Adolf Eichmann, the man in charge of organizing the deportations, offered a deal, probably on the orders of his superior, Heinrich Himmler. Though made through questionable channels, the deal was clear enough: one truck for every thousand Jews, a total of ten thousand trucks to save a million Jewish lives. A combination of understandable mistrust of the Nazi government, a great deal of diplomatic incompetence, the opposition of the British government, and general Allied policies against negotiation undermined the deal. The exchange, trucks for lives, never happened. By July 1944 most of the Jews of Hungary were dead.

Meanwhile, the Allies advanced. In spring 1944, U.S. bombers, starting from bases in Italy, could now reach Auschwitz. On April 4, 1944, a reconnaissance mission took photographs of the oil refineries and rubber works run by I. G. Farben at Auschwitz III (Monowitz). The gas chambers were visible in the corners of the photographs. But they were overlooked. In June 1944 John J. McCloy, then assistant secretary of war, argued against bombing the main camps, stating that bombing would divert "considerable air support," that it would be "of doubtful efficacy," and that it "might provoke even more violent action by the Germans." Nevertheless, in August, September, and December, Auschwitz was bombed. But not the death camp. Rather, American planes dropped tons of explosives on the oil refineries and rubber works of Auschwitz III. The killing process was unaffected.

Large-scale rescues by the Allies may have failed, but smaller-scale rescues, involving great acts of courage, succeeded. In Denmark, the population refused to hand over the Jews for deportation. Instead, the Danish underground arranged for the transport of more than seven thousand Jews to safety in Sweden. One man alone, Aage Bertelson, a teacher, organized a rescue operation that saved seven hundred people. In Bulgaria, the government, though anti-Semitic, similarly refused to turn over the Jews of the older part of the country to the Nazis for deportation. As a result, most of Bulgaria's fifty thousand Jews were saved. Bulgaria did, however, turn over the twelve thousand Jews in the new territories (Thrace and Macedonia) it had acquired in its position as a satellite state of the Third Reich.

Rescue occurred even in Berlin in the heart of Nazi Germany. In late February 1943, the German government rounded up Jewish men married to non-Jewish German women. The wives staged a public protest in front of the Rosenstrasse incarceration facility, where their Jewish husbands were detained. Embarrassed by the public protest, Nazi leaders released the men. The Rosenstrasse incident raises the question whether more such resistance would have stopped the deportations and the killing. Germans had demonstrated against euthanasia with a measure of success.

On August 13, 1941, the Bishop of Münster, Clemens August Count von Galen, delivered a public sermon in which he denounced Nazi killings of people with disabilities (Document 4.3). "Never under any circumstances may a human being kill an innocent person apart from war and self-defense," von Galen admonished. The text of his sermon was printed in thousands of copies and distributed throughout Germany and, by dint of its being printed in excerpts in foreign newspapers, it reached the wider world as well. It may even have had an effect, as the Nazis stopped killing those with disabilities in Germany soon after. Yet historians argue that the Nazis stopped such killings when they effectively reached their quotas. By September 1, 1941, they had killed more than seventy thousand people with disabilities in Germany. After the German invasion of the Soviet Union, many would be killed in the east as well.

Galen's protest raises the question of what was possible. Because the leaders of Nazi Germany did not want to antagonize the Catholic Church, Galen was not arrested (though some of the priests who spread his word were). The protest is revealing when juxtaposed with the widespread silence of October and December 1941, when Jews were made to wear yellow stars and subsequently deported.

But not everyone was silent in the face of Jewish deportation. A village in France showed what compassion could achieve. In the Huguenot village Le Chambon-sur-Lignon, the local population harbored five thousand Jews: for every inhabitant a life saved. Once a persecuted minority themselves, the Huguenots of the village showed compassion because their religion, and their humanity, demanded it (Document 4.4). Or, as they more simply put it: "Things had to be done and we happened to be there to do them. It was the most natural thing in the world to help these people."

There were other stories. In Israel, the Yad Vashem Department for the Righteous Among the Nations, which honors those who helped, currently counts 18,269 people who have been documented as having helped Jews. Yad Vashem honors non-Jewish persons who risked their lives, freedom, or safety "in order to rescue one or several Jews from the threat of death or deportation to death camps without exacting in advance monetary compensation." As of January 1, 2001, the following countries could claim more than one hundred people among the righteous:

Poland	5,503
Netherlands	4,376
France	2,008
Ukraine	1,609
Belgium	1,247
Hungary	530
Russia and Belarus	503
Lithuania	488
Czech Republic and Slovakia	464
Germany	342
Italy	287
Greece	234
Countries of former Yugoslavia	220

But during the long night of the Holocaust, the points of light were still too few. For every person showing compassion, there were many more who turned a blind eye, who eagerly plundered the property the Jews left behind, who energetically assisted not the Jews but their persecutors.

Study of the Holocaust requires that we understand what led people to deeds of malice, to callousness, to indifference, and to an unwillingness to see what was happening before them. It also demands that we try to understand why people lacked the courage to look closer, and, seeing the murder in their midst, why they lacked the courage to care, and then to act.

But we also are obliged to ask another question. As Elie Wiesel has formulated it: "Why did that unknown person choose to stand between a Jewish family and its enemy? What motivated him or her, what made him or her different from so many others?"

Document 4.1. Olga Lengyel, Resister in Auschwitz

Oppression as violent as that under which we lived automatically provokes resistance. Our entire existence in the camp was marked by it. When the employees of "Canada" detoured items destined for Germany to the benefit of their fellow internees, it was resistance. When laborers at the spilling mills dared to slacken their work pace, it was resistance. When at Christmas we organized a little "festival" under the noses of our masters, it was resistance. When, clandestinely, we passed letters from one camp to another, it was resistance. When we endeavored, and sometimes with success, to reunite two members of the same family, for example, by substituting one internee for another in a gang of stretcher bearers—it was resistance.

These were the principal manifestations of our underground activity. It was not prudent to go further. Yet there were many acts of rebellion. One day a selectee wrested a revolver from an S.S. and started to beat him with it. Desperate courage certainly expressed this gesture, but it had no effect except to bring mass reprisals. The Germans held us all guilty; "collective responsibility" they called it. The beatings and the gas chamber explain, in part, why the history of the camp includes few open revolts, even when mothers were forced to surrender their children to death. In December, 1944, the Russian and Polish internees had been ordered to give up their babies. The order said they were to be "evacuated." Pitiful scenes followed: mothers distraught with grief hung crosses or improvised medals around the necks of their infants to be able to recognize them later. They shed bitter tears and abandoned themselves to despair. But there was no rebellion, not even suicide.

But an organized underground thrived. It sought to express itself in countless ways—from the broadcast of a "spoken newspaper," the sabotage practiced in the workshops devoted to war industries, and later to the destruction of the crematory oven by explosives.

We were not heroes, and never claimed to be. We did not merit any Congressional Medals, Croix de Guerre, or Victoria Crosses. True, we undertook dangerous missions. But death and the so-called danger of death had a different meaning for us who lived in Auschwitz-Birkenau. Death was always with us, for we were always eligible for the daily selections. One nod might mean the end for any of us. To be late for roll call might mean only a slap in the face, or it might mean, if the S.S. became enraged, that he took out his Luger and shot you. As a matter of fact, the idea of death seeped into our blood. We would die, anyway, whatever happened. We would be gassed, we would be burned, we would be hanged, or we would be shot. The members of the underground at least knew that if they died, they would die fighting for something.

In the beginning I did not know much of the nature of the enterprise in which I was participating. But I knew that I was doing something useful. That was enough to give me the strength. I was no longer prey to crises of depression. I even forced myself to eat enough to be able to fight on. To eat and not let oneself become enfeebled—that, too, was a way to resist.

We lived to resist and we resisted to live.

Source: Olga Lengyel, *Five Chimneys: The Story of Auschwitz* (Chicago: Chiff Davis, 1947), 154–58. Reprinted by permission of Academy Chicago.

Document 4.2. From Page 12 of the *Nashville Tennessean*, June 30, 1942: 1,000,000 Jews Said Killed by Germans

London, June 29 (AP) —The Germans have massacred more than 1,000,000 Jews since the war began in carrying out Chancellor Adolf Hitler's proclaimed policy of exterminating the race, spokesmen for the World Jewish Congress charged today.

They said the Nazis have established a "vast slaughterhouse for Jews" in Eastern Europe, and that reliable reports showed that 700,000 Jews already have been murdered in Lithuania and Poland, 125,000 in Rumania, 200,000 in Russia, and 100,000 in the rest of Europe. Thus about one sixth of the pre-war Jewish population in Europe estimated at 6,000,000 to 7,000,000 persons, has been wiped out in less than three years.

A report to the Congress said that Jews were being shot by firing squads at the rate of 1,000 daily and that almost another 1,000,000 were imprisoned in ghettos surrounded by eight-foot walls, topped with broken glass and electrified barbed wire.

Additionally, the Germans were said to have set up reserves to which Eastern European Jews are being systematically deported for slave labor. Residents of ghettos and reserves live under the most appalling conditions of poverty, disease and hunger, with food rations about one quarter of that allowed the general Polish population it was charged.

Other spokesmen said the entire male Jewish population in Rumania had been pressed into compulsory labor, and that the executions of hundreds of Jews in Czecho-Slovakia had been a common occurrence even before the assassination of Reinhard Heydrich.

The 800,000 Jews in Hungary were reported to have been driven out of employment, with legislation pending in that country for their deportation. In Italy all Jews are drafted for forced labor, while Spain has restored anti-Jewish legislation of the pre-Republican period, a spokesman said.

Source: William R. Downs, "1,000,000 Jews Said Killed by Germans," *Nashville Tennessean,* June 30, 1942, 12. Reprinted with permission of The Associated Press.

Document 4.3. Bishop of Münster, Clemens August Count von Galen, Protests "Euthanasia" Killings, August 3, 1941

Never under any circumstances may a human being kill an innocent person apart from war and legitimate self-defense. If you establish and apply the principle that you can kill "unproductive" fellow human beings then woe betide us all when we become old and frail! . . . woe betide loyal soldiers who return to the homeland seriously disabled, as cripples, as invalids. If it is once accepted that people have the right to kill "unproductive" fellow humans—and even if it only initially affects the poor defenseless mentally ill—then as a matter of principle murder is permitted for all unproductive people. . . .

Then, it is only necessary for some secret edict to order that the method developed for the mentally ill should be extended to other "unproductive" people, that it should be applied to those suffering from incurable lung disease, to the elderly who are frail or invalids, to the severely disabled soldiers. Then none of our lives will be safe any more. Some commission can put us on the list of the "unproductive," who in their opinion have become worthless life. And no police force will protect us and no court will investigate our murder and give the murderer the punishment he deserves. Who will be able to trust his physician any more? He may report his patient as "unproductive" and receive instructions to kill him. It is impossible to imagine the degree of moral depravity, of general mistrust that would then spread even through families if this dreadful doctrine is tolerated, accepted and followed.

Source: Michael Burleigh and Wolfgang Wippermann, *The Racial State: Germany, 1933–1945* (New York: Cambridge University Press, 1991), 152–53. Reprinted with permission of Cambridge University Press

Document 4.4. Magda Trocmé (of Le Chambon-sur-Lignon) in *The Courage to Care*

A poor woman came to my house one night, and she asked to come in. She said immediately that she was a German Jew, that she was running away, that she was hiding, that she wanted to have shelter. She thought that at the minister's house she would perhaps find someone who could understand her. And I said, "Come in." And so it started. I did not know that it would be dangerous. Nobody thought of that.

But all at once, many people were in the village. When you hear that there are nice people who will receive you in their homes in a certain place, and you think you are in danger—and later when you really are in danger— you will do anything to get there. But there was no advertisement. They just came.

Those of us who received the first Jews did what we thought had to be done—nothing more complicated. It was not decided from one day to the next what we would have to do. There were many people in the village who needed help. How could we refuse them? A person doesn't sit down and say I'm going to do this and this and that. We had no time to think. When a problem came, we had to solve it immediately. Sometimes people ask me, "How did you make a decision?" There was no decision to make. The issue was: "Do you think we are all brothers or not? Do you think it is unjust to turn in the Jews or not? Then let us try to help!"

It was not something extraordinary. Now that the years have gone by, perhaps we exaggerate things a little, although I can tell you that things did get complicated later. But in the beginning, when the first Jew came to my house, I just opened the door and took her in without knowing what would happen later. It was even simpler than one might suppose. . . .

Yes, there were dangers, but up until then, nothing had happened. More and more we would disobey. We had a habit of doing it. One day, finally, the governor—the prefect of the Department of the Haute-Loire—Monsieur Bach, came and said to my husband, "Now you must give the names of all the Jews that are here." It was at that time that the Jews had to put on the sign, the yellow star.

My husband said, "No, I cannot. First, I do not know their names"—they often changed their names—"and I don't know who they are. And second, these Jews, they are my brothers."

"No," Monsieur Bach said, "they are not your brothers. They are not of your religion. They are not of your country."

"No, you are wrong," André responded. "Here, they are under my protection." . . .

I was asked lots of times to speak about these things, to say what the lesson was that we must learn from all of this. The lesson is very simple, I think. The first thing is that we must not think that we were the only ones who helped during these times. Little by little, now that we speak of these things, we realize that other people did lots of things too. Also, we must not be afraid to be discussed in books or in articles and reviews, because it may help people in the future to try to do something, even if it is dangerous. Perhaps there is also a message for young people and for children, a message of hope, of love, of understanding, a message that could give them the courage to go against all that they believe is wrong, all that they believe is unjust.

Maybe later on in their lives, young people will be able to go through experiences of this kind—seeing people murdered, killed, or accused improperly; racial problems; the problem of the elimination of people, of destroying perhaps not their bodies but their energy, their existence. They will be able to think that there always have been some people in the world who tried—who will try—to give hope, to give love, to give help to those who are in need, whatever the need is.

It is important, too, to know that we were a bunch of people together. This is not a handicap, but a help. If you have to fight it alone, it is more difficult. But we had the support of people we knew, of people who understood without knowing precisely all that they were doing or would be called to do. None of us thought that we were heroes. We were just people trying to do our best.

When people read this story, I want them to know that I tried to open my door. I tried to tell people, "Come in, come in." In the end, I would like to say to people, "Remember that in your life there will be lots of circumstances that will need a kind of courage, a kind of decision of your own, not about other people but about yourself." I would not say more.

Source: Carol Rittner and Sondra Myers, eds., *The Courage to Care: Rescuers of Jews During the Holocaust* (New York: New York University Press, 1986), 100–107.

Questions

————

Document 4.1. Olga Lengyel, Resister in Auschwitz

1. What were the central dilemmas of resistance?
2. Why did not more people resist?

LINKS

————

Document 4.2. From Page 12 of the *Nashville Tennessean*, June 30, 1942: 1,000,000 Jews Said Killed by Germans

1. Why do you think the *Nashville Tennessean* placed this Associated Press article on page 12?
2. Research the nearest big city newspaper and try to locate that paper's coverage of the Holocaust. The most likely days of coverage include June 29–30, 1942; November 25, 1942 (when Rabbi Stephen S. Wise, chairman of the World Jewish Congress, announced that two million Jews had already been killed); July 3–9, 1944 (reports on Auschwitz); and August 30–31, 1944 (when foreign correspondents were allowed to see the extermination center at Majdanek, which the Red Army had liberated).

LINKS

Document 4.3. Bishop of Münster, Clemens August Count von Galen, Protests "Euthanasia" Killings, August 3, 1941

1. How do such appeals undermine the "racist state"?
2. What does this document tell you about the possibilities of resistance?
3. Why was such a principled response not forthcoming about the killing of Jews?

LINKS
IV. Ethics   13.4. How Does Good Happen?   239

Document 4.4. Magda Trocmé (of Le Chambon-sur-Lignon) in *The Courage to Care*

1. What is the difference between those who looked the other way and those who, like Magda Trocmé, helped?
2. How is Le Chambon-sur-Lignon like your town or neighborhood? How is it different?

LINKS
IV. Ethics   13.4. How Does Good Happen?   239

Further Reading

Bauer, Yehuda. *Jews for Sale? Nazi-Jewish Negotiations, 1933–1945*. New Haven: Yale University Press, 1994.

Breitman, Richard. *Official Secrets: What the Nazis Planned, What the British and Americans Knew*. New York: Hill and Wang, 1998.

Fogelman, Eva. *Conscience and Courage: Rescuers of Jews During the Holocaust*. New York: Doubleday, 1994.

Hilberg, Raul. *Perpetrators, Victims, Bystanders: The Jewish Catastrophe, 1933–1945*. New York: HarperCollins, 1992.

Lipstadt, Deborah. *Beyond Belief: The American Press and the Coming of the Holocaust, 1933–1945*. New York: Free Press, 1986.

Rittner, Carol, and Sondra Myers, eds. *The Courage to Care*. New York: New York University Press, 1986.

Tec, Nechama. *Defiance: The Bielski Partisans*. New York: Oxford University Press, 1993.

———. *When Light Pierced the Darkness: Christian Rescue of Jews in Nazi-Occupied Poland*. New York : Oxford University Press, 1986.

Wyman, David S. *The Abandonment of the Jews: America and the Holocaust, 1941–1945*. New York: Pantheon Books, 1984.

Timeline

1247	Ritual murder charge at Fulda.
1274	Pope Gregory X refutes the existence of Jewish ritual murder in a papal bull. Nevertheless, the charges continue throughout the medieval period.
1523–44	Martin Luther writes pamphlets, first for, then against, the Jews.
1791	In the throes of the French Revolution, the French National Assembly passes the Emancipation Decree granting Jews equal rights with other French citizens.
1812	First Emancipation Edict making Jews citizens of Prussia is promulgated. Jews are given certain rights in exchange for their assimilation to Christian ways.
1871	Second German Empire established. All Jews are granted equal rights under the law, though in practice discrimination continues.
1873	William Marr publishes a pamphlet that makes popular the word *anti-Semitism,* denoting hatred of the Jews as a separate race rather than as followers of a separate religion.
1881–82	Severe pogroms are undertaken in Russia, leading to the first great migration of European Jews to the United States.
Aug. 1, 1914	World War I begins.
Nov. 9, 1918	Germany capitulates, ending World War I.
Nov. 9, 1923	Adolf Hitler and other Nazis attempt to take over the Bavarian government in Munich in what comes to be called the "Beer Hall Putsch."
Jan. 30, 1933	Hitler takes over the chancellorship of Germany. Prior to the "seizure of power," the Nazi Party had received up to 37 percent of the vote in a free election.

Sept. 15, 1935	The Nuremberg Laws are decreed.
Nov. 9–10, 1938	Crystal Night pogrom takes place in Germany and Austria. Subsequently more than thirty thousand Jews are sent to concentration camps.
Sept. 1, 1939	Germany invades Poland, starting World War II.
Oct. 8, 1939	The first Jewish ghetto in Poland is set up.
Nov. 15, 1940	The Warsaw ghetto is sealed.
June 22, 1941	Nazi Germany invades the Soviet Union.
June 23, 1941	Mobile killing units (*Einsatzgruppen*) begin massacres.
July 21, 1941	Hermann Göring signs an order giving Reinhard Heydrich the authority to prepare a "total solution" to the Jewish question.
Sept. 1, 1941	The euthanasia program, which began in October 1939, is officially ended. Between 70,000 and 93,000 people with disabilities were killed.
Sept. 3, 1941	First experimental gassing is carried out on Soviet prisoners of war at Auschwitz.
Sept. 19, 1941	The Jews of Germany are forced to wear the Star of David.
Sept. 29–30, 1941	At Babi Yar, Einsatzkommando 4a kills 33,771 Jews from Kiev.
Dec. 8, 1941	The systematic extermination of Jews at Chelmno, the first extermination camp, begins.
July 22, 1942	The extermination camp Treblinka is completed and mass deportation of the Jews of the Warsaw ghetto, 265,000 of whom would die at Treblinka, begins.
Sept. 12, 1942	The Battle of Stalingrad begins.
May 2, 1944	The first transport of the Jews of Hungary arrives in Auschwitz.
June 6, 1944	Allies land on the beaches of Normandy.
July 23, 1944	Soviet forces arrive at the extermination camp Majdanek, where 360,000 inmates, mostly Jews, have died. Five hundred people are still alive.
Jan. 17, 1945	Warsaw is liberated. The German SS orders the evacuation of Auschwitz and the "death march" begins.
Jan. 27, 1945	Soviet troops reach Auschwitz.
April 11, 1945	U.S. forces liberate Buchenwald.
May 8, 1945	Allied victory in Europe. World War II ends.

Glossary

Anti-Semitism. Popularized by Wilhelm Marr in 1879, the word refers to racial, as opposed to religious, hatred of Jews.

Concentration camps. Camps in which people were detained without due process of law. The Nazi state ran roughly nine thousand such camps and subcamps, in which prisoners suffered inhumane conditions, brutal guards, and death. The camp system included labor camps, transit camps, prisoner of war camps, and extermination camps.

Crystal Night. Government-instigated pogrom or violence against Jews and their property that took place in Germany and Austria on the night of November 9–10, 1938. It is also referred to as the Night of Broken Glass, the November Pogrom of 1938, and, by its German name, Kristallnacht.

Adolf Eichmann. Responsible for organizing the transport of European Jews to their death in the extermination camps of Nazi-occupied Poland.

Einsatzgruppen. German word for mobile killing units, the heavily armed death squads, staffed mainly by the SS, who killed more than 2.2 million Jews.

Extermination camps. Also called death camps. The phrase refers specifically to six camps in occupied Poland—Chelmno, Belzec, Sobibor, Treblinka, Majdanek, and Auschwitz—whose central purpose was killing Jews.

Final Solution (*Endlösung*). Nazi euphemism for the intention to kill all the Jews of Europe.

Hermann Göring. Nominally the number two man in the Nazi hierarchy, he was also the head of the German Air Force (Luftwaffe) and chief of the Four Year Plan to make Germany ready for war.

Reinhard Heydrich. Head of the SD, the Security Service of the SS, and the right-hand man of Heinrich Himmler. In this capacity, he also organized the mobile killing units (*Einsatzgruppen*) and was central to the implementation of the Final Solution.

Heinrich Himmler. Head of the SS, the "elite" police unit of Nazi Germany, who was in charge of the concentration camps.

Adolf Hitler. Head of the Nazi Party and, from 1933 to 1945, chancellor and de-facto dictator of Germany.

Jewish Councils. Established on the order of the Nazis and made up of Jewish leaders who tried, usually unsuccessfully, to ameliorate the plight of their fellow Jews in Jewish communities throughout Europe.

Mein Kampf. (My Struggle). Book written by Adolf Hitler in 1924 stating his racist views and his program for European domination.

Mischling(e). (racially mixed person[s]) In Nazi Germany a racist term for the son or daughter of interfaith parents.

Nazi Party. The abbreviated term for Hitler's party, the NSDAP (the National Socialist German Workers Party).

Nuremberg Laws. Issued in 1935, the laws defined Jews as a race separate from Germans, deprived them of their civil rights, and outlawed marriage and sexual contact between German non-Jews and Jews.

Pogrom. Russian word that means devastation. The term was used to refer to violent mob attacks, usually against unarmed Jewish civilians.

SA. Abbreviation for Sturm Abteilung (Storm Troopers), also known as Brownshirts, the paramilitary organization of the Nazi Party.

SD. Abbreviation for Sicherheitsdienst (Security Service) of the SS. Many of the officers of the SD served in the *Einsatzgruppen* (mobile killing units).

SS. Abbreviation for Schutzstaffel (Protection Squad). Originally Hitler's body guard, it became the "elite" unit of the Nazi state and was centrally responsible for carrying out the extermination of the Jews of Europe.

Star of David. Beginning in September 1941, the German government forced German Jews to wear the Star of David for easy identification as Jews. The Star of David had been a symbol of Judaism, and in particular Zionism, since the late nineteenth century.

Third Reich (Third Empire). The name Hitler gave to his regime, proclaiming that it would last a thousand years, though it lasted twelve years (1933–45). The purpose of this name, which was taken from the title of a book by Arthur Moeller van der Bruck, was to separate the new German empire from the Weimar Republic, which preceded it, and to place Nazi Germany in the tradition of the Holy Roman Empire (the First Reich) and Imperial Germany, 1871–1918 (the Second Reich).

Wannsee Conference. Conference of Nazi leaders in Berlin that convened on January 20, 1942, to coordinate the extermination of European Jews.

Warsaw ghetto. Largest Jewish ghetto in Poland. Established by the Nazis on October 12, 1940, it contained within its walls nearly half a million people. It was also the site of a heroic Jewish uprising against German forces.

Part II
Representations of the Holocaust
in the Arts

In the epilogue to *Beloved*, her Pulitzer Prize–winning novel about the traumatic history of slavery, Toni Morrison writes, "This is not a story to be passed on." This injunction against storytelling not only undercuts the novel's insistence on speaking the unspeakable but also undercuts Morrison's own act of storytelling. Why would Morrison warn her audience against passing on a tale that she herself has just told? The double meaning of the term *pass on*—to tell again or to pass by—registers the paradoxical dilemma of the novel: slavery is not a tale to be told or a tale to be passed by. The terrors of slavery are simultaneously not to be remembered and not to be forgotten. As Morrison states, "You are condemned to repeat the mistakes [of the past] if you do not fully understand them. And that's true for black people as well as whites. In the move toward a life here, we didn't want to dwell on slavery. You can't absorb it; it's too terrible. So you just try to put it behind you. It's a perfect dilemma. Forgetting is unacceptable. Remembering is unacceptable" (*U.S. News and World Report*, October 19, 1987). The character Beloved becomes the spectral embodiment of this dilemma: she represents a traumatic history that can never be completely spoken or silenced, a history that can never be fully understood. By foregrounding the difficulty of telling this story, Morrison insists that the horrors of history can never be fully represented or assimilated even as she argues for the necessity of bearing witness to this unspeakable past.

Morrison's meditation on the difficulty and necessity of resurrecting the debilitating history of slavery also speaks to the issues involved in representing and remembering the Holocaust and other genocides: can we make meaning in the face of the horrors of the Holocaust? How can we represent events that shatter all meaning? Is it possible to remember historical trauma without being overcome or destroyed by it? What is art's role in re-presenting traumatic history? These are difficult questions with many different answers. In the chapters that follow we provide a wide range of approaches and responses to these questions from different artistic media: language, literature, memorials, photography, and film. In each chapter, we address how the unspeakable gets spoken. The Holocaust challenges art's ability to "make meaning." As an event that defies the imagination, it cannot be encompassed by conventional methods of representation. It constantly exceeds the very frames of reference being used to explain it. For example, when Art Spiegelman finally represents Auschwitz at the end of volume 1 of *Maus*, he breaks the cartoon frame. His picture of Auschwitz seems to spread beyond the borders of the book. His cartoon frames, then, draw our attention to how he is framing the story; his violation of these frames suggests that the story he is telling exceeds any act of explanation or containment. Spiegelman, like many of the other artists we discuss in this part, refuses to simplify the complexity of the traumatic history of the Holocaust by registering the impossibility of making sense of it. His narrative marks its own limits of understanding even as it bears witness to the horror. The Holocaust, like other historical traumas, may remain beyond the reach of meaning but still it must be remembered. As Morrison insists, art may not redeem the traumas of history but it does provide a route toward their articulation.

5
Language and the Holocaust

We often take language for granted. Conventionally we view our words as pictures of the world and as bearers of meaning to be communicated and understood. We assume responsibility for the words we utter because the freedom to speak is not the freedom from responsibility.

When we address the relationship between language and the Holocaust, however, we are confronted by a regime, the Third Reich, that regularly employed language to dissemble, deceive, and deny responsibility. We are also dealing with events that defy description in conventional phrases. How can we speak about the unspeakable?

Consider the address by Heinrich Himmler, the head of the SS, the elite police unit of Nazi Germany, to his officers in Posen on October 1943. During his three-hour speech Himmler devoted ten minutes to the "evacuation of the Jews," which he described as "a glorious page in our history and one that has never been written and can never be written." How do we respond to these words? In the camps, deceit was outright, as when an SS officer stood outside the undressing room, the antechamber to the "disinfection area" (the gas chamber) and said to the soon to be murdered: "Get undressed. Soon you'll get a mug of tea."

The Holocaust also presents problems of language for its victims and their descendants. The writer Elie Wiesel describes his vocation as a paradox: "I write to denounce writing. I tell of the impossibility one stumbles upon in trying to tell the tale." The theologian Emil Fackenheim also proffers a paradox: the Holocaust must be communicated, yet is incommunicable. One survivor says, "I was there" but also "I could not believe my eyes"; others speak of "the need to tell our story to the rest" but express their fear that either they will not be believed or that "the rest" would rather not hear such horror stories. German-Jewish survivors in particular reflect upon the dilemma of describing their experiences in the language of the murderers.

Hearing and reading the words associated with the Holocaust shows us the ways language can be misused and teaches us that how one talks about something affects the listeners' understanding. Language can guide or stop thought. Speakers who use stereotypes, for example, blind themselves and their listeners to the particularity of a person or group, substituting an image of the other for experience. Such speakers can manipulate their listeners to act a certain way toward those being stereotyped. The repeated use of racial or eugenic language can habituate people to certain attitudes. Thus, language has the power to hurt or kill by distancing speakers from the consequences of their actions or by deceiving their listeners about what is meant. Studying the Holocaust reminds us that to be good citizens we must attend to the language of public life.

The discussion that follows focuses on the power of naming, of designation, to shape our understanding of groups of people and of events. Attention is also directed to how language can be manipulated to convey hurtful falsehoods.

5.1. A Comparison of Names

The Holocaust, as an event or a series of events, has been given a variety of names, each with different connotations. What follows is a list of these names and what they mean. The list elaborates names employed in Germany, France, Israel, and the Untied States, as well as names—such as Auschwitz, genocide, and the Holocaust—that are used more broadly.

Die Endlösung der Judenfrage (the final solution of the Jewish question, or problem). This German term represents the culmination of a process that began with the "radical solution to the Jewish problem" and the "international solution," both of which were usually understood as referring to forced emigration. Next came the "final aim" (*Endziel*), which entailed plans for the concentration of Jews into ghettos and camps. Then in June 1940 discussion began on a "territorial final solution." In a communiqué dated July 31, 1941, Field Marshall Göring, nominally second in command to Hitler, spoke of a "total solution" (*Gesamtlösung*). By August 28, 1941, Adolf Eichmann, who would oversee the transport of European Jews to death camps in Poland, referred to an "imminent final solution." Finally, at the Wannsee Conference on January 20, 1942 (Document 3.1), the state bureaucracy and industry confirmed their participation in what they called the Final Solution (*Endlösung*), which entailed the attempted extermination of European Jewry. *The Final Solution* was also the title of the first history of these events in English, published by Gerald Reitlinger in 1953. Beyond its specific history, the term also raises general issues of language. What does it mean to speak of solutions to problems when the problems are conceived of as humans? What does it mean to speak of the existence of a people as a problem? What does it mean to call a solution final? What do such euphemisms do? There are other such euphemisms: *resettlement* [*Umsiedlung*], which meant relocation to a concentration camp or a death camp, and *special treatment* [*Sonderbehandlung*], which meant gassing.

Die Judenvernichtung (the destruction of the Jews). The initial postwar term of choice in Germany, it was also used by the Nazis. It has a detached, scientific feel to it. In Germany buildings and things are *vernichtet*; people are *umgebracht* (killed) or *gemordert* (murdered). By referring specifically to the Jews, *Judenvernichtung* leaves out the many others who were killed by the Third Reich and its collaborators.

La déportation (the deportation). This is the French term of choice. Consider what deportation entails: aliens who are illegally on your land are escorted over the border to who knows what fate; the deporting country is not responsible for that fate.

(The) *Shoah.* This Hebrew term was already in use in 1940 in Poland to describe the Jewish plight. Translations include catastrophe, calamity, desolation, devastation, and disaster—the disaster. The word appears in Psalms, Isaiah, Ezekiel, and Job, where it refers sometimes to collective, sometimes to individual (threat of) destruction or desolation. Biblically it is tied to divine judgment and retribution; it indicates a new relationship between God and history, God and the Jewish people. In modern Hebrew *Shoah* is employed for great natural disasters and, with proper qualifiers, great human disasters—nuclear disaster, for example, is *shoah gar'init*. But by itself and preceded by the definite article, the term *the shoah* was selected in 1955 by Yad Vashem, the Israeli "martyrs' and heroes' remembrance authority," as the descriptive term for situating the event in time. In Israel, the day of commemoration is known as Yom ha-shoah v'ha-g'vurah (day of disaster and heroism).

Churban or *Hurban* (both transliterations of the Hebrew term are acceptable; in Yiddish, *Khurbm*). The Hebrew (and Yiddish) term refers to the destruction of a sacred place (the Temple). When used as the Third *Churban*, it refers to the destruction of European Jewry. It also functions as a form of chronology that begins in C.E. with the destruction of the Second Temple (the destruction of the first and second Jerusalem temples mark, respectively, the first and second Churbans). With the Jewish exile from Israel, the holy community had replaced Jerusalem and the temple as the sacred place and house. Various massacres that befell medieval Jewish communities were dated by the number of years after the Second Churban. (Thus the 1096 massacre at Mainz was dated A.H. 1026 or after the Churban. One problem with Churban is that it links the calamitous events of Jewish history in a seemingly unending chain of Jewish catastrophes (with the implication that the chain would continue and that there would be a fourth Churban.) Because it suggests a lachrymose history and a martyrology of events, many Jews reject the term.

Auschwitz. Auschwitz was the largest camp complex in Nazi Germany —a combination concentration camp, labor camp, and death camp. Auschwitz has become a synecdoche (a trope in which part of something is used to signify the whole) for the destruction of European Jewry. In this use of the term, the systematic murder of the death camp is what makes the actions of Nazi Germany distinctive from other genocides and, in this sense, unique. The use of the term *Auschwitz* also underscores the fate of the Jews, for more Jews died here than anywhere else. An estimated 1.1 million people died in Auschwitz—90 percent of whom were Jews, but there were also Roma and Sinti ("Gypsies"), Jehovah's Witnesses, homosexuals, Poles, and members of other groups. Nevertheless, the monument built at Auschwitz in postwar Communist Poland sought to deemphasize the tremendous loss of Jewish lives. The monument replaced human figures with a triangle evoking the fate of the political prisoners and it consisted of twenty memorial stones in twenty languages, including Hebrew and Yiddish, each bearing the same message about the murder of "4 million Poles and other victims of fascism." The term *Auschwitz* also isolates the event in one place even though there were some nine thousand camps and subcamps throughout Europe, as well as numerous ghettoes. That Auschwitz should possess such symbolic resonance is a comparatively new phenomenon in the United States. For the first twenty years after the Liberation, the concentration camps of Dachau and Buchenwald were the centrally evocative locations in the American imagination as was Bergen-Belsen for Britain. These were the camps liberated by U.S. and British forces. Auschwitz was liberated by the Soviet Army.

Genocide. Raphael Lemkin introduced this term, which combines the Greek word *genos* (race) with the Latin suffix *cide* (killing), in 1943 to describe the events taking place in Europe. Use of the term *genocide* opens up a number of questions about what constitutes a group and what is the nature of the destruction. For example, is there cultural genocide (in which language and institutions are extinguished) as well as physical genocide (mass murder)? While the term *genocide* allows comparison across instances of mass murder, does it diminish the specificity and the horror of every instance? Does the motive to wipe out an entire people affect our understanding of the event? What if genocide happens without explicit genocidal intent? At what point can we call mass murder genocide? When is the percentage of the members of the community murdered sufficiently high to be considered genocide? For example, which is more horrible, the murder of one-third of world Jewry or two-thirds of European Jewry? Here one can see the subtle way in which our language prefigures our response.

Holocaust. The term comes from the Greek *holokaustus*, "burnt whole" and was used to translate *olah* (what is brought up [to sacrifice]) in the Septuagint (the Greek translation of the Torah). Since the term carries the connotation of a ritual victim, the question then becomes: why such a sacrifice? French writers used it in the 1920s in reference to World War I. According to the scholar of Jewish literary responses to catastrophe through the ages, David Roskies, *Holocaust* had no special resonance for American and British ears. Hence it could deal with the inconceivability of the events or the break with the past that the events during World War II represented for the Anglo-American (Jewish) communities. Used with a lower case *h*, the term *holocaust* already appeared in Jewish underground reports in 1940. The historian Gerd Korman locates the use of the term *Holocaust* with an uppercase *h* in the late 1950s. In 1968 it became a subject heading in the Library of Congress catalog. For many Jews, the name *Holocaust* also indicates uniqueness.

Questions

1. Think about your name. Are you named after someone? Do you have your father's last name, your mother's, or both? Does your name signal possible membership in an ethnic group?

2. Consider the hypothetical case of Siegfried Braun or Brunhilde Schmidt in Germany in 1938. Their names do not sound Jewish. The Nazis therefore enacted a law that required all Jewish men without obviously Jewish-sounding names to adopt the middle name "Israel" and all Jewish women without obviously Jewish-sounding names to adopt the middle name "Sara." What does this say about how names code perceptions and shape events?

3. Consider the euphemisms that facilitated the murderous actions of the Third Reich and their collaborators: *resettlement, special treatment, selection, Action, Kristallnacht* (night of broken glass), *Reich Work Group of Sanitariums and Nursing Homes* (the cover for the adult euthanasia program), and *Reich Committee for the Scientific Registration of Serious Hereditary and Congenital Diseases* (the cover for the child euthanasia program). Are there analogies with contemporary euphemisms (*collateral damage, ethnic cleansing, pacification*) and an ambiguous phrase such as *family values?*

3. Consider the following questions from a math test designed for use in the schools of the Third Reich.

    a. The construction of a lunatic asylum costs 6 million marks [the German currency]. How many houses at 15,000 marks each could have been built for that amount?

    b. To keep a mentally ill person costs approx. 4 marks per day, a cripple 5.5 marks, a criminal 3.5 marks. . . . According to conservative estimates, there are 300,000 mentally ill, epileptics, etc., in care. How much do these people cost in total, at a cost of 4 marks per head? How many marriage loans [loans given to recently married couples] at 1,000 marks each . . . could be granted from this money?

    What is the problem with these seemingly objective math questions? How does naming influence the way one might think about these math problems?

4. What are the implications of stereotypical language employed against Jews, such as the epithets *parasite, blood sucker, vermin, bacillus, usurer, egotist,* or *cosmopolitan* or the expression "to Jew someone down"? Have

other societies used such language against other groups? Is such language used in everyday life? Can you provide examples?

5. Examine the meanings of a survivor's silence in the face of those people who, out of either ignorance or malevolence, deny that the Holocaust ever happened. Why do you think that a survivor sometimes falls silent? Is it because (a) nothing indeed happened; (b) it is demeaning to respond to such a falsehood; (c) the living cannot speak for the dead; (d) the experience of the Holocaust is inexpressible; (e) the survivor is fearful of an inadequate response; or (f) the survivor feels shame or guilt over his or her survival? What might other meanings of silence be?

LINKS

6
Literature and the Holocaust

Prose

The Holocaust poses special problems to the writing and reading of literature. Can one represent the murder of European Jewry in fiction? In poetry? Can literature still "make meaning" in the face of the near physical destruction of a people? Does the struggle with the limitations of language not end here—in defeat?

Elie Wiesel, survivor of Auschwitz and the author of *Night*, as well as many other books on the Holocaust, has made the argument most forcefully: "There is no such thing as a literature of the Holocaust, nor can there be." By this, he does not mean that no one can write about the Holocaust. Rather, he suggests that the rules of aesthetic judgment that hitherto governed our approach to literature no longer seem adequate. Yet a compelling and rich body of literature about the Holocaust has emerged. This literature brings us closer to the experience of the Holocaust and challenges our notions of what literature can do and how we read. Lawrence L. Langer, one of the greatest scholars of this literature, has gathered essays, diaries, short stories, dramas, poetry, and sketches in an anthology titled *Art from the Ashes*. He chose this title, "not to proclaim a phoenix reborn from the mutilation of mass murder, redeeming that time of grief, but to suggest a symbiotic bond linking art and ashes in a seamless kinship." Because of the subject matter, we should not allow simple identification or the desire for redemption or the longing for beauty conventionally conceived to guide our appreciation or shape our criticism of this literature. "Whatever 'beauty' Holocaust art achieves," Langer writes, "is soiled by the misery of its theme."

Holocaust literature encompasses a variety of different literary genres including novels, short stories, drama, poetry, diaries, and memoirs. Among the best-known and most widely read pieces are Elie Wiesel's *Night* and Anne Frank's *The Diary of a Young Girl*. These are important books, but there are many others. We include in this chapter a discussion of *Night* (Document 6.1) but focus more attention on *Maus: A Survivor's Tale* by Art

Spiegelman, in particular volume 1 (Document 6.2). The two texts are very different: *Night* is a memoir of a survivor of Auschwitz; *Maus* is the story, narrated as a cartoon, of the author's father, also a survivor of Auschwitz. Both are true stories and both are father-son stories. But *Maus* narrates much more of the pre-Holocaust world of east European Jewry, with all the richness, complexity, and difficulties, even pettiness, that we associate with real life. *Night* evokes the world of east European Jewry but does not describe it, and the evocation is through the eyes of a boy. Moreover, *Maus* explores issues of genre, representation, human motivation, and loss with greater complexity. As such, it can be analyzed at many levels. *Night*, however, is more immediate. In simple language, it reveals the heart of death-camp reality.

We also include analyses of two short stories by Ida Fink and Tadeusz Borowski. The stories are based on the experiences of survivors. Tadeusz Borowski, a non-Jewish Pole, survived Auschwitz and Dachau. Borowski's story, *This Way to the Gas, Ladies and Gentlemen,* is a brutal account of an Auschwitz prisoner who survives by cleaning the trains arriving in the camp (Document 6.3). Ida Fink, a Jewish girl born in Poland in 1921, survived the Nazi occupation of Poland, first in a ghetto, then in hiding. Her story, "The Shelter," is about the experience of hiding, but more important it evokes a world in which the inhumanity of the Holocaust has come to be seen as commonplace (Document 6.4). Both *This Way for the Gas, Ladies and Gentlemen* and "The Shelter" are works of fiction, but they are also documents and are based on direct experience.

Document 6.1. Discussion of Elie Wiesel's *Night*

Elie Wiesel's *Night* is one of the most widely read books on the Holocaust, and for good reason. In sparse prose, utterly shorn of sentimentality, Wiesel tells about Auschwitz as seen through the eyes of a fifteen-year-old boy. It is a wrenching book that raises searching questions about the relationship of man to man and man to God.

Elie Wiesel was born in Sighet, a Rumanian town close to the border of Hungary, on September 30, 1928. In 1940, Hungary annexed the town; four years later German troops, aided by the Hungarian police, took Wiesel and his family and the other Jews of Sighet prisoner and subsequently deported them to Auschwitz. Elie Wiesel's family all died there, except for his father, who died in Buchenwald.

Elie Wiesel vowed not to write about Auschwitz for ten years. Then, in 1956, he published *Und die Velt hot Geshvign* (And the world remained silent), a memoir written in Yiddish and published in Buenos Aires. The book *Night*, which appeared in France in 1958, and in the United States in 1960, is a significantly shortened version of the work originally composed in Yiddish. Wiesel once said that *Night* is "the foundation. . . . All my subsequent books are built around it."

Night is a true story, a testimony, but it is also a literary work, shaped by literary tradition and literary convention. To focus on the literary is not to slight what happened. Rather, it helps us to disclose the more searching questions and the deeper meanings hidden in the text.

The book begins with "They"—the Jewish community of Sighet—and Moshe the Beadle, a deeply pious synagogue helper, a man who studies the spiritual truths of the Kabbalah. Eliezer, himself from a deeply pious family, asks Moshe to teach him the mysteries of the sacred texts. *Night* thus starts in a Jewish community, at the beginning of the boy's spiritual journey, with Eliezer searching for the highest truths about God. The subsequent narrative is not, however, about that journey to higher truths. It is instead about a descent into darkness, into night, into a world where human ties are severed and God is absent.

When Eliezer arrives at the platform in Auschwitz, his mother is separated from him in an instant, never to be seen again. Eliezer now has only one thought: to stay with his father. The struggle of Auschwitz is also the struggle of the son to maintain this tie. But among the men and boys all around him, he sees even this bond coming undone. There is Bela Katz, from Eliezer's hometown, who works for the special unit (*Sonderkommando*) and feeds corpses to the crematoria, his own father's among them. There is a boy in the adjacent labor camp of Buna who beats his father when the old man does not make his bed properly. There is Meier, who on the death march kills his father in a frenzied scramble for bread. And there is the son of Rabbi Eliahou, who runs ahead of his father when the father falters. Rabbi Eliahou was a good man, liked by all, and deeply devoted to his son.

As he is dragged ever deeper into night, Eliezer has more and more difficulty maintaining his devotion, and he prays to a God in whom he no longer believes "never to do what Rabbi Eliahou's son has done" (87). There are trying moments. When Eliezer's father is struck by a Gypsy, Eliezer "had not flickered an eyelid" (37). At Buchenwald the desire to lose his father, "this dead weight," plagues Eliezer, and he is "ashamed forever" (101). He gives his sick and dying father a piece of bread, but "with a heavy heart," and reflects: "No better than Rabbi Eliahou's son had I withstood the test" (102).

Eliezer is at once a boy who acts compassionately but who fears that in the dark reaches of his heart he would also like to be rid of his father. To hold onto his father, to maintain the most basic human tie, is then both a struggle against the outside world of a hellish death camp and a fight against the hunger- and exhaustion-induced faltering of his own heart. It is also a struggle not to be alone. *Night* begins with the word "They"; it ends with "me."

Eliezer is also alone because God has left him. This too is a truth of Auschwitz, which Wiesel conveys by framing central scenes in ways familiar to the Western literary imagination. The first shattering of his faith occurs immediately when he arrives in Auschwitz. As the train nears the camp, a madwoman, Madame Schächter, sees the flames of the furnace. She is the only one to see the obvious, and the others in the boxcar try to calm her. The first night in the camp, Eliezer also sees the flames. They have turned "the little faces of the children . . . into wreaths of smoke." Angered, he pledges: "Never shall I forget those flames which consumed my faith forever" (32). The nineteenth-century German philosopher Friedrich Nietzsche similarly announced the death of God. In one of the most famous passages of his work, a madman enters the marketplace in the light of day carrying a lantern to illuminate the obvious: that God is dead and we have killed him.

But in Auschwitz it is God who has abandoned man. One of the central passages of *Night* involves a hanging framed as a crucifixion. There are "three victims in chains" and in the middle "the little servant, the sad-eyed angel." Eliezer watches as the three mount the chairs. "Where is God? Where is He?" a man behind him asks. The chairs are removed and the three hang, but being lightweight "the sad-eyed angel" dies a slow death, and as Eliezer walks by, the man repeats his question. "Where is He?" Eliezer's inner voice replies, "Here he is—he is hanging here on this gallows" (32–33).

Man has murdered God, again. But here God is also the father who abandons the child. There is therefore no hope of resurrection, as in the martyrdom of Christ, and there is no hope that a ram will be substituted for the sacrifice of the son, as in the story of Abraham. Accordingly, the prayer, or Kaddish, of Rosh Hashanah, the new year, is not a lamentation but an accusation.

> This day I had ceased to plead. I was no longer capable of lamentation. On the contrary, I felt very strong. I was the accuser, God the accused. My eyes were open and I was alone—terribly alone in a world without God and without man. Without love or mercy. I had ceased to be anything but ashes, yet I felt myself to be stronger than the Almighty. (65)

This, then, is the final revelation of Eliezer's spiritual journey. It is not an elevating revelation; it is far from what he hoped for when he spoke with Moshe the Beadle; it is not a revelation about community; it is not about "they." In this sense, too, Eliezer is left with the last lonely word of the book, and from this he must reconstruct life.

———
Source: Elie Wiesel, *Night,* translated by Stella Rodway (New York: Bantam, 1986).

Document 6.2. Discussion of Art Spiegelman's *Maus: A Survivor's Tale*

Art Spiegelman is a cartoonist who tries to come to terms with the story of his father, Vladek Spiegelman, a survivor of Auschwitz. Born and raised in the United States, Art Spiegelman sees his work as both biographical and autobiographical, an account of a lived experience and a narrative that exploits the possibilities of fiction. To represent what he has calls "the central trauma of the Twentieth Century" in a way that is innovative, thought-provoking, and multilayered, Spiegelman has chosen an artistic medium that seems at once very familiar and shockingly inappropriate: the comic book.

In this comic book, the Nazis are cats, the Jews are mice, the Poles are pigs, and the Americans are dogs. At first glance, this device may seem crude. Yet the form succeeds in undermining easy identifications; it also foils simple attempts to turn the Holocaust into a morality tale. Moreover, *Maus* is in part an American story. By interweaving the story of a Holocaust survivor with that of his son, who happens to be a cartoonist in New York, the book situates the Holocaust as a theme in contemporary American life. Artie, the cartoon-artist, is not only trying to figure out what exactly happened to his father and mother and brother in the Holocaust but he is also trying to explore the ways the Holocaust has shaped his own life.

What Is *Maus* About?

Two stories interweave in *Maus Part I: A Survivor's Tale: My Father Bleeds History,* published in 1986. The first story involves Vladek's attempt to save himself and his family from the reign of terror and displacement brought about by the Nazi invasion of Poland and the terror of the Holocaust. It is a story of love and fear, cunning and commitment, and survival. The second story involves Art Spiegelman and his attempt to understand his father and his family: the experiences they went through, the scars they bear, the wounds that still afflict them. Divided into six chapters, *Maus*, volume 1, depicts Vladek as a suitor and lover situated in a rich Jewish life in prewar Poland ("The sheik"); then as a husband, father, and businessman ("The Honeymoon"); thereafter, beginning in 1939, Vladek joins the Polish Army, and is captured ("Prisoner of War"); he returns home only to be confined with his family to a Jewish ghetto ("The Noose Tightens"); then they go into hiding ("Mouse Hole") and are deported in 1944 to Auschwitz ("Mouse Trap"). In the course of all of this, Vladek and his family witness terror and narrowly escape death; they are confined and betrayed; they bribe others; and they survive where others do not. In a sense, they are lucky. But the questions of who are the survivors and does anyone ever survive is also addressed. Art Spiegelman's brother, Richieu, did not survive. And his mother, though she would survive Auschwitz in one sense, did not in another, and committed suicide in New York in 1968, when Art Spiegelman was an adolescent. She had written diaries in Auschwitz, and the diaries survived the war. But after her death, in a moment of depression and rage, Vladek burned her diaries. In the last frame of *Maus I*, Art Spiegelman calls his father "a murderer."

Whereas volume 1 recounts the tribulations of Spiegelman's parents until they are brought to the gates of Auschwitz, *Maus Part II: A Survivor's Tale: And Here My Troubles Began*, published in 1991, is situated in the barracks of Auschwitz, with flashes to the present in the bungalows of the Catskills and the parents' apartments in Florida and Rego Park. Reluctantly, Vladek recounts everyday life in the death camp and how he and his wife survived against all odds. It is a taxing story. In the last frame of *Maus II*, Vladek says to Artie, "I'm tired from talking, Richieu, and it's enough stories for now."

The Issue of Genre

Comics are associated with mass or popular culture, with entertainment, with laughter. Is treating the Holocaust through the medium of comics not sacrilegious? Does it not raise questions about the commodification of the Holocaust?

Spiegelman attempts to break out of the "elitist market of art" to bring a topic to the attention of an audience who might not think or read about the Holocaust. He is fully aware of the dangers of simplification and misrepresentation associated with the genre of cartoons. His anxieties and reservations even become part of the story. For example, toward the beginning of *Maus II*, Artie, the cartoon figure, justly observes: "There's so much I'll never be able to understand or visualize. I mean, reality is too complex for comics. . . . So much has to be left out or distorted" (*Maus II*, 16). On the other hand, Mala, Artie's stepmother, seems equally right when she says:

Figure 6.2a: *Maus I,* front cover. Used by permission of Pantheon Books, a division of Random House, Inc.

Art Spiegelman is co-founder/editor of *Raw*, the acclaimed magazine of avant-garde comics and graphics. His work has been published in the *New York Times*, *Playboy*, the *Village Voice*, and many other periodicals, and his drawings have been exhibited in museums and galleries here and abroad. Honors he has received for *Maus* include a Guggenheim fellowship, and nomination for the National Book Critics Circle Award. Mr. Spiegelman lives in New York City with his wife, Francoise Mouly, and their daughter, Nadja.

Figure 6.2b: *Maus I*, inside flap. Used by permission of Pantheon Books, a division of Random House, Inc.

"It's an important book. People who don't actually read such stories will be interested" (*Maus I*, 133).

Maus has been referred to as documentary art, pictorial literature, novelized comic, graphic novel, and oral history. A vehicle for testimony, a medium for memory work, *Maus* resists simple classification. Is it, for example, fiction or non fiction? Spiegelman himself protested the *New York Times Book Review's* decision to list *Maus* on the fiction list. He stated:

If your list were divided into literature and non-literature, I could gratefully accept the compliment as intended, but to the extent that "fiction" indicates a work isn't factual, I feel a bit queasy. As an author, I believe I might have lopped several years off the thirteen I devoted to my two-volume project if I could have taken a novelist's license while searching for a novelist's structure. . . .

I know that by delineating people with animal heads I've raised problems of taxonomy for you. Could you consider adding a special "nonfiction/mice" category to your list?

Maus is not made up, although it is obviously shaped and constructed. The form of the cartoons is an important part of this construction. For his sketches, Spiegelman chose a rough rather than a finished look, black and white rather than color. This choice suggests an aesthetics of open-endedness and the ill-suitedness of a finished, polished representation of the Holocaust.

The Issue of Animals

Spiegelman uses animal caricatures to address identities. But this technique is not as straightforward as it first appears. The animal caricatures raise questions about the degree to which identities are fixed. Should Artie's French wife, Françoise, for example, who converted to Judaism, be depicted as a mouse, a rabbit, or a frog? The hollowness of racial prejudices, which assume a static sign of racial identity, is further undermined in the second volume. Spiegelman depicts an Israeli Jew not as a mouse but as a porcupine.

The animal drawings also allow Spiegelman to privilege the figurative over the real. The mice, after all, do not really look like actual mice, nor are they merely stylized as humans. Rather, Spiegelman uses the figurative to evoke distinctions of time and documentation. He does this by varying his sketches. In *Maus I* (29), he depicts himself and his father in the present as white mice, his father and grandfather in the past as black. Similarly, if more disturbingly, he blotches out with a dialogue box the smashed skull of a child whose head has been beaten against a wall (108). The dialogue box reads, "This I didn't see with my own eyes." Here Spiegelman uses images and nonimages to raise questions about the documentary character of testimony.

Reading Cartoons

Because cartoons are both visual and textual narratives, they demand specific kinds of reading. As an art form, cartoons allow authors to adjust and break frames, to interrupt texts with images, and to put both texts and images into tension, sometimes even contradiction, with one another. In short, cartoons are extremely malleable, and, in the case of a reflective cartoon like *Maus*, experiments with frames and panels and focus and dialogue boxes invite interpretation and discussion.

The front and back covers of the Pantheon edition are good starting places for interpreting Spiegelman's cartoons. On the cover, Vladek and his wife, Anja, are crouched under the centerpiece of the title page: the swastika with a cat face (Figure 6.2a). Here we are already introduced to the main characters. Whereas Vladek and Anja are individualized by being sketched in softer contours and dressed like human beings, their enemies are referred to through the well-known symbol of swastika and an anonymous cat face, evoking Adolf Hitler. The title appears in the color of blood and, as if to suggest the familiar horrors, bleeds into the white circle and the swastika. These horrors bear down on Vladek and Anja, who are rendered frightened and vulnerable (she more than he).

The back cover can be read as well. The maps of Poland with its neighboring states and of Rego Park, New York, situate the story in present and past. The insertion of Vladek and Artie, the main characters of the story, onto the map further suggests that this is a book about a relationship across time. Inside the book jacket, there are mice, mainly faces and upper torsos, male and female, young and old (though no children), dressed nicely and individually different. The darkness, almost blackness of the image as well as the yellow stars portend an ominous future for a Jewish community still intact, however precariously. Inside of the back jacket, one sees the same figures, but the image is extended, and there is a child at the bottom of the right page. Probably, he is meant to evoke Artie's older brother Richieu, who did not survive. The inside flap (Figure 6.2b), with Artie the cartoonist writing in a camp, his cigarette smoke complicitous with the smoke of the crematorium, folds down over the image of Richieu, suggesting again the importance of the complicated, guilt-ridden relationship of Artie to his dead brother. In the image on the flap, Artie wears a mouse mask. Is he really a mouse like the mice of the Holocaust? In *Maus II*, Spiegelman also sketches mice on the inside of the covers, but their faces are anonymous. They seem alienated from one another. An uncountable mass, they all wear the same striped uniforms of the camps, and the child has disappeared.

Document 6.3. Discussion of Tadeusz Borowski's *This Way for the Gas, Ladies and Gentlemen*

Born in 1922 to Polish parents in Zhitomir in the Soviet Ukraine, Tadeusz Borowski was considered one of the great Polish authors of his generation. Interned in Auschwitz as a young man, he survived the war. But Auschwitz stayed with him, and, in 1951, three days after the birth of his daughter, he committed suicide by turning the gas valves on in his kitchen. He was not yet thirty.

His story, *This Way for the Gas, Ladies and Gentlemen*, is unsentimental and unsparing. Borowski refuses to spiritualize or wrest meaning from the suffering in the death camp. Rather, he narrates in a matter-of-fact way, which has the effect of rendering the horror disorienting, and the dilemmas, for victims then and readers now, unsolvable.

The principle literary innovation of *This Way for the Gas, Ladies and Gentlemen* involves narrative perspective. In thinly disguised autobiography, Borowski writes as a privileged inmate of Auschwitz. He is not slated for the gas chambers and survives by emptying out the boxcars of Jewish prisoners arriving at the ramp. He cleans out the cars and helps herd the Jews into lines, full-well knowing that they will soon be gassed.

In the story, the narrator asks to be assigned to the unit that cleans out the cars because he wants to get a pair of shoes. He is fortunate and receives his assignment. He prepares for the arrival of the trains, opens the doors to the boxcars (which are full to the breaking point with people), sorts the living from the dead, separates inmates, and assists in the selection of those who will be gassed and those who will work. He also cleans out the trampled infants from the floor and the corners of the boxcars. As he does these things, one task after the next, his inner compassion for the Jewish victims diminishes. He becomes detached, even contemptuous. He works mechanically, and loses interest in the pair of shoes. In the end, all he wants is to return to the camp, which seems to offer at least the comfort of an unmattressed bed.

The story considers an inmate who faces a dilemma that was commonplace in the death camps: should he bargain for his life at the cost of helping to liquidate his fellow inmates or face almost certain death? In this story, the reader is drawn into the dilemma. The reader encounters the fate of Jewish victims from the outside, from a distance, precisely analyzed by the narrator, who himself tries to distance himself from the people who are about to be gassed, if they are not already dead. But the narrator himself is also a victim and therefore cannot take on the role, or the views, of the killers,

German SS men. The reader is thus torn, drawn into a maelstrom of empathy with a privileged inmate and complicity in his actions as well as in his descent into detachment and indifference.

The story does not offer hope. Instead, it leaves the reader with a sense of a diminished self. This is why it is so unsparing, and why it poses questions of good and evil in what Primo Levi has called "the gray zone" in terms both radical and honest.

Source: Tadeusz Borowski, *This Way for the Gas, Ladies and Gentlemen* (New York: Penguin, 1976).

Document 6.4. Discussion of Ida Fink's "The Shelter"

Born in Poland in 1921, Ida Fink survived the ghetto and in 1942 went into hiding and in this way lived out the war. In 1957 she emigrated to Israel. Marked by terse, arrestingly simple prose, her stories typically address issues of confinement and apprehension. They also address loss.

"The Shelter" appeared in a collection entitled *A Scrap of Time and Other Stories*. Originally published in Polish in 1983, the collection has since been translated into Hebrew, Dutch, German, and English, and in 1985, the book received the first Anne Frank Prize for Literature. Ida Fink is also the author of *Journey*, which appeared in English in 1992 and chronicles the story of two Jewish sisters trying to use false papers to get out of Poland. More recently still, Ida Fink published a second volume of short stories entitled *Traces*.

The story "The Shelter" is about a Jewish couple who survive the war and then revisit the poor Polish family in whose house (in a storage space) they found refuge from the Nazis. In exchange for shelter, and if they survived the war, the Jewish couple had promised to provide the money that would allow the Polish man, Oleg, and his wife to build a new house. The Jewish couple returned to see the house, and Oleg showed it to them with evident pride. He then showed them "a shelter, as pretty as a picture" that he had built for them, "just in case something happens." The Jewish woman cried.

Source: Ida Fink, "The Shelter," in *A Scrap of Time and Other Stories,* translated by Madeline Levine and Francine Prose (Evanston, Ill. : Northwestern University Press, 1995).

Poems

The philosopher Theodor W. Adorno asserted, "To write poetry after Auschwitz is barbaric." Yet there is poetry, some from survivors of Auschwitz. The poetry of the Holocaust struggles with common difficulties: how to represent an absence that is an individual absence but also a larger absence; how to use images to describe a landscape that no one, except those who were there, could possibly imagine; and how to use metaphor without implying that the Holocaust was like something else. There are further difficulties. The poetry of the Holocaust is not written in a common language; it is written in Yiddish, Hebrew, Polish, French, and, most problematical because it is the language of the killers, German. When we read it, we often read it in translation and thus lose the sound and rhythm essential to poetry. Holocaust poetry also asks us to imagine even as it insists that the Holocaust, as such, is beyond our imagination.

We have included four poems: "The Butterfly" by Pavel Friedmann (Document 6.5), "For My Child" by Abraham Sutzkever (Document 6.6), "Written in Pencil in the Sealed Railway-Car" by Dan Pagis (Document 6.7), and "You Onlookers" by Nelly Sachs (document 6.8). Originally written in Czech, Yiddish, Hebrew, and German, respectively, the poems address loss and, more poignantly still, life never lived—"unsung cradle songs" in the words of Nelly Sachs. The poets are Jewish, and all but Nelly Sachs experienced the camps. Pavel Friedmann died there.

Pavel Friedmann was born in Prague on January 7, 1921, and was deported to Terezin on April 26, 1942. From there he was sent to Auschwitz, where he died on September 29, 1944. "The Butterfly" appears in a collection of poetry and drawings and paintings by children in the special concentration camp of Terezin (Theresienstadt) entitled . . . *I never saw another butterfly* . . .

Abraham Sutzkever, born in 1913, was from Smorogon, a city near Vilnius in Lithuania. The Lithuanian police found him in hiding and took him out to be shot. Taunting him, the police shot above his head, and Sutzkever survived. In the ghetto, his wife, Freydke, bore him a son, but the Germans killed the infant by poisoning. This is the topic of "For My Child." After escaping the ghetto, Abraham Sutzkever and his wife fought with partisan units, often enduring great hardship. In 1947 he and his wife emigrated to Palestine.

Dan Pagis was born in 1930 in the Bukovina (now Romania) and survived camps in Transnistria (now in the Ukraine). He emigrated to Palestine and wrote poems, not in German, his mother tongue, but in Hebrew, his adopted language.

Born in Berlin in 1891, Nelly Sachs was able to emigrate to Sweden in 1940. She stayed in Sweden until her death in 1970. The author of poems and stories, she received, along with Israeli novelist S. Y. Agnon, the Nobel Prize for Literature in 1966.

Document 6.5. The Butterfly by Pavel Friedmann

The last, the very last,
So richly, brightly, dazzlingly yellow.
Perhaps if the sun's tears would sing
    against a white stone. . . .

Such, such a yellow
Is carried lightly 'way up high.
It went away I'm sure because it wished to
    kiss the world good-bye.

For seven weeks I've lived in here,
Penned up inside this ghetto.
But I have found what I love here.
The dandelions call to me
And the white chestnut branches in the court.
Only I never saw another butterfly.

That butterfly was the last one.
Butterflies don't live in here,
    in the ghetto.

———

Source: Hana Volavková, ed., *. . . I never saw another butterfly . . . : Children's Drawings and Poems from Terezin Concentration Camp, 1942–1944,* expanded 2d edition by the United States Holocaust Memorial Museum (New York: Schocken, 1993), 39. Used by permission of Schocken Books, a division of Random House, Inc.

Document 6.6. For My Child by Abraham Sutzkever

Was it from some hunger
or from greater love—
but your mother is a witness to this:
I wanted to swallow you, my child,
when I felt your tiny body losing its heat
in my fingers
as though I were pressing
a warm glass of tea,
feeling its passage to cold.

You're no stranger, no guest,
for on this earth one does not
give birth to aliens.
You reproduce yourself like a ring
and the rings fit into chains.

My child,
what else may I call you but: love.
Even without the word that is who you are,
you—seed of my every dream,
hidden third one,
who came from the world's corner
with the wonder of an unseen storm,
you who brought, rushed two together
to create you and rejoice:—

Why have you darkened creation
with the shutting of your tiny eyes
and left me begging outside
in the snow swept world
to which you have returned?

No cradle gave you pleasure
whose rocking
conceals in itself the pulse of the stars.
Let the sun crumble like glass
since you never beheld its light.

That drop of poison extinguished your faith—
you thought
it was warm sweet milk.

I wanted to swallow you, my child,
to feel the taste
of my anticipated future.
Perhaps in my blood
you will blossom as before.

But I am not worthy to be your grave.
So I bequeath you
to the summoning snow,
the snow—my first respite,
and you will sink
like a splinter of dusk
into its quiet depths
and bear greetings from me
to the frozen grasslands ahead—
        Vilnius Ghetto January 18, 1943

Source: Abraham Sutzkever, *Burnt Pearls: The Ghetto Poems of Abraham Sutzkever*, translated by Seymour Mayne and Ruth R. Wisse (Oakville, Ont.: Mosaic Press, Valley Editions, 1981), 32–3, ISBN 0-8896-21411.

Document 6.7. Written in Pencil in the Sealed Railway-Car by Dan Pagis

here in this carload
i am eve
with abel my son
if you see my other son
cain son of man
tell him that i

Source: Dan Pagis, *Points of Departure*, translated by Stephen Mitchell (Philadelphia: Jewish Publication Society of America, 1981), 23.

Document 6.8. You Onlookers by Nelly Sachs

You onlookers

Whose eyes watched the killing.
As one feels a stare at one's back
You feel on your bodies
The glances of the dead.

How many dying eyes will look at you
When you pluck a violet from its hiding place?
How many hands be raised in supplication
In the twisted martyr-like branches
Of old oaks?
How much memory grows in the blood
Of the evening sun?

O the unsung cradlesongs
In the night cry of the turtledove—
Many a one might have plucked stars from the sky,
Now the old well must do it for them!

You onlookers,
You who raised no hand in murder,
But who did not shake the dust
From your longing,
You who halted there, where dust is changed
To light.

Source: Nelly Sachs, *O the Chimneys*, translated by Michael Hamburger and others (New York: Farrar, Straus and Giroux, 1967), 19. Reprinted by permission of Farrar, Straus and Giroux, LLC.

Questions

Document 6.1. Discussion of Elie Wiesel's *Night*

1. Why do you think Elie Wiesel initially titles the book, "And the World Remained Silent"?
2. Compare the hanging of the "sad-eyed angel" to the crucifixion of Christ as portrayed in the Bible? Where do you see similarities? Where do you see differences? How has the context changed?
3. Describe the relationship of the son, Eliezer, to his father? What do the trials and tribulations of that relationship tell us about the "concentration-camp universe"?
4. What justifies the sparse prose of Night? Can you imagine this book written in a more ornate style?
5. What does Eliezer have left when he has survived?

LINKS

Document 6.2. Discussion of Art Spiegelman's *Maus: A Survivor's Tale*

1. What is gained, what is lost, when the Holocaust is treated in comics?
2. In what sense is *Maus* a work of fiction?
3. In what sense is *Maus* a peculiarly American book about the Holocaust?
4. What issues does the manipulation of cartoon form raise for an understanding of the Holocaust?

LINKS

Document 6.3. Discussion of Tadeusz Borowski's *This Way to the Gas, Ladies and Gentlemen*

1. Is it possible to identify with the plight of the narrator?
2. What would happen if you identified with his plight? Would you be forced to ignore the fate of others?

LINKS

I. History 3. The Killing Process 3.8. German Railway Schedule	61
IV. Ethics 13.3. What Is a Choiceless Choice?	235

Document 6.4. Discussion of Ida Fink's "The Shelter"

1. Why did the Jewish woman cry?
2. What was wrong with Oleg's assumption?

LINKS

I. History 4. Resistance and Rescue 4.4. Magda Trocmé	82
IV. Ethics 13.2. Is Genocide More Than Mass Murder?	232
13.4. How Does Good Happen?	239

Document 6.5. The Butterfly by Pavel Friedmann

1. Why did the poet choose to write about a butterfly? A yellow butterfly?
2. Why do you think "butterflies don't live in here"?

LINKS

I. History 3. The Killing Process 3.2. Images of the Warsaw Ghetto	47
III. Other Genocides 11. Bosnia and Kosova 11.3. Images of War by Children of Former Yugoslavia	190

Document 6.6. For My Child by Abraham Sutzkever

1. A child is lost here. What else?
2. Why does the poet wish to "swallow you, my child"?
3. What is the tone of the poem?

LINKS

I. History 3. The Killing Process 3.5. The Jäger Report	50
IV. Ethics 13.5. What Are the Limits of Forgiveness?	241

Document 6.7. Written in Pencil
in the Sealed Railway-Car by Dan Pagis

1. What is different about the setting of the poem as compared with the original creation story in Genesis 2–4? How does this different setting affect the meaning of the poem? How is it a reflection on the changed meaning of Genesis in a world defined by the Holocaust?
2. Who is the "you" in the fourth line of the poem? (Note that in the original Hebrew version of the poem, "you" is a plural pronoun.) What does this imply about our responsibilities as readers and as persons in a post-Holocaust world?
3. Why can "eve" not finish the poem?
4. What do you imagine comes after the "i" in the last line?

LINKS

I. History   3. The Killing Process   3.8. German Railway Schedule   68
IV. Ethics   13.2. Is Genocide More Than Mass Murder?   232

———————

Document 6.8. You Onlookers by Nelly Sachs

1. Who are the onlookers?
2. What nouns are central to the imagery of the poem?
3. What kind of world does the poet construct from these nouns?

LINKS

I. History   4. Resistance and Rescue   4.2. *Nashville Tennessean*, June 30, 1942   80
IV. Ethics   13.2. Is Genocide More Than Mass Murder?   232

Further Reading

On *Night*

Langer, Lawrence L. *The Holocaust and the Literary Imagination.* New Haven: Yale University Press, 1975.

Roth, John K. *Consuming Fire: Encounters with Elie Wiesel and the Holocaust.* Atlanta: John Knox, 1979.

Rittner, Carol, ed. *Elie Wiesel: Between Memory and Hope.* New York: New York University Press, 1990.

On *Maus*

Doherty, Thomas. "Art Spiegelman's *Maus*: Graphic Art and the Holocaust," *American Literature* 68 (1996): 69–84.

Hungerford, Amy. "Surviving Rego Park: Holocaust Theory from Art Spiegelman to Berel Lang." In *The Americanization of the Holocaust*, edited by Hilene Flanzbaum, 102–24. Baltimore: Johns Hopkins University Press, 1999.

LaCapra, Dominick. "'Twas the Night Before Christmas': Art Spiegelman's *Maus*." In *History and Memory After Auschwitz*, 139–79. Ithaca: Cornell University Press, 1998.

On *This Way for the Gas, Ladies and Gentlemen*

Borowski, Tadeusz. *This Way for the Gas, Ladies and Gentlemen.* New York: Penguin, 1976.

Levi, Primo. "The Gray Zone." In *The Drowned and the Saved,* 36–69. New York: Summit Books, 1988.

On Poetry

Langer, Lawrence L. ed. *Art from the Ashes: A Holocaust Anthology.* New York: Oxford University Press, 1995.

Volavkova, Hana, ed. *. . . I never saw another butterfly . . . : Children's Drawings and Poems from Terezin Concentration Camp, 1942–1944.* Expanded 2d edition by the United States Holocaust Memorial Museum. New York: Schocken, 1993.

7
Monuments and Memorials

Monuments and memorials are sites where individuals and nations go to remember and bear witness, where individuals go to mourn and nations attempt to work out their relationship to their historical past. They are places of individual as well as national memory. The Vietnam Veterans Memorial, for instance, offers visitors an intense, personal experience as they examine the names on the wall; its location among other monuments and memorials on the Mall in Washington, D.C., places it within a larger narrative of national identity. Pointing from its axis to both the Washington Monument and the Lincoln Memorial, the Vietnam Veterans Memorial references a larger national context. As Marita Sturken points out in *Tangled Memories: The Vietnam War, the AIDS Epidemic, and the Politics of Remembering* (Berkeley and Los Angeles: University of California Press, 1997), the wall, made of black granite and set horizontally in the ground, works in opposition to the vertical monuments made of white stone on the Mall; yet its polished granite surface, which reflects the visitor's face as well as the Washington Monument, also mirrors the national setting. Hence, the Vietnam Veterans Memorial works both within and against national memory even as it offers a place for personal reflection. Its chronological list of names, for instance, personalizes and individualizes the memorial experience; yet, read in their entirety, the names offer a larger narrative of the war (the heaviest days and years of battle, for instance). The seemingly endless list of names, as well as the fact that names continue to be added to the wall, suggests the way that Vietnam continues to remain an open wound in the national psyche.

The extensive and heated debate over the political and aesthetic vision of the Vietnam Veterans Memorial underscores the complex historical, political, and aesthetic context in which national memory is constructed and in which a monument or memorial is understood. The V-shaped wall of black granite set into the earth has been seen alternately as a black gash of shame (a boomerang, a tombstone, a degrading ditch) and as a healed wound. For some, its modernist form endows it with a more flexible and hence a greater meaning; for others, the form turns the memorial into a monument to defeat. The political compromise to place a traditionally realistic statue of three soldiers by the site along with an American flag exemplifies how aesthetic issues can carry national meaning.

The complex contexts of a memorial affect how it is experienced and understood. A memorial's location, its visual and verbal cues, the political and historical circumstances of its origin, as well as the visitors who happen to be there at any given time all affect its meaning. Visiting the Vietnam Veterans Memorial wall when no one else is there is a very different experience from visiting it when people are there making rubbings of names or leaving personal mementos. The meaning of the memorial will be different also once the generation who experienced the Vietnam War is dead. Similarly, the Boston Holocaust Memorial is endowed with a particular national perspective because it is a stop on the Freedom Trail. Like the U.S. Holocaust Museum, on the Mall in Washington, D.C., the Boston Memorial asks visitors to situate the Holocaust within a U.S. narrative of national identity. The heroic iconography of Nathan Rapoport's monument, Liberation, and its location near the Statue of Liberty and Ellis Island places the Holocaust within a U.S. national narrative of liberty and justice for all. Here, the United States is once again the place of refuge for the immigrant; unlike Vietnam, the Holocaust can reinforce rather than challenge U.S. identity. For those countries who acted as perpetrators rather than liberators in the Holocaust, the act of national remembering inherent in any memorial is even more vexed.

Besides understanding the various contexts that inform a memorial's meaning, it is also important to understand how a memorial can simultaneously provide meaning and enable forgetting. By publicly marking a historical trauma, a memorial may relieve the viewer of his or her burden to remember and become a substitute for memory. Once a traumatic event has been officially dealt with—once it has been marked in solid stone—it can seem to offer closure to the event that in turn can lead to forgetting that event. Paradoxically, as James Young observes in *The Texture of Memory: Holocaust Memorials and Meaning* (New Haven: Yale University Press, 1993), healing can lead to forgetting. The Holocaust monument in Hamburg-Harburg, he points out, foregrounds this dilemma (28–37). Often called the sinking monument, Hamburg-Harburg's Monument Against Fascism, built in 1986, enacts this process of forgetting. Located in the commercial center of Harburg near a shopping mall, the monument, a twelve meter high and one meter square pillar, forces viewers to bear the burden of memory. The plaque at its base reads: "We invite the citizens of Harburg, and visitors to the town, to add their names here to ours. In doing so, we commit ourselves to remain vigilant. As more and more names cover this 12 meter tall lead column, it will gradually be lowered into the ground. One day it will have disappeared completely, and the site of the Harburg Monument Against Fascism will be empty. In the end, it is only we ourselves who can rise up against injustice." Ironically, as Young points out, the more actively visitors participate in remembering by signing the monument, the more quickly the monument disappears (30). In the end, the visitor is left with only a memory of the monument. Having been sunk completely into the ground, the monument itself is then covered by a tombstone that marks its absent presence. Like the traumatic history to which it bears witness, this memorial vanishes. In effect it becomes a countermemorial that points up the danger of all memorials: in the act of remembering memorials also enable forgetting.

Memorials take many forms. They do not necessarily have to be commissioned works of art or take the traditional form of the tombstone; they can be informal and ad hoc, like the memorials that often occur on roadsides at the site of deadly accidents or at the homes of celebrities who have been tragically killed. Nor do memorials have to be made of stone. In Sarajevo, a man goes to play the cello at the site of his family's death every day. In Israel in the Martyr's Forest a tree will be planted for each victim of the Holocaust. Also in Israel the whole country comes to a halt for two minutes of silence on Holocaust Remembrance Day. People become living monuments, enacting an ephemeral, performative memorial. In Berlin, a memorial consists of a simple sign in front of the Wittenbergplatz subway station reads, "Places of Terror That We Should Never Forget" above a list of the concentration camps. Destroyed buildings also stand—in their very ruins— as memorials. Despite the different forms they may take, memorials exist as a sacred space through which to remember.

Memorials are built to bear witness to that which we should not forget. In contrast, it is often argued, monuments, such as the Arc de Triomphe in Paris, honoring the victories of Napoleon, are built to commemorate triumphs. Nevertheless, the two terms are often used interchangeably: the most traditional form of monument, the tombstone, for instance, marks a site of mourning. The slight distinction between these terms may be useful to keep in mind when comparing the monument and memorial we discuss below.

From hundreds of possible Holocaust memorials, we have chosen two for our focus, both in Poland: Nathan Rapoport's Warsaw Ghetto monument (Document 7.1) and the memorial at Treblinka (Document 7.2). Each has a very specific location that shapes the meaning of the memorial and each approaches the question of representation and remembering in very different ways: Rapoport's monument is realistic, while the memorial at Treblinka is more abstract. Both evoke a wide range of interpretations. The comparison between the two is meant to underscore the different ways a single nation has responded to the Holocaust and the many meanings any single monument or memorial may have. Throughout this section we are indebted to James Young's *Texture of Memory*, especially pages 155–89, for facts and interpretive insights.

Document 7.1. Warsaw Ghetto Monument

The Warsaw Ghetto Monument, sculpted by Nathan Rapoport, a Polish Jew who escaped the Holocaust in the Soviet Union, bears witness to the largest and longest armed resistance against the Nazis, the Warsaw ghetto uprising. The monument was unveiled on April 19, 1948, the fifth anniversary of the uprising. Trained in the heroic school of realism, Rapoport uses epic realism to memorialize and mythologize the revolt. The monument is a freestanding wall of roughly hewn stone that represents the ghetto wall that divided Warsaw's Jews from the rest of the city. It also looks like a tombstone and evokes the Western Wall in Jerusalem. On the front side are seven figures symbolizing the various stages of life. They are strong yet skeletal. They carry the weapons of resistance—a rock, dagger, rifle, grenade—and appear to be coming toward the viewer, breaking out of the imprisoning ghetto wall through the frame of a doorway. The flames in the background signify the burning down of the ghetto and the fallen youth in the lower right-hand corner is a reminder of the ultimate failure of the resistance fighters. Despite these signifiers of the final destruction of the Warsaw ghetto, the vertical and raised position of the figures emphasizes their resistance.

While the front of the monument affirms the resistance fighters, the back laments their defeat. In a reference to the Arch of Titus, which depicts a triumphal procession led by the Emperor Titus after the destruction of Jerusalem and the Jewish exile, twelve stooped and shrouded figures, referring to the twelve tribes of Israel, move across the back of the monument. These figures signify the archetype of Jews in exile. But the presence of the Nazis, whom Rapoport dehumanizes and strips of individuality by representing them through their helmets and bayonets, places this exile in the specific historical context of the Holocaust. In contrast to the composition on the front, which is vertical and raised, the composition on the back is horizontal and recedes into the rock. The rabbi, holding the Torah scroll, is the only figure looking up, as if to ask the heavens for help; the rest look down, as if resigned to their fate. The two sides, however, work in concert with each other. On the back the final figure at the end of the line is looking backward, forcing our eyes around to the other side of the monument; the fallen figure on the front echoes the stooped figures on the back. The inscription, which is written in Hebrew, Yiddish, and Polish, echoes the dual meaning of the two compositions, celebration and mourning: "To the Jewish People—Its Heroes and Its Martyrs." The use of a menorah, a candelabrum used in Jewish worship since ancient times, on each side makes clear the specifically Jewish context of this memorial.

The changing character of the monument's location has, however, altered its meaning. Some of the meaning the monument conveyed when it was first built amid the ruins of the Warsaw ghetto changed when it became surrounded by apartment buildings. Whereas before it was the only solid structure in the area, now it is one square block among many, and where it once stood alone, it is now part of a larger memorial path. It also has taken on national significance by becoming the site of other resistances. Most notably, it was a gathering place for the Polish grass-roots resistance movement Solidarity in the 1980s. Also, it has been reproduced in Israel, and both Poland and Israel use an image of the monument on postage stamps and postcards. This monument, then, has become part of a larger national identity of resistance in each country.

Figure 7.1. Warsaw Ghetto Monument. From James E. Young, *The Texture of Memory: Holocaust Memorials and Meaning*, Yale University Press, 1993.

Document 7.2. Treblinka

What to do with the concentration and death camps has been a pressing issue. Should the camps be left to fall into ruins? Should they be restored and maintained? What does it mean to turn these places of death into tourist sites? The memorial at Treblinka attempts to deal with these issues.

In Treblinka 850,000 Jews were gassed and burned. The death camp was destroyed in 1944 by the Germans, who plowed it under and planted it over with pine trees and grain fields. The memorial at Treblinka was dedicated in 1964. Designed by the sculptor Franciszek Duszenko and the architect Adam Haupt, it consists of 17,000 granite shards set in concrete around a twenty-six-foot obelisk. Concrete railroad ties form a path leading to the memorial, reminding the visitor of the trains that brought prisoners to the camps. The lack of parallel tracks, however, insists that no train can ever go there again. Several hundred of the slabs bear the names of Jewish communities in Poland destroyed during the Holocaust; a separate row of granite stones stands in front of the clearing and names the countries of origin of the Jews who perished in Treblinka. A menorah is located at the cap of the obelisk. In this memorial, dedicated to registering the vast numbers of men, women, and children killed at the camp rather than accounting for particular individuals, the only individual commemorated is a Polish-Jewish hero, Janusz Korczak, who, as the head of a Jewish orphanage, chose to accompany his charges to Treblinka. The granite shards resemble gravestones and the entire field looks like a Jewish graveyard. The shards, along with the obelisk, which is cleaved from top to bottom, reflect the Jewish funerary tradition of layering tombstones and the Nazi desecration of Jewish graveyards. The theme of brokenness also reflects the fragmentary nature of remembering such horror. The past remains in ruins and Jewish culture has been destroyed. The Holocaust cannot be represented or remembered as a whole: it is too incomprehensible and memory is incomplete. The stone motif also reflects the Jewish tradition of laying stones at tombstones as an act of remembrance. By foregrounding the fragmentary nature of any act of remembrance, the memorial at Treblinka refuses to offer any easy meaning. The only narrative that is offered to the visitor is on a plaque at the base of the obelisk. It reads "Never Again" in Yiddish, Russian, English, French, German, and Polish.

Figure 7.2. Treblinka. From James E. Young, *The Texture of Memory: Holocaust Memorials and Meaning*. Yale University Press, 1993.

Questions

———

1. Look at the images of the Warsaw Ghetto Memorial and the memorial at Treblinka. What do you see? Consider the background information in the text. How does knowing the background influence your perception of the two memorials? Compare and contrast the two memorials. Which one seems more meaningful? Why?
2. Visit and research monuments and memorials in your area. In the American South, for example, Civil War memorials, including the Confederate flag, may be especially useful for generating discussions of the historical, political, and aesthetic contexts of memory, for as V. S. Naipaul states in *A Turn in the South* (New York: Knopf, 1989), the South has a "monumental culture" precisely because of its history of defeat.
3. Choose a historical event and design a memorial or monument (out of clay or other materials) that speaks to the issue the event raises.

8
Photographs

O ne has only to search online with the key words *Holocaust* and *photogra-phy* to discover that there are hundreds of thousands of photographic records of the Holocaust. Photography, whether in still photos or in 8-millimeter film, was a unique medium during the mid-twentieth century. Because it seemed to capture reality, photography convinced people of the authenticity of the events of the Holocaust when words sometimes faltered.

Each of the thousands of photographs was an attempt to record an event from the photographer's perspective. Some photographs were taken by ama-teurs, some by professionals, some were damaged as they were smuggled in and out of hiding places, some were discarded, ignored, even doctored. Yet the sheer quantity of photographs, the consistency of their subject matter, and the many different sources of photographs conveyed something of the magnitude of the Holocaust to an incredulous world.

Photographs are especially powerful conveyors of meaning. They can be looked at over and over again to reinforce memory, to re-experience an emotion, to learn more, or to reinterpret. Unlike the original event, the images are there for the viewer who chooses to look. Moreover, many pho-tographs have captions, and these can help interpret or carry the meaning. Sometimes the caption adds significantly to the power of the picture. In Figure 8.1, the caption tells the story of the older woman carrying the little boy. Without the caption, the picture would still be striking but would not convey so well these people's desperation. With the caption, the photograph portrays a particular fate that would otherwise get lost in the staggering statistics of victims.

The act of photographing images of the Holocaust, with its devastating consequences, presented special challenges to photographers. Photographs try to tell a story, to create meaning. For the practiced photographer, deci-sions about how to do this are deliberate. Those who took photographs during and after the Holocaust had to make decisions about what to docu-ment, whether they wanted to shock or appeal to understanding, to concen-trate on one aspect of the event or to capture a panorama, a symbol of something larger or a realistic portrayal. They also had to decide whether to assume the perspective of perpetrator, victim, bystander, or witness.

Figure 8.1. Selection of Hungarian Jews for extermination, on the ramp at Auschwitz. At the left is Rosa Goldenzeil, shortly before she was murdered in the gas chambers with her grandson Dani Jakubovitch. She had learned that young women with children were immediately gassed, and convinced her unknowing daughter to give her the baby, thereby saving her daughter's life. Visitors hear this story in the U.S. Holocaust Memorial Museum's *Testimony* film. Yad Vashem, Jerusalem, courtesy of the United States Holocaust Memorial Museum.

According to Barbie Zelizer, in her book *Remembering to Forget* (Chicago: University of Chicago Press, 1989), there are three periods of Holocaust photography, roughly corresponding to pre-Holocaust photographs, the early phases of the Holocaust, and photographs from the liberation of the camps.

Before the Nazis began their persecution and killing of Jews and other groups they considered undesirable, people in central Europe lived in villages and towns and went about their daily activities, taking care of business, tending to their households, and watching their children. Photos, taken primarily of individuals and family events, such as weddings and picnics, became part of the family history or the memories of a town. A moving example of such photographs can be seen in the Tower of Faces exhibit at

Figure 8.2. Tower of Faces. Photo courtesy of the United States Holocaust Memorial Museum Photo Archives.

the Holocaust Memorial Museum in Washington, D.C. (Figure 8.2). They were all collected by Yaffa Eliach (Document 3.7), who before the war was a young Jewish girl living in the Lithuanian village (shtetl) of Eishyshok, a town that had been in existence since the early eleventh century. Her grandparents had brought some cameras and other photographic equipment from New York and had become the village photographers. They spent many hours taking pictures of the people who lived there as they went about their lives. Of the four thousand Jews who lived in Eishyshok, only twenty-nine, including the four-year-old Yaffa, survived the mobile killing squads on September 25, 1941. Eliach visited the site of her shtetl as an adult and realized that unless something was done the memory of the Jewish village would be gone. Jews no longer lived there, and fewer and fewer people knew that Jews had ever lived there. She decided to rescue the memory of her shtetl from oblivion by collecting the photographs her grandparents had taken. After many years of searching, her collection was brought together in the Tower of Faces. The curators of the museum accepted her photographs because they elicit nostalgia while capturing the complex, evolving life of a shtetl. They also personalize the Holocaust. Because they were taken before the Holocaust, they show people with an identity other than that of victim.

In the early phases of the Holocaust, the atrocities committed by the

Nazi policies were relatively inaccessible to Allied photographers. The few photographs that did emerge were provided by individuals who had entry to the camps and who were present during the internment and killings of the victims, including members of the underground, people who escaped from the camps or the mobile killing units, sympathetic civilians who themselves were not victims, soldiers who took souvenir pictures with their personal cameras to send home, and the members of the German propaganda units. Most of the photographs from the early years of the Holocaust were taken by the Nazis themselves. They were documenting the units' activities, the medical experiments, the routines, the architecture, or the commandant's household. For many Nazis, there was such pride in the excellent execution of duty that the subject matter of the confinement, humiliation, and even slaughter of innocent victims was just part of the efficient administration of the camp. The Nazis photographed themselves at work to document their observance of duty. Many of these photographs took a long time to surface, and the few that reached Western hands during the early years of the war were treated unevenly. At first many newspapers downplayed the pictures of atrocities with the excuse that war always creates atrocities, or that the portrayed atrocity was an isolated event, or that the pictures were too horrible for the public to see. The scarcity of photographs and the self-censoring by the news media no doubt delayed the public's awareness of the Holocaust and helped to blunt its outrage.

The second round of photographs of the Holocaust was provided by the Allied forces when they liberated the death camps. With the army and its official photographers came a host of news photographers. In the final phase of the Holocaust, there was little left but to photograph the suffering. For these photographers there were no instructors, no guidelines. No one had ever before had the overwhelming assignment to try to document an event of such magnitude, emotional impact, and horror. Not only was the assignment overwhelming, but the effect of what they saw was almost paralyzing. Margaret Bourke-White, one of the best-known photographers of the Liberation, claimed that she took pictures from a self-imposed stupor and that she often did not know what she had taken until she had seen the prints. The photographers had to decide where to place the evidence of atrocity in the picture, whether to depict many or few victims, how to portray survivors, and whether to show survivors or the bodies that were the objects of torture.

Two types of photograph emerged from this period. The first depicts survivors, often emaciated, whose sense of hopelessness shows in their blank expressions. These pictures came to symbolize the Nazi's brutality. The second type, depicting the industrialization of mass slaughter, symbolizes the impersonal, callous nature of the atrocities. These are pictures of open

Figure 8.3. General Dwight Eisenhower and other officers examine corpses at Ohrdruf, April 12, 1945. Photo courtesy of National Archives at College Park.

furnaces with human remains inside, hanging ropes suspended from ceilings, piles of artificial limbs taken from handicapped victims, and heaps of human hair. Unfortunately, these scenes sometimes had the effect of numbing the viewers to the personal aspects of the atrocities, leaving them with an impression of numbers but not with empathy or a sense of the personal tragedy and trauma.

Many photographs show people bearing witness. These include reporters and soldiers looking at piles of bodies, as well as German civilians who were brought into the camps to view the remains and victims and be photographed doing so. In one photograph, General Dwight Eisenhower is shown looking at corpses at Ohrdruf, Germany (Figure 8.3); afterward he proclaimed, "Let the world see." His proclamation opened the door for the publication and posting of photographs of Holocaust atrocities. The addition of witnesses in pictures added a whole new layer of credibility to photographs. The media became more aggressive about showing pictures of the Holocaust. What was once considered too horrible to show in a newspaper began appearing on the front pages of newspapers and in whole sections of news magazines.

As the photographic evidence for the Holocaust accumulated, its role changed. The myth that the atrocities were isolated incidents vanished. The accuracy of the documentation and credits for the photographs became secondary. Respect for the dignity of the victims who appeared in the photographs was lost in the need to inform and affect the public. The thousands of photographs began telling the broad story, portraying the scope and the horror of the Holocaust in images often calculated to jar the imagination.

Questions

1. Consider the role of photography in past wars and disasters. How has it helped communicate the nature of the events?
2. Consider the compositions in the pictures in Figures 8.1 and 8.3. What is the message in each? Which picture is the most compelling?
3. Try to imagine yourself as the liberator of a concentration camp. What would you photograph? What message would you want to send to the readers of newspapers and news magazines?
4. Is it possible to become habituated to atrocity? Why do you think this might happen?

LINKS

Further Reading

Eliach, Yaffa. *There Once Was a World: A Nine-Hundred-Year Chronicle of the Shtetl of Eishyshok*. Boston: Little, Brown, 1998.

Gilbert, Martin. *The Holocaust: Maps and Photographs*. New York: Hill and Wang, 1970.

Keller, Ulrich, ed., *The Warsaw Ghetto in Photographs: 206 Views Made in 1941*. New York: Dover, 1984.

Linenthal, Edward. *Preserving Memory: The Struggle to Create America's Holocaust Museum*. New York: Viking, 1995.

Swiebocka, Teresa. *Auschwitz*. Bloomington: Indiana University Press, 1993.

Williams, Val. *Warworks: Women, Photography, and the Iconography of War*. London: Virago, 1994.

Zelizer, Barbie. *Remembering to Forget: Holocaust Memory through the Camera's Eye*. Chicago: University of Chicago Press, 1998.

9
Film

Leaders of the Third Reich used films to mobilize support for their rule and to inculcate the German people with the Nazi racial-eugenic worldview. In the wake of the Holocaust, film has been employed for other purposes: to document, to bear witness, to mitigate or reduce the import of the Holocaust, to provide meaning, to unmask attempts to mystify or suppress the past, to explore relationships between those events and contemporary societies, to say the unsayable, and to examine the life of the traumatized victim. Although these films often represent themselves as narratives of events that happened and were witnessed, it is important to recognize that such films (especially quasi-memoirs and documentaries) are not transparent windows onto the past. In this regard we consider Louis Malle's *Au revoir les enfants* (Good-bye children) (Document 9.1) and Alain Resnais's *Nuit et Brouillard* (*Night and Fog*) (Document 9.2). The first film is especially suitable for those confronting issues raised by the Holocaust for the first time; the second is for more advanced students.

Viewing these films allows us to consider not just who the perpetrators and the bystanders were but also to realize that we might act as perpetrators or bystanders under similar conditions (or at least share their attitudes and values). To situate the Holocaust as a past event that occurred merely "there" and "then" renders it either an awful object of fascination or so much of what Charlotte Delbo calls "useless knowledge." Asking "How would I have acted back then?" can often be no more than self-indulgent speculation, and learning the so-called lessons of the Holocaust can neither resurrect the dead nor self-evidently prepare us to confront different situations. The killers, after all, may not announce themselves with a brass band playing the anthem of the Nazi Party, "The Horst Wessel Song."

Some films transcend these abstractions by forcing us as viewers to assume the role of perpetrator or bystander, compelling us to confront Charlotte Delbo's "useless knowledge." Delbo indicates with this phrase that the nonutilitarian violence of the Holocaust, the killing that served no rational purpose, offers no lessons; rather the sheer fact of it rips a hole in the naturalness of the world that calls each individual to be here now and attend to what is happening: to whom, by whom (what), and how. In other words, one cannot unproblematically employ film as the primary means to tell the story. Documents, witness accounts, and historical reconstructions and analyses bear the bulk of that responsibility. Film and discussion about film can, however, turn our attention to the different ways the story is told. It can also add insight to the motivation for telling stories in a certain way, forcing us to examine the contemporary interests and concerns that condition certain depictions of the Holocaust.

Document 9.1. Discussion of *Au revoir les enfants* (Good-bye Children)

Louis Malle's *Au revoir les enfants* (France, 1987, 104 minutes) is the director's quasi memoir of his school days in German-occupied France. It provides insights into the power of stereotypes, the active ignorance of the bystander, accidental complicity, and the responsibility of memory. Although this film about hidden identities does question the transparency of representations of one's past, it also conveys some sense of the different forms of collaboration, resistance, and rescue that took place in German-occupied France during the Holocaust. The film is effective not because it is didactic but because it is a genre film, a coming-of-age story, with which students can identify. But the film also allows for the possibility of moving beyond the familiar in order to reach a deeper understanding of the film and of ourselves. Further, since it is presented as a thinly disguised reenactment of the director's childhood, *Au revoir les enfants* carries the authority of witness.

The plot is simple. Julien Quentin leaves Paris and returns to his Catholic boarding school in January 1944. The brightest kid in his class, he is surprised to discover that he now has a rival, the newly enrolled Jean Bonnet, who is really Jean Kippelstein, a Jewish boy being hidden by Father Jean, the school's headmaster. The first half of the film involves the now-threatened Julien's attempt to get the goods on his new competitor; the second deals with their friendship, which is interrupted by the arrival of the Gestapo and the arrest of Bonnet, two other Jewish youths in hiding, and Father Jean. It concludes with the director's voice-over indicating the fates of the deportees (as the French refer to the hundreds of thousands of individuals sent to concentration and death camps) and informing his audience that he witnessed and has never forgotten what happened at his school. Malle's film receives the title from Father Jean's—and the film narrative's—last words as the priest is being led off by the Gestapo.

Thirteen years before the release of *Au revoir les enfants,* Malle had co-written and directed *Lacombe, Lucien,* a film about an adolescent peasant in rural France who, rebuffed by the Resistance, becomes a member of the Miliz, the French paramilitary collaborationist militia that helped the Germans round up Jews. He produced this film two years after Marcel Ophuls's *Le chagrin et la pitié* (The sorrow and the pity) had shattered French myths about mass participation in resistance to the Germans and their anti-Jewish policies (actually only a small fraction of the French population participated in the Resistance). The film also undermined the illusory distinction between France and Vichy (the French collaborationist government under Marshal Pétain and Pierre Laval). *Lacombe, Lucien*'s focus on the ignorant, resentful youth appeared to suggest that collaboration was limited to such individuals and that, but for the caprice of events, the average Frenchman would have joined the Resistance. These implications led to the film's condemnation by the newly sensitized French press. With *Au revoir les enfants,* Malle drew a different picture of wartime France and its inhabitants for a new audience that was gripped by the very public trial of the newly captured German war criminal Klaus Barbie. Known as the Butcher of Lyon, Barbie had been responsible for, among other atrocities, the rounding up, deportation, and death of forty-four Jewish children hidden in a school in Izieu, France.

Certain background facts about France during World War II set the stage for the film's plot. France surrendered six weeks after the German invasion of June 1940. It was then divided into two sections: Paris and the North under German rule aided by French collaboration, and the South, named after its capital at Vichy and led by World War I hero Marshal Pétain. In November 1942, the German occupied the South while retaining the Pétain regime as the nominal government. Under Pétain, the French government extensively collaborated in the legal restrictions on Jewish life and later in the deportation of Jews, especially those not born in France. When the film begins all of France is still occupied by the Germans.

Early in the film Julien picks up one of Jean Bonnet's books and reads the title, *The Memoirs of Sherlock Holmes.* This signpost almost begs the viewer to imitate Julien and become a detective trying to find out Bonnet's true identity, indeed to get one up on him. Whereas Quentin is limited by being a participant in the story, the viewer has the advantage of picking up the clues that the director has left for the audience. They are numerous: most obvious perhaps is the constant reference to Jews. Stereotypical depictions (including some quasi-positive ones such as the association of Jews with high intelligence) are readily offered by Quentin's fellow students and by Joseph, the lame kitchen worker at the school who, after being fired by Father Jean, returns triumphant at the end as a Gestapo informer. Perhaps

most telling is Julien's not-so-innocent questions of his older brother—
"What's a Kike?" and "What exactly do people blame them for?"—and his
dissatisfaction with his brother's answers to both. Most, if not all, of the
characters' statements about Jews are made by persons who may never
knowingly have met a Jew in their lives or whose hypocrisy is evident.
There is also a scene in a restaurant in which the audience observes a distinction made by the French between different Jews: there is the native
French Jew, the "decent" Israelite who has always been there and hence has
a right to remain there; and the foreign Jew, the "dirty" Jew (*juif*), who is the
proper object of deportation.

Another telling scene takes place in the public bathhouse. A large sign is
posted in front: THIS ESTABLISHMENT IS PROHIBITED TO JEWS. Also, when
Father Michel assigns students to public showers or private baths, he makes
a point of directing Bonnet to the tubs because in the shower rooms his
circumcision would have revealed his Jewishness to his classmates as well
as to German soldiers. Some viewers may see in this an ironic reference to
the Auschwitz gas chambers that masqueraded as showers. This reference
was probably not Malle's intention; nevertheless, it would be consonant
with Malle's showing Jewishness rather than verbalizing it. Later, when the
Gestapo raids the school, the audience sees that circumcision is a telling
marker of male Jewishness as the soldier orders Julien and the other boys in
the infirmary to pull down their pants. This scene also depicts another
Jewish stereotype when one of the soldiers begins sniffing and says, "There
is a Jew here, I just know it"—the so-called telltale Jewish stench. Jewish
presence is also signified by the film the boys see one evening: Charlie
Chaplin's *The Immigrants*, which is about Jews coming to America. Both the
boys and the viewers of Malle's film observe the immigrant's desired freedom signaled (ironically) by that famous gift from France, the Statue of
Liberty, which greets them upon their ship's arrival in New York. Also, it
was wrongly held by many, including Third Reich propagandists, that Charlie
Chaplin was Jewish.

Other scenes to which Julien himself is privy include Jean's strange
bedside prayers and actions, his refusal to eat paté (pork), and his nonparticipation in Communion—initially because he claims to be Protestant.
Later in the film Father Jean refuses Bonnet when, desperately trying to
allay suspicions about his identity, he attempts to take Communion. This
last scene raises the question, Why does Father Jean, who has hidden Bon-
net/Kippelstein in his school, risk revealing the boy's Jewish identity by
refusing him Communion? Father Jean is caught in a dilemma: it is one
thing to disobey the immoral laws of the state and another to transgress the

laws of the Church, and hence of God, by offering Communion to a nonbeliever.

The initial nonparticipation also places the focus on a key marker of identity: names. Quentin doubts Bonnet's claim to be Protestant because his family name is usually found among Catholics. The relationship between name and identity is played out through the entire film. For example, the name Jean Kippelstein written in one of Bonnet's books inspected by Quentin suggests that its owner is Jewish, although he does not realize at the time that Kippelstein is a Jewish name. In a key scene in which he acts out his confusion over the persecution of the Jews and the apparent universal indifference to their fate, Quentin baits his mother by pointing out how their Alsatian relatives bear a name usually borne by Jews, Reinach, and hence his family may be Jewish.

Malle also describes a French collaborationist society. One character, the ignorant Joseph, who is attempting to get even with those whom he feels treated him unfairly, is reminiscent of the resentful youth in *Lacombe, Lucien*. In *Au revoir les enfants,* Malle also casts Julien's never-seen father, a collaborating manufacturer, as well as all of the schoolchildren's parents, whom Father Jean excoriates in his sermon and who have managed to preserve or even increase their wealth under German occupation. Then there is the most crucial scene of the film: the Gestapo agent Doctor Müller asks Quentin's class, "Which one of you is Jean Kippelstein?" and Julien cannot help looking in Bonnet's direction for a fraction of second. He does not intend to betray his friend, but he is convinced that he has. Moreover, the viewer of the film is also tempted to look in Bonnet's direction, as Julien did, and is thus complicitous in Julien's betrayal. The film ends with a final voice-over in which the narrator—purportedly Louis Malle—says, "Over forty years have passed, but I will remember every second of that January morning until the day I die." Thus, the film is presented as a way for the director to atone for what he considers his betrayal and hence his role in the murder of Bonnet/Kippelstein. The viewer might also wonder whether the film is a form of penance and, if so, how does telling this story perform an act of atonement? Indeed, might Julien have acted otherwise?

Consider first, that the young schoolboy Louis Malle, unlike Julien Quentin, did not befriend Kippelstein; he had minimal contact with him. Although the roundup of the hidden Jewish students did leave its mark on his memory, what troubled Malle the most was his ignorance of what was going on around him. After making the film, Malle discovered that for forty years he had been convinced that the kitchen boy, the film's Joseph, had been the informer; in actuality, the kitchen boy was another Jewish boy hidden by the priests at the school.

Document 9. 2. Discussion of *Night and Fog (Nuit et brouilliard)**

The first major documentary about the Holocaust, Alain Resnais's *Night and Fog* (France, 1955, 32 minutes) was commissioned by the French government to depict Nazi atrocities. The title derives from Hitler's Night and Fog Decree, issued in December 1941, which called for rounding up political prisoners (Resistance fighters, illegal journalists) in the foggy dead of night and either executing them or giving them a summary trial and then deporting them to the concentration camps, where they disappeared. Since the film's production in 1955, this documentary has been employed in U.S. schools, churches, and synagogues to speak the unspeakable. *Night and Fog* combines black-and-white newsreels, stills, and scenes from *Triumph of the Will*, Leni Riefenstal's film of the 1934 Nazi Party rally in Nuremberg, to detail a chronology. It follows the "Nazi machine" from its assumption of power to its building of concentration camps, from the rounding up, deporting, and gassing of the victims to the liberation of the survivors. It then concludes with the Nuremberg trials and the perpetrators' cries of "I am not responsible." Documentary black-and-white footage is juxtaposed with scenes, filmed in color, of the present-day (1955) ruins of the concentration-labor-death camp Auschwitz.

Why subject people to this unspeakable horror, shocking even to those who have seen films or stills of the dead or the piles of shoes, bowls, hair, and bones that the Americans, British, and Soviets encountered when liberating a concentration or death camp? Those piles leave their impression. Often viewers fail to register—or, more properly, forget that they had registered—that the film alternates black-and-white footage with scenes in color. The film presents other, often discordant, juxtapositions—between the words of Jean Cayrol's text (he had been a non-Jewish Resistance fighter who had been among those interned under the Night and Fog Decree) and the images, between Hanns Eisler's soundtrack (Eisler was a Jewish Communist who had fled Germany after Hitler's seizure of power) and both text and images. These often jarring juxtapositions are meant to provoke the audience to reflect upon what is being presented: what is juxtaposed, what is contrasted, what is mentioned, and what is not.

When viewers are asked what the film is about, they often reply, "the murder of the six million Jews." But whom does the narrative describe as

---

*Because of the graphic depiction of concentration camp victims, high school teachers who show the film may need to secure parents' and guardians' permission.

victims? In the translation of the screenplay, one can search mightily and futilely for mention of the Jews. Only Stern, "a Jewish student from Amsterdam," is described as Jewish (and in the original English-subtitled print even this mention is left out). The only nationality of the dead mentioned in the film is Spanish, specifically the three thousand Spanish prisoners at Mauthausen quarry (where Cayrol was himself imprisoned for a time). The film notes the triangular insignia of the various concentration camp prisoners: the political prisoners' red and the criminals' green, but not the Jews' yellow stars let alone the homosexuals' pink or the black of Roma and Sinti ("Gypsies"). One may counter that many of the stills show deportees with stars on their sleeves being loaded on trains. Indeed, this disconnection between narrative and image generates a moment to think: why is nothing spoken about the Jews? Is that proper? A similar issue arises with respect to the perpetrators. Neither the German people nor the French but only the Nazis are mentioned. The French government, moreover, threatened to prevent the general release of the film unless the director concealed the complicity of the French police in the deportation of Jews to Auschwitz by airbrushing the brim of the military cap *(kepi)* worn by the French gendarme guarding the transit camp at Pithiviers. Resnais searched his conscience for three months until he finally decided that the whole was more significant than any one part. The government also asked Cayrol never to refer to Germans since France and West Germany were at the time beginning a rapprochement. The film also raises issues about memory (especially the final evocation of memory and forgetfulness), about the responsibility of the audience, and about the responsibility of the filmmakers, as well as about the filmmakers' conception of the Holocaust. What aspects of the Holocaust did the filmmakers leave out? What indeed is the film about: an event that took place ten years before; or the possibility of its happening again; or the ongoing maintenance of the institutions, structures, and values that contributed to the Holocaust? When asked in 1962 what the film was about, Resnais himself said that it is about Algeria and the violent French measures employed to suppress the Algerians' call for their independence.

Questions

————

Document 9.1. Discussion of *Au revoir les enfants* (Good-bye Children)

1. Why did Julien not realize that Jews were being hidden in his school and why did he not befriend them? What is our responsibility for what we do not know but perhaps should know? Is ignorance in such situations always active ignorance—a conscious or unconscious effort not to know?
2. How, in this film, do names signify identity?
3. What does it signify when Julien's mother, a character otherwise viewed lovingly by son and director, demonstrates hypocrisy by declaring that some Jews are decent and that she has nothing against Jews in general, yet is quick to confute Julien's baiting question, "Aren't we Jewish?"?
4. What does it reveal when viewers look in Bonnet's direction as Julien did in response to Doctor Müller's question, "Which one of you is Jean Kippelstein?"?
5. How might Julien have acted otherwise?
6. Why did Malle not realize that the kitchen boy was Jewish?

LINKS

I.   History   2. The Creation of a Racist Society   2.1. Signs of Racism, Symbols of Segregation   18
      4. Resistance and Rescue   4.4. Magda Trocmé   82
IV. Ethics   13.4. How Does Good Happen?   239

————

Document 9.2. Discussion of *Night and Fog (Nuit et brouillard)*

1. What are the consequences of not mentioning the Jews by name in the film?
2. Who is portrayed as the perpetrator? What is the effect of not mentioning the Germans or the French?
2. What does the film suggest about the way memory is constructed within the context of contemporary history and politics? Does this make memory less legitimate?

LINKS

I.   History   3. The Killing Process 3.8. German Railway Schedule   61
III. Other Genocides   10. The Armenian Genocide   10.7. Starting Over?   169
IV. Ethics   13.5. What Are the Limits of Forgiveness?   241

Other Films

The Diary of Anne Frank: George Stevens, 1959, U.S.A. (170 minutes). The
director, George Stevens, reproduces the claustrophobic feel of the attic
hiding place, but the characters of the film verge on Jewish stereotype
even as their Jewishness is underplayed. Anne Frank is thoroughly
Americanized (a *Shikse*). Furthermore, as the concluding voice-over of a
line in her diary underscores, she is represented as an overly optimistic
young girl and a benign figure for identification. "I still believe," she
says "in spite of everything that people are truly good at heart." Her
seven months in concentration camps, which culminated with her death
from typhus, is thus glossed over. To better illustrate how the film
altered the tone, content, and characterizations of the diary, it could be
compared with *The Diary of Anne Frank: The Definitive Edition* (New
York: Anchor Books, 1995).

Europa, Europa: Agnieszk Holland, 1990, Germany/France/Poland (100
minutes). This coming-of-age film brings up questions of identity and
stereotype as well as marginalization.

Image Before My Eyes: Josh Waletzky, 1980, U.S.A. (90 minutes). This film
about Jewish life in prewar Poland emphasizes that Jews were not just
victims but people with a rich culture that was irrevocably destroyed.

Jud Süss: Veit Harlan, 1940, Germany (100 minutes). This is a Nazi film,
loosely based on the life of Joseph Süss Oppenheimer, who was executed in 1738 for alleged treason while serving as financial advisor to
the Duke of Württemberg. It suggests the power of anti-Semitic propaganda and the manifold forms of Jewish representation.

Life Is Beautiful: Robert Benigni, 1997, Italy (125 minutes). This Oscar-
winning Italian film raises the question whether comedy is an appropriate vehicle for representing the Holocaust. Unfortunately, especially for
audiences who have no other exposure to the history of the Holocaust,
the film's benign representation of the concentration camp and of life in
the camps is extraordinarily unrealistic.

Lodz Ghetto: Alan Adelson and Kathy Taverna, 1989, U.S.A. (156 minutes).
This documentary provides insight into ghetto life.

The Nasty Girl: Michael Verhoeven, 1990, Federal Republic of Germany (94
minutes). The story of one German girl coming to grips with her town's
past and the town's attempts to avoid its past. It shows an adolescent
full of spunk overcoming preconceptions.

One Survivor Remembers: HBO, 1995, U.S.A. (39 minutes). An Oscar-winning
film, this is a moving memoir of Gerda Weissmann Klein's journey from

adolescence through the camps to liberation and a new life in the United
States.

The Quarrel: Eli Cohen, 1990, Canada (90 minutes). The film is based on
Chaim Grade's short story "My Quarrel with Hersh Rasseyner," in
When Night Fell: An Anthology of Holocaust Short Stories, edited by Linda
Linda Schomer Raphael and Marc Lee Raphael (New Brunswick, N,J.:
Rutgers University Press, 1999). It dramatizes contrasting theodicies as
well as the split between the religious and the secular Yiddish cultures
of prewar Poland.

Schindler: Jon Blair, 1992, Great Britain (122 minutes). This is a documentary
about *Schindler's List.* See also *Anne Frank Remembered*: Jon Blair, 1995,
Netherlands, U.S.A., Great Britain (117 minutes). For the purposes of
contrasting the documentaries with the feature films, it is most effective
to view *Schindler's List* and *Anne Frank* first.

Schindler's List: Steven Spielberg, 1993, U.S.A. (197 minutes). Steven Spielberg's Oscar-winning film was the first feature film to represent the
Holocaust before a mass audience. It offers a picture of life in the ghetto
and in a labor camp rather than in a death camp; it also displays the
important role greed and self-interest played in the Holocaust. Unfortunately, the film descends into schmaltz with the invention of Schindler's
lachrymose departure scene, while the soundtrack sometimes slips into
the maudlin.

Shoah: Claude Lanzmann, 1985, France (570 minutes). Claude Lanzmann's
epic documentary brings together on-site interviews with survivors,
perpetrators, bystanders, and witnesses.

Sophie's Choice: Alan J. Pakula, 1982, U.S.A. (150 minutes). An Auschwitz
doctor offers Sophie, a Polish Catholic woman, a choice: to save one of
her children in exchange for sending the other to its death.

The Wave: Alexander Grasshof, 1981, U.S.A. (46 minutes). This film shows a
striking dramatization of a high school experiment in the corruption of
power. You do not have to be German to be a potential perpetrator.

Wannsee Conference: Heinz Schirk, 1984, Federal Republic of Germany (87
minutes). This recreation of the conference in real time with verified
citations is most effectively viewed after a reading of the protocol of the
meeting (see Document 3.1).

Weapons of the Spirit: Pierre Sauvage, 1988, U.S.A. (90 minutes; 38 minutes).
Made up mainly of interviews, this film, which shows the matter-of-
factness of rescue, portrays the people of Le Chambon-sur-Lignon who hid
Jews in their village. The longer version is preferable.

Part III
Other Genocides

G *enocide* is a relatively new word. In 1943 in the course of writing *Axis Rule in Occupied Europe*, Raphael Lemkin combined the Greek word *genos* (nation or tribe) with the Latin suffix *cide* (killing) to describe German atrocities. According to his definition, genocide consists of "a coordinated plan of different actions aiming at the destruction of essential foundations of the life of the national groups, with the aim of annihilating the groups themselves." Lemkin was a Jewish refugee from Poland and also a lawyer who sought more than merely to describe a specific phenomenon. He wanted to punish and prevent a specific crime. Owing in no small part to his efforts, the United Nations, formed in the aftermath of World War II, recognized genocide as a crime under international law in 1948. Article II of the 1948 Convention on the Prevention and Punishment of the Crime of Genocide defines genocide as follows:

> In the present Convention, genocide means any of the following acts committed with intent to destroy, in whole or in part, a national, ethnic, racial or religious group, as such: a) killing members of the group; b) causing serious bodily or mental harm to members of the group; c) deliberately inflicting on the group conditions of life calculated to bring about its physical destruction in whole or in part; d) imposing measures intended to prevent births within the group; e) forcibly transferring children of the group to another group.

In the years since the convention was passed, references to genocide have become commonplace, and the use of the term today is much wider than either Lemkin's original definition or that of the convention. In some instances current usage is frivolous, careless, or misguided. In many others, however, it is simply ambiguous. Did the near-total decimation of the original population of the Western Hemisphere, largely through disease but also through brutal wars of conquest, constitute genocide? To what extent could the word also be applied to the trans-Atlantic slave trade, which caused the death of millions over several centuries? What term does one use to describe the murder of millions, without reference to ethnicity, in the Soviet Union under Joseph Stalin, in China under Mao Zedong, or in Cambodia under the Khmer Rouge? And how appropriate is it to refer to the recent "ethnic cleansing" in the former Yugoslavia as genocide?

There are no straightforward answers to these questions. Perhaps the questions themselves are often misplaced. Mass atrocities, whatever their designation, should be resisted and, when possible, prevented. Their victims should be remembered, their survivors assisted, and their long-term consequences addressed. The fundamental lessons of the Holocaust concern the value of all human life, the prejudices that endanger it, and the processes by which such prejudices become murderous. In this context, any of the historic crimes mentioned above, and many more, might be appropriately considered along with the Holocaust in learning about genocide.

Here we focus on three atrocities of the past century: the Armenian genocide in the Ottoman Empire during World War I, the campaigns of "ethnic cleansing" in the former Yugoslavia, and the 1994 genocide in Rwanda. The first two cases have been officially recognized by international organizations as crimes of genocide: the Armenian genocide has been recognized as such by the European Parliament, and the Rwandan genocide by the United Nations. The issues and dynamics of both, moreover, allow clear points of comparison with the Holocaust. The third case, that of Bosnia and Kosovo, is more ambiguous. Notwithstanding the enormous problems facing these regions, the danger of genocide in the Balkans appears less imminent than in the past. In their decision to intervene here, however, international leaders were clearly motivated by events, images, and issues that vividly recalled the crimes of Hitler's Germany in World War II.

The three chapters in this part are designed to be used together or separately. Each contains several questions for reflection, a timeline, a glossary of terms and abbreviations, and suggestions for further reading. The centerpiece of each chapter is a detailed narrative supplemented by documentary texts. To illustrate parallels among the three cases, each narrative examines the nature of "life before," with an emphasis on the presence or absence of preexisting prejudice, events and ideologies that created the conditions necessary for mass murder, the system of mass murder and the experiences of victims, the moral choices and responsibilities of individuals, the response of the international community, and the issues facing survivors.

Our aim in placing these cases side-by-side is to consider genocide not as an isolated or distant tragedy but rather as a recurring problem of our civilization. The details of the tragic events presented in these chapters, less familiar to most than the history of the Holocaust, have often presented a barrier to thinking more deeply about them. We hope that these chapters can help to remove that barrier.

10
The Armenian Genocide

The Armenian genocide was carried out between 1915 and 1923 in what is now Turkey. Less prominent internationally than the Holocaust or more recent campaigns of mass murder and ethnic cleansing, the systematic killing of Armenians during World War I is nevertheless recognized by many scholars as the first genocide of the past century or even the first of its kind in history. Beneath the political complexities accompanying the end of the Ottoman Empire and the birth of modern Turkey, the Armenian genocide anticipated fundamental issues and questions that reemerged in the context of the Holocaust and continue to weigh heavily in the present.

The efforts of the Young Turk government to eliminate the Armenian minority in the Ottoman Empire during World War I predate the Holocaust by over two decades, and some scholars have seen in these events a direct precedent for Hitler's genocidal policies. Germany was the most important ally of the Ottoman Empire in World War I, and German leaders of the Nazi period, including Hitler, were certainly aware of what had transpired there just a few years earlier. Preparing military leaders for the brutal subjugation of Poland on the eve of World War II, Hitler even referred to the Armenian genocide directly. "Who," he asked, "still remembers today the annihilation of the Armenians?" Although there is no evidence that Nazi leaders generally seized upon the Armenian genocide as a model for the Final Solution, parallels are unmistakable. Radical nationalism, the manipulation of religious prejudice, the use of deportations and concentration camps, and the pretext of war are some of the factors common to both events.

Yet the Armenian genocide should also be considered on its own terms. When addressing World War I, very few commentators give even superficial attention to what was widely regarded as the war's greatest atrocity. Similarly, in presenting the dissolution of the Ottoman Empire, its defeat in World War I, and the emergence of modern Turkey, historians often neglect the human dimensions of these colossal developments. For the Armenians, certainly, the replacement of a collapsing multiethnic empire by a young national state had cataclysmic consequences. Considering this transformation from their perspective, one can question more critically the claims of ethnic identity, so portentous in our own day, and the mythology that typically surrounds national histories.

The Armenians in the Ottoman Empire

The Armenians are the ancient inhabitants of a western Asian region that today includes eastern Turkey, the Republic of Armenia, and areas of several bordering states. By the sixteenth century most of this region, which suffered repeated invasions and warfare during much of its history, was incorporated into the Ottoman Empire. The Armenians were one of the empire's many Christian minorities, separated from the majority Turkish Muslim population by language as well as religion. Although Armenians enjoyed considerable freedom in everyday life, they also faced official discrimination.

Religious prejudice was clearly a factor in the Armenian genocide. The role of religion and religious difference in Armenian history, however, is by no means straightforward. For much of the Ottoman Empire's history Jews and Christians enjoyed a tolerance toward religious minorities scarcely conceivable in Europe during the same period. Coming to see another religious group as "damned" or worthless can certainly contribute to a process of dehumanization, and this kind of prejudice, as evident in the religious roots of anti-Semitism, is at work in genocide. In the Armenian case, however, it is not a sufficient explanation in itself. For hundreds of years, the Ottoman sultan recognized the Armenians, as well as the Jews and the Greeks, as semi-autonomous religious communities, or millets, within his empire. This system of administration asserted the superiority of Islam while reflecting the Koran's acknowledgment of Jews and Christians as "people of the book."

Systematic persecution of Armenians began only with the Ottoman Empire's rapid disintegration during the 1800s, under the force of national independence movements, many of which were supported by the intervention of European powers. Although Armenians enjoyed a reputation as the sultan's sadik millet, or "faithful community," the Ottoman government came to view them as a threat. The concentration of a minority Christian population on the empire's eastern border with an expanding Russia seemed especially ominous.

At the same time, moreover, many Armenians began to challenge their subordinate status in Ottoman society. This challenge was in part attributable to a national awakening typical of the nineteenth century and was characterized among Armenians by a new appreciation for the Armenian language, the establishment of Armenian schools, and the publication of Armenian books and newspapers. Hand in hand with this awakening of national pride came dramatic changes in the formal legal position of Armenians within the empire. Pressured by European powers and spurred on by liberal reformers, the Ottoman state undertook a "reorganization" of society that lent its name to a whole period of Ottoman history—the so-called Tanzimat era from 1839 to 1876. Although new laws recognized the Armenians as full citizens, the changes remained largely a matter of theory rather than practice where the Armenian population was concerned.

It was apparently with the idea of returning Armenians to "their place" that they were massacred in such large numbers—estimates run as high as three hundred thousand deaths—between 1894 and 1896. This campaign of violence, driven by armed troops and erupting across great distances more or less simultaneously, seems to have been consciously implemented by the government of Sultan Abdul Hamid, who was under international pressure for reform at the time. These events, along with a similar massacre of over twenty thousand Armenians in 1909, undoubtedly established a precedent for the later genocide. As brutal and destructive as these massacres were, however, they did not represent a state attempt to eliminate all Armenians.

More important, however, was the problem of continuity. Confronted with issues still very present in our own day, the Ottoman Empire faced three possible courses of action. One course, embodied imperfectly by the Tanzimat reforms, was to move from a system of subordination and oppression to a truly multicultural society. This was the road not taken, and it would be worthwhile to consider why. The second course, attempted by Abdul Hamid, was essentially to restore the old order, but in this instance requiring an enormous application of violence. The third course was to create yet another kind of new order, and one that had no place for the Armenian minority at all.

The Armenians Under the Young Turks

In 1908 a military coup d'etat brought to power a revolutionary group known as the Committee of Union and Progress (CUP) or, more popularly, the Young Turks. This movement initially enjoyed the enthusiastic support of the Armenians and promised a new era of solidarity among the peoples of the empire. Hearkening back to the abandoned reforms of the Tanzimat era, the Young Turks forced Abdul Hamid to accept a written constitution and, particularly important for the Armenians, proclaimed an end to religious discrimination. When an attempted countercoup in 1909, accompanied by the aforementioned violence against Armenians, failed to reestablish the old order, the Young Turks deposed Abdul Hamid and at least officially denounced the massacres.

In the years that followed, however, the government of the CUP became increasingly authoritarian and nationalistic. This shift, which led ultimately to the genocide against the Armenians, was in part attributable to the rapid disintegration of the Ottoman Empire during this period, anticipating its final demise in World War I. As Ottoman authority collapsed, most notably in the Balkans but also in northern Africa, proponents of radical nationalism among the Young Turks gained in influence. In its most extreme expression, generally referred to as Pan-Turkism, this nationalism looked beyond Ottoman traditions and institutions to a mythic Turkish past and envisioned, in place of the lost empire, a state unifying Turkish peoples across the Asian continent.

Although some Young Turk leaders had espoused such ideas earlier, a useful reference point for the establishment of radical Turkish nationalism as a government ideology is the 1913 coup within the CUP that brought to power the radical nationalists who ruled the country during the genocide. Most important among these figures were Talaat Pasha, the minister of the interior, Enver Pasha, the minister of war, and Djemal Pasha, the minister of the navy. (Note: Surnames became common in Turkey only following a 1934 law requiring their use.) Document 10.1, an excerpt from the memoirs of the Henry Morgenthau, U.S. ambassador to the Ottoman Empire from 1913 to 1916, offers his account of a visible shift in Turkish politics during this period away from the cosmopolitan ideas of the 1908 revolution.

In reading this text, one can easily recognize the overt prejudice and ethnocentrism that Morgenthau brings to his interpretation of the growing nationalism he observed. Horrified by the genocidal policies he had witnessed firsthand, Morgenthau sought to explain the crimes of the Young Turk leaders partly in terms of longstanding Western stereotypes concerning the brutality of "the Turk." His explanations, of course, fail to address adequately the wider occurrence of genocide and may simply perpetuate a cycle of prejudice.

Beneath such national stereotypes, however, this text reveals much about workings of nationalism and raises the problems inherent in Morgenthau's own bifurcated vision. In particular, Morgenthau's contrast between democracy, on one hand, and nationalism on the other, as well as his characterization of Pan-Turkism as an "atavistic reversion" rather than a modern ideology seems too simplistic, especially given the parallels between the situations he describes and the circumstances of life in Germany after Hitler's rise to power in the early 1930s.

Genocide

On November 2, 1914, the Ottoman Empire formally entered World War I on the side of Germany and Austria-Hungary against Great Britain, France, and Russia. Sultan Mehmet V, notwithstanding the secular character of both the war and the Young Turk government, proclaimed the conflict a *jihad*, or Islamic "holy war" against the Allies. Although Armenian leaders, realizing that their homelands near the Russian border would become a major battle-ground, had urged neutrality, their position at the outset of the war was essentially loyal. Armenian soldiers in the Ottoman Army served with distinction precisely in this eastern theater, and no less a figure than Minister of War Enver Pasha, one of the leaders later held principally responsible for the genocide, commended their service to the Armenian patriarch, the head of the Armenian Church. As Ottoman forces began to suffer serious set-backs in the early months of 1915, however, the Young Turk government openly identified the Armenians as an internal enemy and ordered that they be disarmed and deported from their homes.

Although these "deportations" had begun even earlier, Armenians normally commemorate April 24 as the beginning of the genocide. On the night of April 23–24, hundreds of Armenian political, religious, and cultural leaders were arrested in the Ottoman capital of Constantinople and from there they were then deported and, for the most part, put to death. These deportations from a cosmopolitan urban center, far from the eastern front, made the aims of the government abundantly clear. At the end of May, moreover, this policy found formal expression in the Temporary Law of Deportation, which authorized the relocation of persons suspected of treason or espionage, a charge ultimately extending to the entire Armenian population.

Deportation, in this as in other genocides, was another word for annihilation. Armenians serving in the Ottoman military were segregated, disarmed, worked to exhaustion, and executed, in some instances after being forced to dig their own graves. Men not serving in the military were often either arrested and killed prior to the deportations or separated and shot early in the course of the death marches. It was thus largely a defenseless population of women and children, leaving their homes under the pretext of temporary resettlement, who fell victim to the protracted horrors of the deportations: starvation, thirst, exposure and exhaustion, rape, and murderous attacks both by armed marauders and by the gendarmes supposedly charged with their protection.

The route of the deportation marches (or in some instances rail transports) was generally southward, and their stated destination was a series of camps in the Syrian and Iraqi deserts. Only a small percentage of deportees, however, ever reached these camps, and many of those who did survive the journey were subsequently murdered outright or simply left there to die. Although lacking the technological efficiency of the Nazi deportations and death camps, this system of genocide resulted in an estimated one million to two million deaths.

Document 10.2 is an account of the deportations by a lieutenant in the Turkish military that includes a graphic depiction of brutalities against the Armenians. It reveals the systematic nature of the genocide and illustrates the lethal effectiveness of deportation as a means of mass murder. The report also raises questions about the psychological and political reasons for referring to genocide as "deportation" (Document 5.1) or the ways in which the circumstances of "resettlement" make perpetrators more ruthless and victims more vulnerable.

Perpetrators, Bystanders, Rescuers

The account by the Turkish lieutenant in Document 10.2 suggests some of the ambiguity of responsibility and complicity in genocide. Was this officer a perpetrator? Was he instead, as the tone of his report suggests, primarily an onlooker? Or might he appropriately be described, at least according to his own version of events, as a rescuer?

Emphasizing individual leaders in mass atrocities, such as Adolf Hitler, Joseph Stalin, Pol Pot, and Mao Zedong, simplifies complex events and focuses moral outrage. On the other extreme, the attribution of "collective guilt"—to the Serbs, the Germans, or "the white man," for example—accomplishes the same simplification. In analyzing the Armenian genocide, writers have typically identified as the perpetrators the Young Turk triumvirate—Talaat, Enver, and Djemal—that essentially ruled the Ottoman state during World War I. All were later tried and convicted as war criminals and sentenced to death in absentia. More frequently, however, Armenians and others simply speak of the genocide committed by "the Turks."

There can be no doubt that the Armenian genocide was ordered and organized by the Young Turk leadership in Constantinople. Ambassador Morgenthau's account of a conversation with Talaat Pasha, the Ottoman minister of the interior, excerpted in Document 10.3, and the reports of German diplomats that follow (Documents 10.5 and 10.6) are just a few of the many sources that document this important fact. These government figures may have been the perpetrators, but clearly here as elsewhere, genocide required the participation of thousands, or perhaps even hundreds of thousands, of individuals.

Documents 10.3 and 10.4 allow readers to consider issues of moral responsibility from opposing vantage points. Of all the texts in this section on the Armenian genocide, most readers will likely find the conversation re- called in Document 10.3 the most accessible, illuminating, and thought- provoking. The passage is remarkable above all for the frankness and even levity with which Talaat discusses the murderous policies of his govern- ment. Cordial in his relationship with the U.S. ambassador and seemingly reasonable in other matters, Talaat nevertheless moves between contempt and hatred in his attitude toward the Armenians and is defensively dismiss- ive of any reminders of their humanity.

Document 10.4 is very different, both in its view of the genocide "from below" and in its emphasis on the compassion shown to some Armenians by their Turkish neighbors. The account comes from an oral history collec- tion of survivor testimony at the University of California at Los Angeles and describes the efforts of a Turkish military officer to shelter an endangered Armenian family. Richard Hovannisian, who has analyzed the whole collec- tion of taped interviews, included this example in one of his essays to illus- trate what he refers to as "shades of altruism" during the genocide.

Because this narrative is simple and straightforward, one can only guess at the motives and attitudes of the Turkish officer in the story. He and his family do not seem, however, to have been outspoken critics of the mea- sures against the Armenians or even to have been "rescuers" in any idealis- tic sense. Furthermore, the Armenians' conversion to Islam that is men- tioned in the text, although apparently urged in this instance out of concern for their safety, naturally represented a kind of coerced assimilation not entirely removed from the aims of the genocide. Notwithstanding these ambiguities, however, one should note that many Armenians were spared through precisely such complex cases of intervention on their behalf.

International Response

At the time of the Armenian genocide, the Ottoman Empire was already at war with the Allied Powers of Great Britain, France, and Russia, soon to be joined by the United States. As in the Holocaust, therefore, the question of military intervention was partly preempted by the fact of a world war. To the extent that military operations assisted the Armenians—as in the spec- tacular rescue of the besieged defenders of Musa Dagh by a French warship on patrol in the Mediterranean—this effect was for the most part incidental.

The international community did, however, recognize the genocide as an atrocity distinct from the general conduct of the war. And despite con- cerns that formal protests by countries at war with the Ottoman government might serve to worsen the suffering of the Armenians, the Allied powers ultimately decided to condemn the massacres against them openly. In a joint declaration on May 24, 1915, Great Britain, France, and Russia denounced what they described as "new crimes against humanity and civilization" and warned that the leaders of the Ottoman government would be held personally responsible for the persecution of the Armenians.

The unique relationship of Ambassador Morgenthau with the government in Constantinople must be understood in the context of U.S. neutrality, which lasted until April 1917. During the early years of the war, the administration of President Woodrow Wilson received wide political support for its faithfulness to a long tradition of American neutrality and its refusal to allow the United States to be drawn into a European war. Under such circumstances, military intervention on behalf of the Armenians was never a serious option. Instead, Morgenthau used his "neutral" position to its fullest—in protesting to the Ottoman government, in bringing the genocide to world attention, and not least in opening channels for humanitarian aid.

Of all the major powers, however, Germany undoubtedly exercised the greatest influence on the Ottoman government and thus had the greatest potential for effective intervention against the genocide. It is not surprising, however, particularly given the assignment of "war guilt" to Germany at the end of World War I and its own genocidal policies during World War II, that many have accused the German government of direct complicity in the atrocities of its Ottoman ally.

There is some truth to this claim. German officers were closely involved in the activities of the Turkish military at the time of the genocide, and the German government, in its efforts to censor any information that could serve the propaganda purposes of its enemies, clearly attempted to conceal Turkish atrocities from the public. Despite its repeated protests against the genocide through private channels, moreover, the German government remained, throughout the war, the most important ally of a government engaged in the systematic murder of its own people.

Johannes Lepsius, a German pastor, was the most prominent of several German citizens who, outraged at the treatment of the Armenians, urged political and humanitarian measures on their behalf. After the end of the war, Lepsius published a collection of German government documents entitled *Deutschland und Armenien* (Germany and Armenia), seeking to demonstrate the extent of the genocide and to prove that his government had taken efforts to prevent it.

Documents 10.5 and 10.6 are translated from Lepsius's documentation. Although hardly sufficient in themselves to establish or refute the charge of

German complicity in the genocide, they do give insight into the resolve with which Young Turk leaders were willing to carry out their policies regardless of world opinion. In reading these texts, moreover, one can also identify and analyze some of the rationalizations through which the German government sought to justify its position. These rationalizations, one should note, bear some resemblance to those later used by leaders in the United States and other countries who wished to prevent the issue of the genocide from troubling their own relations with Turkey.

The aftermath and legacy of the Armenian genocide have been characterized above all by unresolved issues. This can be said of many atrocities, and there are all too many injured communities today still in search of understanding, recognition, and justice. No formal declaration or material restitution has the power to undo a genocide. For members of the surviving Armenian community, nevertheless, the quest for "resolution" has remained particularly elusive. Uprooted from their historic homeland and dispersed across the globe, many Armenians today face complex choices concerning their cultural identity and their relationship to the past.

International concern over the genocide, reflected to some extent in the documents that follow, proved remarkably short-lived even among the wartime enemies of the Ottoman Empire. The settlement after World War I provided for both the trial of perpetrators and the establishment of an independent Armenia. The Turkish nationalists who overthrew the postwar Ottoman government and established the Republic of Turkey in 1923, however, rejected these terms and indeed continued the persecution and expulsion of the Armenians. Preoccupied with other strategic concerns, Britain, France, and the United States ultimately reconciled themselves to these developments.

In the end, only a very small number of Armenians remained in what is now Turkey. The largest group of Armenians today is located in the Republic of Armenia, formerly a part of the Soviet Union, but sizeable diasporas exist in the former Soviet Union, throughout Europe and the Middle East, and in the United States. Survivors of the genocide and their descendants have had essentially no alternative but to adapt, with varying degrees of eagerness or reluctance, to their new circumstances. The unresolved issues of the past have not prevented Armenians from living in the present and looking to the future.

Integration into a new society, however, also involves intentional and unintentional transformations of identity. This dilemma, more or less common to immigrants everywhere, is heightened for some Armenians by the fact of the genocide. The preservation of Armenian identity and Armenian culture, in this context, becomes an assertion of human dignity against an event that attempted to efface a whole history and way of life.

The Armenians have also tried to protect the memory of the genocide against systematic campaigns of denial. Even now, the Turkish government continues to deny that the genocide against the Armenians occurred and to promote this claim abroad. Although scholars can easily refute the denial on the basis of archival documents, press accounts, and survivor testimony, the political and financial resources available to deniers raise concerns for many Armenians, especially because interest in historical events typically diminishes with the passage of time.

Document 10.7, exploring some of the issues confronting survivors, is taken from the book *Black Dog of Fate* by the Armenian American poet and writer Peter Balakian. Balakian's memoirs, in which he recounts his gradual awakening to the significance of his Armenian ancestry, are probably the single most accessible and informative resource for high school and college students wanting to read more about the Armenian genocide and the lives of Armenian survivors in the United States.

In the excerpt, Balakian reflects on the life of his grandparents and their adjustment to life in the United States. Standing alone, the text perhaps presents more questions than answers: Why did Balakian's family choose to remain silent about their traumatic past? How did this past nevertheless remain with them and shape their identity? How did they pass this identity on to their children and grandchildren? In considering these questions, one can gain a better appreciation for the issues facing genocide survivors and, more generally, the way that seemingly remote events shape the lives of "ordinary" individuals.

Document 10.1. Pan-Turkism: Excerpt from *Ambassador Morgenthau's Story* by Henry Morgenthau

Long before the European War began, the Turkish democracy had disappeared. The power of the new Sultan had gone, and the hopes of regenerating Turkey on modern lines had gone also, leaving only a group of individuals, headed by Talaat and Enver, actually in possession of the state. Having lost their democratic aspirations these men now supplanted them with a new national conception. In place of a democratic constitutional state, they resurrected the idea of Pan-Turkism; in place of equal treatment of all Ottomans, they decided to establish a country exclusively for Turks. I have called this a new conception; yet it was new only to the individuals who then controlled the destiny of the empire, for, in reality, it was simply an attempt to revive the most barbaric ideas of their ancestors. It represented, as I have said, merely an atavistic reversion to the original Turk. We now saw that the Turkish leaders, in talking about liberty, equality, fraternity, and constitutionalism, were merely children repeating phrases; that they had used the word "democracy" merely as a ladder by which to climb to power. After five hundred years' close contact with European civilization, the Turk remained precisely the same individual as the one who had emerged from the steppes of Asia in the Middle Ages. He was clinging just as tenaciously as his ancestors to that conception of a state as consisting of a few master individuals whose right it is to enslave and plunder and maltreat any peoples whom they can subject to their military control. Though Talaat and Enver and Djemal all came of the humblest families, the same fundamental ideas of master and slave possessed them that formed the statecraft of Osman and the early Sultans. We now discovered that a paper constitution and even tearful visits to Christian churches and cemeteries could not uproot the inborn preconception of this nomadic tribe that there are only two kinds of people in the world—the conquering and the conquered.

When the Turkish Government abrogated the Capitulations, and in this way freed themselves from the domination of the foreign powers, they were merely taking one step toward realizing this Pan-Turkish ideal. I have alluded to the difficulties which I had with them over the Christian schools. Their determination to uproot these, or at least to transform them into Turkish institutions, was merely another detail in the same racial progress. Similarly, they attempted to make all foreign business houses employ only Turkish labour, insisting that they should discharge their Greek, Armenian, and Jewish clerks, stenographers, workmen, and other employees. They ordered all foreign houses to keep their books in Turkish; they wanted to furnish employment for Turks, and enable them to acquire modern business methods. The Ottoman Government even refused to have any dealings with the representative of the largest Austrian munition maker unless he admitted a Turk as a partner. They developed a mania for suppressing all languages except Turkish. For decades French had been the accepted language of foreigners in Constantinople; most street signs were printed in both French and Turkish. One morning the astonished foreign residents discovered that all these French signs had been removed and that the names of streets, the directions on street cars, and other public notices, appeared only in those strange Turkish characters, which very few of them understood. Great confusion resulted from this change, but the ruling powers refused to restore the detested foreign language.

Source: Henry Morgenthau, *Ambassador Morgenthau's Story* (New York: Doubleday, Page, 1918), 283–85. The entire text of Morgenthau's memoirs is available online at www.ukans.edu/~libsite/wwi-www/morgenthau/MorgenTC.htm.

Document 10.2. The Deportations: Excerpt from the Report of Lieutenant Sayied Ahmed Moukhtar Baas, December 26, 1916

In April 1915 I was quartered at Erzeroum. An order came from Constantinople that Armenians inhabiting the frontier towns and village be deported to the interior. It was said then that this was only a precautional measure. I saw at that time large convoys of Armenians go through Erzeroum. They were mostly old men, women and children. Some of the able-bodied men had been recruited in the Turkish Army and many had fled to Russia. The massacres had not begun yet. In May 1915 I was transferred to Trebizond. In July an order came to deport to the interior all the Armenians in the Vilayet of Trebizond. Being a member of the Court Martial I knew that deportations meant massacres. . . .

Then the deportations started. The children were kept back at first. The Government opened up a school for the grown up children and the American Consul of Trebizond instituted an asylum for the infants. When the first batches of Armenians arrived at Gumush-Khana all able-bodied men were sorted out with the excuse that they were going to be given work. The women and children were sent ahead under escort with the assurance by the Turkish authorities that their final destination was Mosul and that no harm will befall them. The men kept behind, were taken out of town in batches of 15 and 20, lined up on the edge of ditches prepared beforehand, shot and thrown into the ditches. Hundreds of men were shot every day in a similar manner. The women and children were attacked on their way by the ("Shotas"), the armed bands organised by the Turkish Government who attacked them and seized a certain number. After plundering and committing the most dastardly outrages on the women and children they massacred them in cold blood. These attacks were a daily occurrence until every woman and child had been got rid of. The military escorts had strict orders not to interfere with the "Shotas."

The children that the Government had taken in charge were also deported and massacred. The infants in the care of the American Consul of Trebizond were taken away with the pretext that they were going to be sent to Sivas where an asylum had been prepared for them. They were taken out to sea in little boats. At some distance out they were stabbed to death, put in sacks and thrown into the sea. A few days later some of their little bodies were washed up on the shore at Trebizond.

In July 1915 I was ordered to accompany a convoy of deported Armenians. It was the last batch from Trebizond. There were in the convoy 120 men, 700 children and about 400 women. From Trebizond I took them to Gumish-Khana. Here the 120 men were taken away, and, as I was informed later, they were all killed. At Gumish-Khana I was ordered to take the women and children to Erzinjian. On the way I saw thousands of bodies of Armenians unburied. Several bands of "Shotas" met us on the way and wanted me to hand over to them women and children. But I persistently refused. I did leave on the way about 300 children with Moslem families who were willing to take care of them and educate them. The "Mutessarrif" of Erzinjian ordered me to proceed with the convoy to Kamack. At the latter place the authorities refused to take charge of the women and children. I fell ill and wanted to go back, but I was told that as long as the Armenians in my charge were alive I would be sent from one place to the other. However I managed to include my batch with the deported Armenians that had come from Erzeroum. In charge of the latter was a colleague of mine Mohamed Effendi from the Gendarmerie. He told me afterwards that after leaving Kamach they came to a valley where the Euphrates ran. A band of Shotas sprang out and stopped the convoy. They ordered the escort to keep away and then shot every one of the Armenians and threw them in the river.

At Trebizond the Moslems were warned that if they sheltered Armenians they would be liable to the death penalty.

Government officials at Trebizond picked up some of the prettiest Armenian women of the best families. After committing the worst outrages on them they had them killed.

Cases of rape of women and girls even publicly are very numerous. They were systematically murdered after the outrage.

The Armenians deported from Erzeroum started with their cattle and whatever possessions they could carry. When they reached Erzinjian they became suspicious seeing that all the Armenians had already been deported. The Vali of Erzeroum allayed their fears and assured them most solemnly that no harm would befall them. He told them that the first convoy should leave for Kamach, the others remaining at Erzeroum until they received word from their friends informing of their safe arrival to destination. And so it happened. Word came that the first batch had arrived safely at Kamach, which was true enough. But the men were kept at Kamach and shot, and the women were massacred by the Shotas after leaving that town.

The Turkish officials in charge of the deportation and extermination of the Armenians were: At Erzeroum, Bihas Eddin Shaker Bey; At Trebizond; Naiil Bey, Tewfik Bey Monastirly, Colonel of Gendarmerie, The Commissioner of Police; At Kamach; The member of Parliament for Erzinjian. The Shotas headquarters were also at Kamach. Their chief was the Kurd Murzabey who boasted that he alone had killed 70,000 Armenians. Afterwards he was thought to be dangerous by the Turks and thrown into prison charged with having hit a gendarme. He was eventually executed in secret.

Source: British Archives, Public Records Office (London), Foreign Office Records FO 371/2768/1455/folios 454–58, electronic files, the Armenian National Institute, Sample Documents, at www.Armenian-genocide.org (retrieved November 2001).

Document 10.3. Talaat: Excerpt from *Ambassador Morgenthau's Story* by Henry Morgenthau

He went from one emotion to another as lightly as a child; I would find him fierce and unyielding one day, and uproariously good-natured and accommodating the next. Prudence indicated, therefore, that I should await one of his more congenial moments before approaching him on the subject that aroused all the barbarity in his nature. Such an opportunity was soon presented. One day, soon after the interview chronicled above, I called on Talaat again. The first thing he did was to open his desk and pull out a handful of yellow cablegrams.

"Why don't you give this money to us?" he said, with a grin.

"What money?" I asked.

"Here is a cablegram for you from America, sending you a lot of money for the Armenians. You ought not to use it that way; give it to us Turks, we need it as badly as they do."

"I have not received any such cablegram," I replied.

"Oh, no, but you will," he answered. "I always get all your cablegrams first, you know. After I have finished reading them I send them around to you."

This statement was the literal truth. Every morning all uncoded cablegrams received in Constantinople were forwarded to Talaat, who read them, before consenting to their being forwarded to their destinations. Even the cablegrams of the ambassadors were apparently not exempt, though, of course, the ciphered messages were not interfered with. Ordinarily I might have protested against this infringement of my rights, but Talaat's engaging frankness about pilfering my correspondence and in even waving my own cablegrams in my face gave me an excellent opening to introduce the forbidden subject.

But on this occasion, as on many others, Talaat was evasive and noncommittal and showed much hostility to the interest which the American people were manifesting in the Armenians. He explained his policy on the ground that the Armenians were in constant correspondence with the Russians. The definite conviction which these conversations left upon my mind was that Talaat was the most implacable enemy of this persecuted race. "He gave me the impression," such is the entry which I find in my diary on August 3d, "that Talaat is the one who desires to crush the poor Armenians." He told me that the Union and Progress Committee had carefully considered the matter in all its details and that the policy which was being pursued was that which they had officially adopted. He said that I must not get the idea that the deportations had been decided upon hastily; in reality, they were the result of prolonged and careful deliberation. To my repeated appeals that he should show mercy to these people, he sometimes responded seriously, sometimes angrily, and sometimes flippantly. . . .

One reason why Talaat could not discuss this matter with me freely, was because the member of the embassy staff who did the interpreting was himself an Armenian. In the early part of August, therefore, he sent a personal messenger to me, asking if I could not see him alone—he said that he himself would provide the interpreter. This was the first time that Talaat had admitted that his treatment of the Armenians was a matter with which I had any concern. The interview took place two days afterward. It so happened that since the last time I had visited Talaat I had shaved my beard. As soon as I came in the burly Minister began talking in his customary bantering fashion.

"You have become a young man again," he said; "you are so young now that I cannot go to you for advice any more."

"I have shaved my beard," I replied, "because it had become very gray—made gray by your treatment of the Armenians."

After this exchange of compliments we settled down to the business in hand. "I have asked you to come today," began Talaat, "so that I can explain our position on the whole Armenian subject. We base our objections to the Armenians on three distinct grounds. In the first place, they have enriched themselves at the expense of the Turks. In the second place, they are determined to domineer over us and to establish a separate state. In the third place, they have openly encouraged our enemies. They have assisted the Russians in the Caucasus and our failure there is largely explained by their actions. We have therefore come to the irrevocable decision that we shall make them powerless before this war is ended."

On every one of these points I had plenty of arguments in rebuttal. Talaat's first objection was merely an admission that the Armenians were more industrious and more able than the dull-witted and lazy Turks. Massacre as a means of destroying business competition was certainly an original conception! His general charge that the Armenians were "conspiring" against Turkey and that they openly sympathized with Turkey's enemies merely meant, when reduced to its original elements, that the Armenians were constantly appealing to the European Powers to protect them against robbery, murder, and outrage. The Armenian problem, like most race problems, was the result of centuries of ill-treatment and injustice. There could be only one solution for it, the creation of an orderly system of government, in which all citizens were to be treated upon an equality, and in which all offenses were to be punished as the acts of individuals and not as of peoples. I argued for a long time along these and similar lines.

"It is no use for you to argue," Talaat answered, "we have already disposed of three quarters of the Armenians; there are none at all left in Bitlis, Van, and Erzeroum. The hatred between the Turks and the Armenians is now so intense that we have got to finish with them. If we don't, they will plan their revenge."

"If you are not influenced by humane considerations," I replied, "think of the material loss. These people are your businessmen. They control many of your industries. They are very large tax-payers. What would become of you commercially without them?"

"We care nothing about the commercial loss," replied Talaat. "We have figured all that out and we know that it will not exceed five million pounds. We don't worry about that. I have asked you to come here so as to let you know that our Armenian policy is absolutely fixed and that nothing can change it. We will not have the Armenians anywhere in Anatolia. They can live in the desert but nowhere else."

I still attempted to persuade Talaat that the treatment of the Armenians was destroying Turkey in the eyes of the world, and that his country would never be able to recover from this infamy.

"You are making a terrible mistake," I said, and I repeated the statement three times.

"Yes, we may make mistakes," he replied, "but"—and he firmly closed his lips and shook his head—"we never regret."

I had many talks with Talaat on the Armenians, but I never succeeded in moving him to the slightest degree. He always came back to the points which he had made in this interview. He was very willing to grant any request I made in behalf of the Americans or even of the French and English, but I could obtain no general concessions for the Armenians. He seemed to me always to have the deepest personal feeling in this matter, and his antagonism to the Armenians seemed to increase as their sufferings increased. One day, discussing a particular Armenian, I told Talaat that he was mistaken in regarding this man as an enemy of the Turks; that in reality he was their friend.

"No Armenian," replied Talaat, "can be our friend after what we have done to them."

One day Talaat made what was perhaps the most astonishing request I had ever heard. The New York Life Insurance Company and the Equitable Life of New York had for years done considerable business among the Armenians. The extent to which this people insured their lives was merely another indication of their thrifty habits.

"I wish," Talaat now said, "that you would get the American life insurance companies to send us a complete list of their Armenian policy holders. They are practically all dead now and have left no heirs to collect the money. It of course all escheats to the State. The Government is the beneficiary now. Will you do so?"

This was almost too much, and I lost my temper.

"You will get no such list from me," I said, and I got up and left him. . . .

Talaat's attitude toward the Armenians was summed up in the proud boast which he made to his friends: "I have accomplished more toward solving the Armenian problem in three months than Abdul Hamid accomplished in thirty years!"

Source: Henry Morgenthau, *Ambassador Morgenthau's Story* (New York: Doubleday, Page, 1918), 332–33, 336–39, 342.

Document 10.4. An Ambiguous Rescue Story: Excerpt from the Testimony of Aram Kilichjian

My brother's commander, Zia Bey, whose word the Turks respected, came and said, "Give this boy to me." When the man saw that my mother and sister didn't want to give me up, he summoned a Turk he knew, gave him a donkey, and told my mother, "Go with him and see what they are doing to young Armenians." My mother went to the place called Giulasar and saw that many Armenians had died there and were being ripped apart by vultures. Finally, my mother was persuaded and delivered me to that man. Zia Bey took me to his village near his family. They were not my mother and father, but the people loved me and looked after me. . . . The man had a grown daughter, who would take me in her lap and cuddle me.

After a month, I saw that there was a commotion in the house and that preparations were being made. . . . I thought it was something like a wedding. It was a circumcision ceremony for Zia Bey's son. They came and found me, too, and tried to circumcise me at the same time. I fled to the garden and hid, but they came and found me and did it to me. Afterwards, Zia Bey's son lay on one side of the room and I lay on the other—but the man liked me very much. And they gave me the name Said.

It was a time of famine. . . . There was a bread that was called "vasika" bread. One room of this man's house was filled with flour. This man's wife, whom I called abla [auntie], would say, "Get up and take these breads to your mother and family." In those difficult days our family was well-fed. That woman was very good and liked to help. If I say she was better than my mother, believe me. . . . The woman and her daughter would get cloth from their store and sew clothes for my mother and sisters, who by that time had been Islamicized at the urgings of the family that had taken me. My sisters had married Turkish boys. Naturally my mother wept and said, "I'll die but I won't become a Turk." Zia Bey said, "Don't cry, no one will take your religion from you, but I want you on the surface to show yourself to be Turkish, so that they won't kill you."

Source: Testimony of Aram Kilichjian, excerpted in Richard G. Hovannisian, "Intervention and Shades of Altruism During the Armenian Genocide," in *The Armenian Genocide: History, Politics, Ethics*, edited by Richard G. Hovannisian (New York: St. Martin's Press, 1992), 190–91. Reprinted by permission of Macmillan Ltd.

Document 10.5. Report to the German Government: Letter from Ambassador Wolff-Metternich to Chancellor Bethmann-Hollweg, July 10, 1916

The persecution of the Armenians in the eastern provinces has reached its final stages.

In the carrying out of its program, the solution of the Armenian question through the extermination of the Armenian race, the Turkish government has refused to be daunted, either by our interventions or by the interventions of the American embassy and papal delegates, or by the threats of the Entente Powers, and least of all by considerations of public opinion in the western world. It is now preparing to dissolve and disperse the last clusters of Armenians that survived the first deportations.

At issue here are Armenians who stayed behind in northern Syria (Marasch, Aleppo, Ras-ul-Ain) and in some of the larger localities in Asia Minor (Angora, Konia), namely, those who were sent there in the transports or migrated there earlier. But they are also clearing out among the local population and among the Catholic and Protestant Armenians, although the Porte had always guaranteed that the latter would be spared.

Some of these remnants are being sent to Mesopotamia; others are being Islamicized. . . .

Finally we must mention the measures of the Porte against the institutions that were maintained to this point by American and German organizations on behalf of the Armenian population in these regions—namely, orphanages, hospitals, schools, and the like. The few institutions that are not already closed are threatened daily by the authorities with the deportation of Armenian personnel, schoolchildren and orphans, and with other regulations. Individual exceptions to which the government still agreed last year have been withdrawn, and there is little hope that these institutions will be able to resume their previous level of activity after the war. The Turkish government has correctly recognized that the schools and orphanages directed by foreigners have had a great influence on the awakening and development of national feeling among the Armenians. From their standpoint it is only consistent that they impose strict controls on them or dissolve them entirely. . . .

As much as we must lament that we have not succeeded in directing the Armenian policy of the Porte along other lines, neither our enemies nor the neutral powers have the right to criticize us for this. We have done our best to ease the lot of the unfortunate Armenian nation, both through influence on the government and through humanitarian aid.

Source: Johannes Lepsius, *Deutschland und Armenien, 1914-1918: Sammlung Diplomatischer Aktenstücke* (Bremen: Donat & Temmen, 1986), 280–82. Reprinted by permission of Edition Temmen.

Document 10.6. Germany's Interests: Meeting of the Imperial Budget Committee, September 29, 1916, Notes of the State Secretary

In the Armenian question, we have intervened energetically with the Porte from the very beginning. Perhaps later after the war, when our position is no longer so precarious, we will publish all of our negotiations. I can tell you confidentially that our ambassador has gone so far as to incur personally the resentment of the minister of the interior. After his first three months in his post, the ministers concerned said that the ambassador apparently had nothing better to do than to annoy them constantly on the Armenian issue.

In light of the recent complaints that the Armenian orphanages are being dissolved and that Armenian girls and boys are being brought into harems and Turkish orphanages and forced to become Mohammedans, I personally raised serious objections with the Turkish Foreign Minister, who is currently here in Germany. I pointed out that these measures would be extraordinarily embarrassing not only for the Turks but also for us and that we would have to request urgently that methods and means be found to alleviate this situation.

I can only say that we have done everything that we could. The only course left would have been to break our alliance with Turkey. You will understand that we could not bring ourselves to do this. As much was we lament the lot of the Armenians from a purely human standpoint, we must think first of our sons and brothers who are having to shed their precious blood in the fiercest battles and who are partly dependent on the support of the Turks. The Turks, after all, are doing us a great service in covering our southeastern flank. You will agree with me that, having already embittered the Turks with our constant interventions in the Armenian question, we could not go so far as to renounce the alliance.

Source: Johannes Lepsius, *Deutschland und Armenien, 1914-1918: Sammlung Diplomatischer Aktenstücke* (Bremen: Donat & Temmen, 1986), 294.

Document 10.7. Starting Over? Excerpt from *Black Dog of Fate: An American Son Uncovers His Armenian Past* by Peter Balakian

Except for those infrequent and awkward moments when my father made some kind of gesture that was directed at the meaning of the Genocide, no one in my family considered the events of Armenia's recent nightmare a reality suitable for conversation or knowledge. The scalding facts of the Genocide had been buried, consigned to a deeper layer of consciousness, only to erupt in certain odd moments, as when my grandmother told me a story or a dream. What my parents did, often in unconscious and instinctual ways, was to make sure that my brother and sisters and I were Americans first. Free. Unhampered, unhaunted, unscarred by the unspeakable cruelties of Armenian history. Perhaps that was how it should have been. Perhaps that was a gift my parents gave us. A gift that enabled me to discover the past for myself from the secure vantage of my upper-middle-class American life, where in some sense, too, the small bit of Armenianness I understood gave me a feeling of having a slightly more substantial sense of identity than many of my peers. If my parents were so capable of freeing us from the past, it seemed to me that they were able to do that because their parents had done their best to close the stone door on their own pasts. My grandmother Nafina Aroosian had witnessed mass murder and endured a death march into the desert with her two babies, the death of her first husband, and the disease-filled refugee quarter of Aleppo. At the age of twenty-five she lost her nation, her home, her family. And my grandfather Diran Balakian had tended the massacred and the dead in Adana, witnessing "one of the most savage bloodbaths of human history." My paternal grandparents had seen their friends disappear at the hands of Turkish executioners in April 1915. They had watched from Constantinople as Armenia was destroyed, and then became nationless refugees.

How did they all survive such catastrophe without some form of confession, release, therapeutic unburdening? Psychologists, psychiatrists, and those who study trauma agree about the importance of coming to terms with loss and grief in order to regain health; did each of my grandparents live close to disintegration, collapse, and breakdown? Outwardly, they carried out productive, humanly engaged lives. They enjoyed their work, raised families with gusto, and found life in America good.

In the case of my grandmother, Nafina, I'll never know of her inner life in the years following the Genocide. Perhaps no one did. After the Genocide, she was silent for more than two decades until the dam broke and she had a breakdown in the wake of the Japanese attack on Pearl Harbor in 1941. The U.S. entry into World War II triggered genocide flashbacks. But after the electroshock treatment worked, she returned to silence. Her friends and family concur that she was quite a pragmatic, level-headed woman, interested in people, popular culture, the stock market, the family business, always focused on the potential of the future. Was there a space behind the space from which she saw you, a space where no one was permitted? Did she ever go there? If my grandmother did not often go to that inner place of the deep wound, it may have been in good part because she lived in a state of numbness. Numbing, Robert Lifton suggests, is a process by which the self distances itself from traumatic experience. It is not repression, which excludes and denies the past, because in numbing one still has the potential for insight and some reclamation of the nightmarish past.

I've come to see my grandmother's numbed response to the Armenian Genocide as a necessary way of survival. What did it mean to be a survivor in an era before the Holocaust and the civil rights movement gave rise to a human rights movement in the United States? What was it like to be a survivor before there was a popular culture of psychology and therapy, whose goal was to help victims achieve a voice and the courage to affirm the moral significance of their wound and trauma? Without social and political movements there can be no public meaning. The word genocide didn't exist until Raphael Lemkin coined it in 1943 and the UN made it a crime against humanity in 1948. In the 1920s, '30s, and '40s, if you were Armenian, you had been torn from your home and land and plunked down in some country in which you landed. Most likely you came home to an Armenian family in which there was a common understanding of the unspeakable secret. But for the most part, you came home to silence. From there you started life over again.

Source: Peter Balakian, *Black Dog of Fate: An American Son Uncovers His Armenian Past* (New York: Broadway Books, 1997), 285–87.

Questions

_____

The Armenian Genocide, Chapter Introduction

1. How were Armenians discriminated against as a religious minority? What would be some similar situations today? Is religious discrimination inevitable, or can different religious groups live together in full mutual respect?
2. How did the challenge of the Armenians to "their place" in Ottoman society result in violence against them? Is it possible to challenge discrimination without violent consequences?
3. Religion has often been a factor in "ethnic cleansing" or genocide. Why? How can religion become a force for evil?

_____

Document 10.1. Pan-Turkism: Excerpt from _Ambassador Morgenthau's Story_ by Henry Morgenthau

1. Why did the Armenians initially support the Young Turks? Considering Morgenthau's account, why do you think the Young Turks abandoned their earlier platform to embrace radical nationalism?
2. As the Ottoman Empire moved toward its final collapse, were there constructive solutions to the problems faced by the Young Turk government?
3. How does the ideology of Pan-Turkism resemble National Socialism in Germany?
4. Did boycotts against Armenian establishments contribute to the conditions necessary for genocide, and if so, how does this dynamic work?

LINKS

I. History   1. From Religious Prejudice to Racism   1.3. Statement by Adolf Hitler   10

Document 10.2. The Deportations: Excerpt from the Report of Lieutenant Sayied Ahmed Moukhtar Baas, December 26, 1916

1. Was the Ottoman Empire's situation in World War I a cause of the genocide? How do circumstances of war enable mass atrocities of this kind?
2. To what extent do you believe that this genocide was planned?
3. Why do you think that perpetrators of genocide select "deportation" as a means of mass murder? Did this make killing large numbers of people "easier"?
4. What did the Young Turks want to accomplish by implementing the genocide? What was their ultimate goal?
5. Why were so many Armenians willing to follow the orders of the Turkish government? Should they have offered more resolute resistance, or would this have merely resulted in more certain death?

LINKS

―――――――

Document 10.3. Talaat: Excerpt from *Ambassador Morgenthau's Story* by Henry Morgenthau

1. What picture of Talaat emerges from Morgenthau's account? Is it possible to "understand" such a person? To whom is Talaat referring when he says "we"?
2. Describe the relationship between Morgenthau and Talaat. What arguments does Morgenthau use in his attempt to dissuade Talaat from a policy of genocide? How does Talaat respond?
3. Talaat reportedly says, "No Armenian can be our friend after what we have done to them." Is this true? How does Talaat use this statement as an argument for genocide?

LINKS

Document 10.4. An Ambiguous Rescue Story: Excerpt from the Testimony of Aram Kilichjian

1. How were such large numbers of people persuaded to participate in massacres against the Armenians?
2. What motivated individuals who refused to participate in the murder of the Armenians? To what extent is the question of motive important?
3. Why did some Turks take Armenian children into their homes? Were attempts to convert these children to Islam part of the effort to destroy Armenian culture, or is there a sense in which conversion was normal or natural?
4. How was it possible for some individuals to participate in both murder and rescue of victims?

LINKS

Document 10.5. Report to the German Government: Letter from Ambassador Wolff-Metternich to Chancellor Bethmann-Hollweg, July 10, 1916

Document 10.6. Germany's Interests: Meeting of the Imperial Budget Committee, September 29, 1916, Notes of the State Secretary

1. Could the Allies have acted earlier to prevent the genocide? Why or why not?
2. How did the United States respond to the genocide? What do you believe were its obligations?
3. Do you find the arguments of the German government concerning its own position with respect to the Turks and the genocide persuasive? Could Germany have stopped the massacres against the Armenians?

LINKS

Document 10.7: Starting Over? Excerpt from *Black Dog of Fate: An American Son Uncovers His Armenian Past* by Peter Balakian

1. Do survivors of the Armenian genocide and their descendants have a responsibility to their culture? If so, what is this responsibility?
2. Why does the government of Turkey, so many years after the genocide, deny that this atrocity against the Armenians occurred? Given the amount of evidence documenting the genocide, should Armenians be concerned about campaigns of denial?
3. Why is it important to Armenians today that Turkey acknowledge the genocide? Why does it matter? How could reconciliation between Armenians and Turks be brought about today?
4. Is it appropriate for some Armenians to seek reparations and advocate the return of lost territory, or is this quest a potential cause of more violence? Are there other ways in which the present government of Turkey might acknowledge responsibility for the genocide?
5. Why have some in the United States resisted the official recognition of the crime against the Armenians as a genocide? Is it appropriate to weigh considerations of "national interest" in these kinds of decisions?

LINKS

Timeline

1839–76	The reforms of the Tanzimat era, enacted under international pressure, bring legal rights to Armenian Christians and other religious minorities in the Ottoman Empire.
1876–1908	Sultan Abdul Hamid rules the Ottoman Empire in reaction against the Tanzimat reforms.
1895–96	Pogroms claim the lives of up to two hundred thousand Armenians.
1908	A military coup, welcomed by the Armenians, brings to power the Committee of Union and Progress, popularly known as the Young Turks. Abdul Hamid is forced to rule as a constitutional monarch.
1909	A conservative countercoup is defeated by the Young Turks and Abdul Hamid is deposed. More than twenty thousand Armenians are massacred in the region of Cilicia. The Young Turks attribute the massacres to their political enemies.
1913	A coup within the Committee of Union and Progress brings the government under the control of radical Turkish nationalists.
Nov. 1914	The Ottoman Empire enters World War I on the side of Germany and Austria-Hungary against Britain, France, and Russia.
Feb. 1915	The first deportations of Armenians occur near the Russian front.
Apr. 23–24, 1915	Hundreds of Armenian leaders are arrested in Constantinople. Most are deported and killed.
May 24, 1915	Allied powers declare that the Ottoman government will be held responsible for "new crimes of Turkey against humanity and civilization."
May 30, 1915	The Young Turk Cabinet approves the "Temporary Law of Deportation."
1915–18	Virtually all Armenians within the Ottoman Empire are deported or killed.
Oct. 30, 1918	The armistice ending the war between the Ottoman Empire and the Allies provides that surviving Armenians are to be returned to their homes.

June 1919   An Ottoman military court convicts and condemns to death in absentia the leading government figures held responsible for the crimes against the Armenians.

Aug. 1920   The Treaty of Sévres between Turkey and the Allies recognizes an Armenian Republic including former Ottoman and Russian territories.

1920–22   Turkish nationalists led by Mustafa Kemal reconquer ceded territories and drive the remaining Armenian population into exile.

July 1923   The Treaty of Lausanne recognizes the territorial gains of the new Republic of Turkey without reference to the Armenians.

Glossary

Abdul Hamid. The sultan of the Ottoman Empire from 1876 to 1909. He reversed many of the Tanzimat reforms and was believed to share responsibility in early massacres against the Armenians.

CUP. The Committee of Union and Progress. This was the official name for the leadership of the Young Turks.

Djemal Pasha. Leader in the CUP and minister of the navy during World War I and the Armenian genocide.

Enver Pasha. Leader in the CUP and minister of war during World War I and the Armenian genocide.

millet. The Ottoman term for religious groups within the empire. The Armenians comprised one millet. Others included Muslims, Jews, Greek Orthodox Christians, and Roman Catholics.

Morgenthau, Henry. U.S. ambassador to the Ottoman Empire at the beginning of World War I. He became one of the most important figures in denouncing the genocide against the Armenians.

Mustafa Kemal. The founder of modern Turkey, also known as Atatürk. He was the leader of Turkish nationalist forces that sought successfully to defy the terms imposed on Turkey after its defeat in World War I.

Pan-Turkism. A nationalist ideology that advocated the unification of Turkish peoples across Asia and became directed against non-Turkish subjects of the Ottoman Empire.

Talaat Pasha. Leader in the CUP and minister of the interior during World War I and the Armenian genocide.

tanzimat. Turkish for "reorganization." The word came to stand for a period of reform in the Ottoman Empire that included recognition of civil rights for ethnic and religious minorities.

Young Turks. The popular term for the leaders of the Ottoman Empire after 1908. The Young Turks came to power with the support of Armenians but would direct the genocide against them during World War I.

Further Reading

Books

Armenian National Committee. *The Armenian Genocide, 1915–1923: A Handbook for Students and Teachers*. Glendale, Calif.: Armenian National Committee, 1988.

Balakian, Peter. *Black Dog of Fate: An American Son Uncovers His Armenian Past*. New York: Broadway Books, 1997.

Dadrin, Vahakn N., *The History of the Armenian Genocide: Ethnic Conflict from the Balkans to Anatolia to the Caucasus*. Oxford: Berghahn, 1995.

Hartunian, Abraham H. *Neither to Laugh nor to Weep: A Memoir of the Armenian Genocide*. Boston: Beacon, 1968.

Hovannisian, Richard G., ed. *The Armenian Genocide: History, Politics, Ethics*. New York: St. Martin's, 1992.

Kherdian, David. *The Road from Home: The Story of an Armenian Girl*. New York: Greenwillow Books, 1979.

Melson, Robert. *Revolution and Genocide: On the Origins of the Armenian Genocide and the Holocaust*. Chicago: University of Chicago Press, 1992.

Peroomian, Rubina. *Literary Responses to Catastrophe: A Comparison of the Armenian and the Jewish Experience*. Atlanta. Ga.: Scholars Press, 1993.

Vassilian, Hamo B. *The Armenian Genocide: A Comprehensive Bibliography and Library Resource Guide*. Glendale, Calif.: Armenian Reference Books, 1992.

Videos

The Great War and the Shaping of the Twentieth Century. Cassette 2, episode 3, *Total War*. A KCET/BBC co-production available from PBS Home Video.

The following films, produced by Michael J. Hagopian, are available from the Armenian Film Foundation in Thousand Oaks, Calif.: *Cilicia . . . Rebirth; The Armenian Genocide: Annihilation of the Population of the Ottoman Empire, 1915–1923; The Forgotten Genocide; Where Are My People?* and *Historical Armenia, Mandate for Armenia: American Military Mission to Turkey and Armenia, 1919*.

11
Bosnia and Kosovo

Nearly fifty years after the defeat of the Third Reich, Europe was once again confronted with images of sealed railway cars full of civilians, skeletal men desperately gazing from behind the barbed wire of camps, and horrific accounts of the rape, forced expulsion, and slaughter of civilians. The promise "Never again" was met by the reality of "Again—here and now." Moreover, in the 1990s communications and media made ignorance impossible. The world knew, and the world watched, as the worst human rights abuses in Europe in half a century unfolded. A report by Human Rights Watch summarizes what occurred in Bosnia.

> The Bosnian Serb army—with the active assistance of the Yugoslav Army and paramilitary groups from Serbia proper— began a drive to "ethnically cleanse" all non-Serbian inhabitants from much of Bosnia. As part of its "ethnic cleansing" campaign, Bosnian Serb forces used tactics such as siege warfare, systematic persecution involving widespread torture, murder, rape, beatings, harassment, de jure discrimination, intimidation, forced displacement of people, confiscation and destruction of property, and the destruction of cultural objects such as mosques and Catholic churches. . . . The abuses perpetrated during the "ethnic cleansing" of eastern Bosnia constitute war crimes and crimes against humanity as that term was defined at the Nuremberg trials and within the meaning of customary international law.

How could this have happened? Did we learn nothing from the Holocaust? How could the highly integrated groups comprising a cultured and sophisticated country split along primitive lines of communal identity? How could soldiers shell cities where they had lived and where they still had friends and even family? How could neighbors suddenly drive out neighbors, schoolmates capture and rape schoolmates, friends kill friends? And how could the world once again witness the beginnings of genocide and fail to act effectively to stop it?

At the deepest level, answers to all these questions remain elusive. But we can approach an understanding by studying the particulars of the situations in Bosnia, the ways in which political opportunism and propaganda tore people and institutions apart, and the misinterpretations of Bosnian history and culture that contributed to the international community's lengthy failure to act.

Bosnia's war ended with the 1995 signing of the Dayton Accords, a deeply flawed agreement that ended the fighting but has proved inadequate to insure national unification and refugee return or to provide the basis for a strong peace. The Dayton Accords also failed to address the increasingly untenable situation in Kosovo. By 1998, Serbian attacks on Kosovo civilians had become so open and so vicious that there were calls for action to prevent another genocidal attack in the Balkans. This time NATO acted by launching air strikes against Serbian positions in Kosovo and against Serbia. After an air war of approximately two months, Serbia pulled its troops out of Kosovo, which remains today in effect an international protectorate.

For people of all ethnicities in the Balkans, the wounds of the recent conflicts remain largely unhealed. Efforts to rebuild and reintegrate Bosnian society have far to go, while the situation in Kosovo may be even less hopeful. For the rest of the world too, the wounds of these conflicts remain open. When we ask who we are at the end of the twentieth century and the beginning of the twenty-first, images of Sarajevo burning and of the slaughtered civilians of Srebrenica must loom large in any answer we can give.

Background

Many Americans have a highly distorted image of the Balkans as a primitive, perpetually strife-torn part of the world. The truth is more complex. The former Yugoslavia was made up of many nationalities, foremost among them Serbs, Croats, Slovenes, Bosnian Muslims, Macedonians, and Albanians. Each of these groups had developed in the course of the nineteenth century a sense of their ethnic and national identities. Yet before World War I, only Serbia emerged as an independent nation. Previously, Serbs had been subjects of the Ottoman Empire or the Habsburg monarchy, where they dwelled primarily in the border regions known as the Military Frontier. Following a war with Turkey and the subsequent Treaty of Berlin, Serbia achieved independence in 1878. The other major nationalities were also subjects of either the Ottoman Empire or the Austro-Hungarian Empire. Albanians and Macedonians belonged to the former, Croats and Slovenes to the latter. The inhabitants of the area of modern-day Bosnia, which has long been the home to various ethnic groups, were subjects of the

Ottoman Empire until after the Congress of Berlin in 1878, when the region came under Austro-Hungarian occupation. Despite this division and a current of nationalism, a movement emerged in the nineteenth century to unite the Yugoslavs (literally, South Slavs). This common Yugoslav ideology formed the basis for the first unified Yugoslav state, which was created in 1918 as the Kingdom of Serbs, Croats, and Slovenes and later renamed Yugoslavia.

Yugoslavia was a multiethnic or multinational state, like Canada (divided between English speakers and French speakers) and Switzerland (divided among German, French, and Italian speakers). To some extent people thought of themselves as Yugoslavs, but they also retained their ethnic identities. In Yugoslavia, these identities coexisted, usually. But when Nazi Germany invaded Yugoslavia in 1941, the Nazis dismembered the country and exploited national tensions between groups. In particular they enlisted extreme Croat nationalists against the Serbs, the most powerful nationality in Yugoslavia. Extreme Croat nationalists committed atrocities against the Serbs that the Serbs never forgot. Nevertheless, a multi-ethnic fighting force under Josip Broz Tito, a Communist leader of Croat and Slovene background, fought back against the Germans and eventually expelled the Nazis from Yugoslav territory. With Tito as its leader, the Yugoslavia that emerged from World War II was a Communist country, though a comparatively open one and one based on a complex multiethnic federalism. In this and in other ways it differed from other Eastern European countries. Citizens of the former Yugoslavia had the freedom to travel, and their standard of living was high, especially in the cities. The recrudescence of nationalism, far from simply being an ancient hatred, began in earnest in 1980, after Tito died. Subsequent struggles for power shifted the balance to Serbia and to extreme Serbian nationalists dissatisfied with Yugoslavia's federalism.

This complex background was often misunderstood by observers and the media, who frequently interpreted the conflicts of the 1990s as the inevitable result of ancient and intractable hatreds. Outsiders were especially prone to misunderstanding the nature of Islam in the area, assuming that Balkan Muslims were Islamic fundamentalists. In fact, Bosnian Muslims are secular Europeans who lived for many years in a multiethnic society with a rich blend of cultures. While Kosovo Albanian life retains certain traditional features, American popular conceptions of Islam in its fundamentalist form are misleading.

Genocide

Accounts by survivors of the Bosnian conflict consistently emphasize the close personal relationships between perpetrators and victims. The words of young refugees interviewed by Doug Hostetter and recorded in his article "Sarajevo U.S.A." are typical.

> After my parents were sent off to the concentration camp, it was the neighbor with whom my father had coffee every afternoon who stole everything from our home before burning it to the ground.

> My next-door neighbor, who took care of me while mother was working as I was growing up, now lives in our home. They use everything that once belonged to us.

> It was three days before my best friend could finally talk. She had returned after being yanked from my side as we slept in the women and girls section of the concentration camp. She said she had been raped all night by seven Serbian soldiers. One of them was our high-school classmate.

Even if one does not subscribe to the theory of "ancient ethnic hatreds," it comes as a surprise to learn how well Bosnians knew one another, how thoroughly their lives were intertwined, and how many things drew them together. Scholars have tried to understand the extremes of violence by looking at variables such as depersonalization, bureaucratic efficiency, and the emotional and even physical separation of the victim from the killer. While these explanations are probably valid for some situations, they do not fit what happened in Bosnia. The genocide in Bosnia was perpetrated upon colleagues, neighbors, friends, and even family members.

Genocide is preceded by a period in which the victims are vilified and dehumanized by the perpetrators. In the case of the Balkans, virulent nationalist speech resurfaced in the early 1980s and continues to the present. There are several important elements to the ideology that precedes genocide. Typically, ideology dignifies the perpetrators' group by pointing to a long and exceptional history, often marked by great suffering. It glorifies the perpetrators' group by assigning to that group a special historical or religious mission. It demeans the victims' group by assigning to its members many negative and often nonhuman characteristics. It purports to demonstrate that the perpetrators' group is under severe and immediate threat from the victims' group. It calls for extreme action and excuses the action as necessary in a time of crisis to protect the perpetrators' group and their special mission. Unfortunately, assertion often substitutes for critical evaluation of evidence, and authority can override experience. In Bosnia, where there was an underdeveloped tradition of objective journalism and government ownership of much of the media, propaganda often proved especially effective, even though it contradicted the daily experience of people living in an integrated society. To an outsider, some of the specific assertions of Serbian propaganda were so excessive as to seem comical (Document 11.1). Yet there was nothing comical about the degree to which propaganda twisted people's perceptions of their neighbors. Moreover, these twisted perceptions led to unspeakable violence.

More than any other event, the massacre of Srebrenica demonstrated the ruthlessness of the attackers, the helplessness of the victims, and the utter failure of the international community. The horrific events that occurred in Srebenica during July 1995 have been thoroughly documented. Because events in Kosovo are more recent, there is less printed documentation available on the experiences of victims and survivors. Since the area was under Serbia's control until June 1999, journalistic access was severely restricted, and thus there are fewer detailed accounts by journalists than there are for Bosnia

There is, however, a wealth of material available on the siege of Sarajevo, including survivors' and journalists' accounts. Film footage of the siege is also readily available. Although not as much has been written about them, other cities in Bosnia sustained sieges as well, often with less international humanitarian aid finding its way to them.

Sieges involved constant fear, chronic hunger, lack of water and electricity, severe cold in winter, lack of communication with loved ones outside the city or neighborhood, lack of medical care, confinement to basements and shelters, and the constant threat of a violent death. People in besieged cities, however, did not experience capture, confinement in camps, torture, rape, and expulsion. Those experiences were part of what was euphemistically known as "ethnic cleansing."

"Ethnic cleansing" is at the center of the assault on Bosnians and Kosovo Albanians. Ethnic cleansing is an attempt to gain territory for one ethnic group by expelling residents of other groups. Mass killings are often a part of ethnic cleansing, but they tend to be used as a way of terrorizing others into leaving, rather than a systematic attempt to exterminate an entire group. Ethnic cleansing in the Balkans has been marked by extreme brutality but it has little to do with an outbreak of madness or of ancient hatred between groups. Instead, this brutality reflects a careful political calculation: the quickest and most efficient way to expel large numbers of people and to ensure that they will not want to return is to use terror, torture, and rape, as well as murder.

Ethnic cleansing was common in rural areas of Bosnia and in small towns and villages that were unable to resist attack. There is less detailed information available on the experience of ethnic cleansing than there is on the experience of siege. Careful examination of what happened in specific towns is important, because it reveals both the extreme brutality and the calculated nature of the attacks (Document 11.2).

Perpetrators, Bystanders, Rescuers

One of the central aspects of the experience of victims in Bosnia was bewilderment, first that they could be suffering such attacks, especially from people they had lived with all their lives, and second, that the world did not intervene to stop what was happening. There are many excellent accounts of the experiences of victims and survivors in Bosnia, including several writings by young people and children (Document 11.3).

Because so many of the perpetrators were personally acquainted with their victims, there was an intimate aspect of betrayal to the Bosnian genocide. Closely related was the remarkable resistance of many of the aggressors to confronting the moral implications of their actions and their seeming inability to understand them (Document 11.4). Despite this moral opacity, there were many instances in Bosnia of people of one ethnic group rescuing people from another group. In some of the areas where the attacks on Muslims were most vicious, for example, the Prijedor area in late spring and summer 1992, many Muslim survivors tell stories of being helped at some point by Serbs. Those who did not receive such help often did not survive. Despite the undoubted courage of many rescuers, it would be an error to think of all of them as heroes. There are examples of people who rescued certain favored Muslims, while participating in or even directing attacks on other Muslims.

International Response

The critical bystanders in the Bosnian conflict were not so much other Bosnians as the rest of the world (Document 11.5). The attack on Bosnia in 1992 was extensively covered in the media of Western countries, and the horrific assaults on civilians were widely known to Western governments and citizens by late summer 1992, if not before. Yet no effective action was taken until late summer 1995. A substantial literature documents the failure of the efforts of the international community and the United Nations in Bosnia. Some of these failures were so egregious (e.g., turning Muslim civilians over to Serb soldiers at Srebrenica) that one may be tempted to condemn everyone who was a part of the international presence in Bosnia. It should be emphasized that individual "peacekeepers" often risked injury and death in their work in Bosnia. The failure of international efforts was not so much a failure of the individuals who worked in Bosnia as an overall failure of political vision and will at the very highest levels.

The genocide in Bosnia was played out before the eyes of the world. It occurred on television and on the Internet. There could be no excuse of not knowing. The only ignorance possible was a willful refusal to know. It was not difficult to distinguish the victims from the perpetrators in this conflict, and the victims deserved far more help than they received.

The Western powers made at least two critical errors in the way they approached the Bosnian conflict. The first was treating ethnic cleansing as though it were a type of natural disaster—that is, aiding survivors and moving them to safer areas, without regard to the reasons they were fleeing their homes. This response put the United Nations and other international agencies in the unintended position of actually assisting the perpetrators by moving members of the targeted ethnic groups from the areas where they lived. The second great error was treating the perpetrators and victims as moral equals and trying to negotiate between them. The perpetrators in Bosnia and Kosovo benefited greatly from negotiations, because negotiations legitimized their power and gave them time to continue their attacks. Gradually, the Western powers came to realize that the Serb leaders were not negotiating in good faith, as they consistently violated every agreement they made. Resolutions, denunciations, and constantly repeated threats to intervene were not followed by effective action, a pattern that encouraged the perpetrators to grow even bolder in their attacks, culminating in the attack on Srebrenica.

With the slaughter of thousands of unarmed civilian men and boys at Srebrenica, the Serb leaders finally went too far. Soon afterward, NATO began air strikes and a combined Bosnian and Croat ground force launched an offensive that regained territory held by the Serbs. Within weeks the Serb leadership was ready to sign a peace agreement. The speed of their capitulation raises questions about what might have happened had intervention come much earlier.

The worst of Bosnia's suffering ended in 1995, but Kosovo's anguish still lay ahead. The Dayton Peace Accords, which ended the fighting in Bosnia, did not so much as mention Kosovo. Serb repression in Kosovo escalated into attacks on civilians and then into full-scale massacres reminiscent of spring and summer 1992 in Bosnia. After an initial pattern of hesitation, negotiation, and threats, NATO intervened with air strikes in March 1999, and within two months the Serb military pulled out of Kosovo. International troops remain in Kosovo; they have been less successful in ending violence there than in Bosnia. The principal victims of violence in Kosovo after the withdrawal of the Serb military have been Serb and Roma ("Gypsies") civilians. It is to be hoped that with the support of the international community, stable and democratic governments will be established in all parts of the former Yugoslavia, and violence will cease. It is unrealistic, however, to expect that this will be accomplished without a serious and lengthy commitment of resources on the part of the international community.

Many practical problems still face the people of Bosnia and Kosovo. The collapse of the economy during the conflict means that jobs are scarce, and salaries are very low, when workers are paid at all. Talented young people often respond to such situations by leaving to work abroad. Daily life in many parts of Bosnia and Kosovo is complicated by the widespread presence of landmines and unexploded ordnance, which continue maiming and killing long after the end of the conflict.

The return of refugees and displaced persons to their homes is one of the essential requirements for a stable and lasting peace. Because Kosovo is under international control, most refugees have been able to go back to their homes. In Bosnia, however, much of the country remains under Serb control. Despite the guarantee of the right to return contained in the Dayton Accords, returning home for Bosnians is fraught with dangers and difficulties. In many areas of Bosnia, property was systematically destroyed. This destruction went far beyond the damage inflicted by shelling and fighting. Houses were burned and dynamited to ensure that their owners, should they survive, would not try to reclaim them. People who return to their homes often find only a pile of rubble where their houses once stood. All their possessions have been destroyed or stolen. Refugees who have no money and no access to construction equipment are confronted with a problem they cannot solve alone. Several international organizations are constructing houses for refugees, but it will require years for them to complete rebuilding even in selected locations.

In addition to all these problems, returning home may place refugees and displaced persons in the distressing situation of having to encounter and deal with the very people responsible for their plight. They may have to face neighbors who actively participated in their persecution, or who witnessed it and did nothing. Some returning people may meet the torturers and murderers of their family members in the streets and shops. Women may encounter their rapists. For all returning persons, there is sure to be a heavy weight of bitter memories of expulsion, fear, and flight.

There are few people in Bosnia or Kosovo who came through the recent conflicts without experiencing severe trauma. Massive individual and collective trauma can debilitate a society for many years. Counseling and services that might be of help are not readily available, particularly in culturally appropriate forms and in the local languages. Related to these problems is the continuing fear, distrust, and even hatred existing between groups. It remains to be seen whether people from different groups will be able to live together again. In some areas, such as Sarajevo, there is reason for hope. In other parts of Bosnia, particularly those under Serb control, and in Kosovo, the future does not look bright in this regard.

There is an overwhelming need in both Bosnia and Kosovo for justice, enforced through the rule of law. The International Tribunal for the former Yugoslavia has the potential to contribute much, despite its late start and the slow pace of its prosecutions. Yet the electoral victory of Vojislav Kostunica over Slobodan Milosovic in September 2000 and Milosovic's subsequent fall from power give rise to hope. The arrest of Slobodan Milosovic on April 1, 2001, and his extradition to the Hague two months later in order to stand trial on war crimes charges also provides grounds for optimism. The court cannot bring back the dead but it can serve as a warning that genocide will not be tolerated.

Document 11.1. Peter Maass in Conversation with a Serbian Woman

I asked . . . whether the fighting in the village was heavy.

"Why, no, there was no fighting between Muslims and Serbs in the village," she said." Then why were the Muslims arrested?"

"Because they were planning to take over the village. They had already drawn up lists. The names of the Serb women had been split into harems for the Muslim men."

"Harems?"

"Yes, harems. Their Bible says men can have harems, and that's what they were planning to do once they had killed our men. Thank God they were arrested first." She wiped her brow.

"How do you know they were planning to kill the Serb men and create harems for themselves?"

"It was on the radio. Our military had uncovered their plans. It was announced on the radio." . . .

"How do you know the radio was telling the truth?" . . .

"Why," she demanded to know, "would the radio lie?"

I had to give up. It was the polite thing to do, even though Vera translated my silence as confirming the verity of the harem report. She took a triumphant puff on her Marlboro.

"Did any of the Muslims in your village harm you?" I asked, softly.

"No."

"Did any Muslim ever do anything bad to you?"

"No."

She seemed offended.

"My relations with Muslims in the village were always very good. They were very nice people."

Source: Peter Maass, *Love Thy Neighbor: A Story of War* (New York: Alfred A. Knopf, 1996), 113–14. Reprinted by permission of Random House, Inc.

Document 11.2. Chronology of "Ethnic Cleansing"

April 30, 1992 Serbs in Prijedor took over city government. They removed democratically elected mayor and police chief and replaced them with extremist Serbs. Roadblocks were set up in Prijedor.

May 9, 1992 Serbs gave Muslim leaders in Kozarac seven days to sign loyalty oath or be considered a "paramilitary terrorist organization."

May 14, 1992 Telephone service in Kozarac was cut and roadblocks put up. The town was sealed off.

May 16, 1992 A tank arrived in Kozarac. There were convoys on the highway and Serb military mobilization.

May 24, 1992

1:00 P.M. Residents told to get out by 6:00 P.M.

2:12 P.M. Shelling began from twelve directions.

3:45 P.M. Radio announced a half hour pause in shelling, but shelling resumed in fifteen minutes.

May 25, 1992, A.M. People fled from the town while shelling continued. Many civilians were killed while fleeing.

May 26, 1992, A.M. All attempts at resistance ended. Civilians were ordered to go to the football field, and about four thousand gathered there. The shelling continued. Community leaders were identified and separated. Some were killed on the spot; others disappeared; others were taken to concentration camps.

June 9, 1992, Hundreds of Kozarac refugees arrived in Banja Luka in sealed cattle cars on their way to a Muslim area. Serb guards refused them water.

June–July 1992 Looting and killings continued in a more chaotic manner. Many residents of Kozarac were detained in concentration camps at Omarska, Keraterm, and Trnopolje.

November 1992 *Washington Post* reporter visited Kozarac and found "the ruins of Kozarac are still sealed, guarded by heavily armed and hostile Serb soldiers."

Source: Mary Battiata, "A Town's Bloody 'Cleansing,' " *Washington Post*, November 2, 1992.

Document 11.3. Images of War by Children of Former Yugoslavia

In my dreams,
I walk among the ruins
of the old part of town
looking for a bit of stale bread.

My mother and I inhale the fumes of gunpowder.
I imagine it to be the smell of pies, cakes, and kebab.
A shot rings out from a nearby hill. We hurry.
Though it's only nine o'clock, we might be hurrying
toward a grenade marked "ours."

An explosion rings out in the street of dignity.
Many people are wounded—
sisters, brothers, mothers, fathers.

I reach out to touch a trembling, injured hand.
I touch death itself.

Terrified, I realize this is not a dream.
It is just another day in Sarajevo.

—Edina, 12, from Sarajevo

I had a new tricycle, red and yellow and with a bell. . . .
Do you think they have destroyed my tricycle too?

—Nedim, 5, refugee

War is the saddest word that flows from my quivering lips.
It is a wicked bird that never comes to rest. It is a deadly
bird that destroys our homes, and deprives us of our childhood.
War is the evilest of birds, turning the streets red
with blood, and the world into an inferno.

—Maida, 12, from Skopje

If I were President,
the tanks would be playhouses for the kids.
Boxes of candy would fall from the sky.
The mortars would fire balloons.
And the guns would blossom with flowers.
All the world's children
would sleep in a peace unbroken
by alerts or by shooting.
The refugees would return to their villages.
And we would start anew.

—Roberto, 10, from Pula

When I walk through town, I see strange faces, full of
bitterness and pain. Where has our laughter gone?
Where is our happiness? Somewhere far, far away
from us. Why did they do this to us? We're their kids.
All we want is to play our games and see our friends.
And not to have this horrible war.

There are so many people who did not ask for this
war, or for the black earth that is now over them.
Among them are my friends.
I send you this message: Don't ever hurt the children.
They're not guilty of anything.

—Sandra, 10, from Vukovar

The soldiers ordered us out of our house and then burned it
down. After that, they took us to the train, where they ordered
all the men to lie down on the ground.

From the group, they chose the ones they were going to kill.
They picked my uncle and a neighbor!
Then they machine-gunned them
to death. After that, the soldiers put the women
in the front cars of the train and the men in the back. As the
train started moving, they disconnected the back cars and took
the men off and to the camps. I saw it all!

Now I can't sleep. I try to forget, but it doesn't work. I have
such difficulty feeling anything anymore.

—Alik, 13, refugee

Source: *I Dream of Peace: Images of War by Children of Former Yugoslavia* (New York: HarperCollins, 1993). © 1994 UNICEF.

Document 11.4. The Mind of the Perpetrators

It was the habit, when the phones were working, for Serbs in the hills [around Sarajevo] to occasionally call Muslim and Croat friends in the city below. People on the receiving end of these calls tended to be dumbstruck by them, particularly when it became clear that those making the calls were not at all ashamed of what they were doing, had not called to apologize or explain themselves, but were only concerned, and on a strictly private basis, for their Muslim friends' welfare, and nostalgic for contact with people from whom they had been separated. As a friend of mine put it, "I can accept that my old schoolmates are shooting at me, but how dare Vlado ring up just to say hello? I couldn't believe it. It was as if he had no responsibility at all for what was happening. He asked about my family. He even asked if I remembered a holiday we all took on the coast in the early eighties."

Source: David Rieff, *Slaughterhouse: Bosnia and the Failure of the West* (New York: Simon & Schuster, 1995), 105. Excerpted with the permission of Simon & Schuster.

Document 11.5. Days in the Life of Bosnian Inmates, 1992

Moharema Menkovic, 42, whose husband and two brothers are still at Omarska, said she was taken to Trnopolje camp after she was ordered to bury the body of a young Muslim neighbor. She said the throat of Mustafa Kilic, 22, from her village of Kamincani, was slashed open in front of her by a Serb neighbor wielding a "very large butcher knife."

She told her story at a Travnik primary school where about 40 refugees sleep in each classroom. As she spoke, she broke down in tears and could not catch her breath. She seemed as furious as she was sad, and kept asking why the West was allowing the camps to exist.

"I apologize," she said, choking on her tears, "but I must ask you where the world is."

Source: Blaine Harden, "Days in the Life of Bosnian Inmates," *Washington Post*, August 7, 1992.

Questions

_____

Document 11.1. Peter Maass in Conversation with a Serbian Woman

1. If you lived in this village, how might you have responded to the Serbian woman?
2. How can people have extreme prejudice against their neighbors and at the same time claim to be on friendly terms with them?

LINKS

_____

Document 11.2. Chronology of "Ethnic Cleansing"

1. What does "ethnic cleansing" really entail?
2. How is "ethnic cleansing" similar to what occurred in Armenia? Are there parallels to the Holocaust?
3. In what ways were the events that occurred in Bosnia between 1992 and 1995 genocide?

LINKS

_____

Document 11.3. Images of War by Children of Former Yugoslavia

1. How do the poems of children help give us an understanding of the magnitude of what happened in the former Yugoslavia?
2. What do you think the legacy of violence will be for the next generation?
3. How do the poems influence your analysis?

LINKS

Document 11.4. The Mind of the Perpetrators

1. How would you describe the moral universe of Vlado and the Serbs in the hills of Sarajevo shelling their former neighbors in Sarajevo?
2. In retrospect, warning signs for genocide often seem clear-cut and obvious. Why might the signs of increasing danger be ignored by potential victims? Why might people choose to remain where they are even if they clearly understand the danger?

LINKS

Document 11.5. Days in the Life of Bosnian Inmates, 1992

1. What were the responsibilities of foreign governments and international organizations with regard to Bosnia's situation? Did they live up to their responsibilities?
2. The International Tribunal's greatest difficulty has been that of gaining custody of suspects. How much support, if any, should the United States, other powers, and international organizations give to capturing the suspects?
3. Although western Europe, the United States, and other countries took in many Bosnian refugees during the war, most displaced persons were not offered refuge outside of Bosnia. It can be argued that prosperous and stable countries should accept and protect every person whose life is in danger from genocidal attack. Yet, if all Muslims had fled Bosnia, the Serb leaders would have achieved their goal. How should the rest of the world respond to refugees fleeing threatened genocide?

LINKS

Timeline

1878	Serbia, previously part of the Ottoman Empire, achieves independence.
	Austria-Hungary occupies Bosnia-Herzegovina.
1908	Austria-Hungary annexes Bosnia-Herzegovina.
1912	Balkan Wars. Serbia conquers Kosovo and part of Macedonia.
1914	After the assassination of the Austrian archduke in Sarajevo on June 28, and the ensuing "July Crisis," Europe falls into what will become known as World War I.
1918	Dissolution of Austro-Hungarian and Ottoman Empires at the close of World War I. Formation of first Yugoslav state.
1941	Germany, Italy, Hungary, and Bulgaria invade Yugoslavia. Semi-independent state of Croatia proclaimed under German auspices. Massacres of Serbs and Jews in Croatian state. Massacre of Muslims and Croats at the hands of extremist Serbs.
1941–45	Successful partisan warfare against occupying powers led by Josip Broz Tito.
1945	Creation of Communist Yugoslavia under the leadership of Tito.
1980	Death of Tito.
1981	Albanian demonstrations in Kosovo put down by Serbian and Yugoslav security forces.
1989	As president of Serbia, Slobodan Milosovic abolishes autonomous status of Kosovo and Vojvodina.
1991	Croatia and Slovenia declare independence in June. Yugoslav forces attempt to halt declarations. In September, United Nations imposes an arms embargo on Yugoslavia.
Mar. 1992	Bosnians vote for independence in a referendum boycotted by Serbs. Bosnia declares independence and is recognized by the United States and the European Union.
Apr. 1992	Siege of Sarajevo and "ethnic cleansing" begins.
Aug. 1992	Journalists publish photographs and reports from concentration camps in Bosnia.

Feb. 1994	A Bosnian Serb shell kills sixty-eight people in Sarajevo. NATO threatens air strikes, and Bosnian Serbs pull back weapons.
May 1995	Bosnain Serbs shell Sarajevo. NATO threatens air strikes, and Serbs take 350 UN peace-keepers hostage.
July 1995	Bosnian Serbs overrun the "safe area" of Srebrenica. UN peace-keepers abandon the city, and Serb forces kill more than five thousand unarmed civilian men and expel many thousands of women and children.
Aug. 1995	NATO planes bomb Serb targets in Bosnia. A ground offensive by Bosnian and Croat troops regains territory from the Serbs.
Nov. 1995	Peace talks begin in Dayton, Ohio.
Dec. 1995	Dayton Peace Accord signed.
1996	The International Tribunal for the former Yugoslavia begins the trial of its first case.
1998	Human rights situation deteriorates in Kosovo. Several massacres of Kosovar civilians by Serbian forces.
Mar.–May 1999	NATO bombs Serbia and Serb positions in Kosovo. Serbs kill and expel Albanian civilians in Kosovo.
June 1999	Serb troops leave Kosovo.
Sept. 2000	Moderate Serb leader Vojislav Kostunica wins Yugoslav election against Slobodan Milosovic.
Dec. 2000	Milosovic falls from power.
Apr. 2001	Milosovic arrested by Yugoslav police.
June 2001	Milosovic extradited to the Hague in order to stand trial on war crime charges.
Nov. 2001	UN tribunal indicts Milosovic for genocide.

Glossary

Dayton Accords. A peace accord reached in Dayton, Ohio, in December 1995. The Dayton Accords stipulate that although Bosnia-Herzegovina retains its territorial integrity, it will henceforth be divided into a Bosnian-Croat federation in the west and a Bosnian Serb Republic in the north and east. The Dayton Accords marked the end of large-scale violence in Bosnia and regulated the return of refugees.

Ethnic cleansing. The organized, violent assault by one ethnic group whose aim is to remove from an area all members of another ethnic group. Ethnic cleansing was practiced by Serbian forces in Bosnia and Kosovo; it has, however, a much longer history and is becoming increasingly standard practice in nationality conflicts throughout the world.

Vojislav Kostunica. Serbian politician who defeated Slobodan Milosovic in September 2000 election to become new Yugoslav president. When Milosovic refused to acknowledge the results of the election, popular uprisings in Belgrade brought about his fall on October 5, 2000. While certainly a Serbian nationalist, Kostunica is associated with a policy of making Yugoslavia "an ordinary, average state" again.

Omarska Camp. A temporary concentration camp set up by Serbian forces in summer 1992. More than three thousand Bosnian Muslims and Bosnian Croats were confined here in inhumane conditions. Prisoners were routinely beaten, assaulted, mistreated, and killed.

Slobodan Milosevic. President of Serbia from 1989 to 2000 and of the Yugoslav Federal Republic from 1997 to 2000. He was an advocate of Serbian hegemony over the constituent republics of former Yugoslavia and, to this end, supported the intervention of the Yugoslav army in Slovenia and Croatia in 1991–92. He also supported Bosnian Serbs in their attempts at ethnic cleansing in 1992–95, as well as the more recent attempt at ethnic cleansing in Kosovo. In November 2001, the UN war crimes tribunal indicted Milosovic for the crime of genocide.

Srebrenica: Site of the worst massacre in Europe since the Holocaust. Srebrenica is a Bosnian village that had been declared a "safe area" by the United Nations. But when Western allies refused to defend it from attacking Serb forces, Srebrenica was overrun by Serbian troops and at least five thousand Muslim men were murdered and their bodies dumped into mass graves.

Josip Broz Tito. Leader of Communist Yugoslavia from 1945 to 1980. A Croat by origin, he organized the partisan forces that expelled Nazi Germany from Yugoslav territory. He also resisted Joseph Stalin's attempt to exercise control over Yugoslavia and emerged as a major force among the nonaligned nations during the Cold War. Finally, under his leadership Yugoslavia became a highly federated, multiethnic state whose standard of living was often higher than neighboring eastern European countries. After his death in 1980, the federal solution slowly came undone.

Further Reading

Anzulovic, Branimir. *Heavenly Serbia: From Myth to Genocide*. New York: New York University Press, 1999.

Bringa, Tone. *Being Muslim the Bosnian Way: Identity and Community in a Central Bosnian Village*. Princeton: Princeton University Press, 1995.

Cohen, Roger. *Hearts Grown Brutal: Sagas of Sarajevo*. New York: Random House, 1998.

Genocide Research Project. *Genocide: Resources for Teaching and Research*. Links page 2. Available at www.people.Memphis.edu/~genocide.

Glenny, Misha. *The Balkans: Nationalism, War, and the Great Powers, 1809–1999*. New York: Penguin, 2000.

Guttman, Roy. *A Witness to Genocide*. New York: Macmillan, 1993.

Hall, Brian. *The Impossible Country: A Journey Through the Last Days of Yugoslavia*. Boston: David R. Godine, 1994.

Hukanovic, Rezak. *The Tenth Circle of Hell: A Memoir of Life in the Death Camps of Bosnia*. New York: Basic, 1996.

Maass, Peter. *Love Thy Neighbor: A Story of War*. New York: Alfred A. Knopf, 1996.

Malcolm, Noel. *Bosnia: A Short History*. New York: New York University Press, 1994.

———. *Kosovo: A Short History*. New York: New York University Press, 1998.

Mertus, Julie. *Kosovo: How Myths and Truths Started a War*. Berkeley: University of California Press, 1999.

Rohde, David. *Endgame: The Betrayal and Fall of Srebrenica*. New York: Farrar, Straus and Giroux, 1997.

Sells, Michael A. *The Bridge Betrayed: Religion and Genocide in Bosnia*. Berkeley: University of California Press, 1996.

Silber, Laura, and Allan Little. *Yugoslavia: Death of a Nation*. Rev. ed. New York: Penguin, 1997.

UNICEF. *I Dream of Peace: Images of War by Children of Former Yugoslavia*. New York: HarperCollins, 1993.

Weine, Stevan M. *When History Is a Nightmare*. New Brunswick, N.J.: Rutgers University Press, 1999.

12
Rwanda

The genocide in Rwanda took place in spring 1994. Many deaths, although by no means all, took place in April, "the month that would not end." The best-known monument to this genocide is a church and church-yard littered with decaying bodies. Left as they fell, the skeletons have become a gruesome reminder that genocide is still with us. In Rwanda, approximately one million people were killed in about thirteen weeks, so many that ultimately the United Nations would officially label the event a genocide. The United Nations Human Rights Commission had previously refused to discuss the case of Rwanda in open session, but in May 1994, at the insistence of the Canadian delegates and after a day and a half of testimony, a special reporter was named whose findings resulted in the designation of the killings in Rwanda as genocide and the establishment of an international tribunal.

Although the genocide in Rwanda of Tutsis by the Hutu Power movement took place in a post-Holocaust world that had loudly declared "Never again," its progress can be looked at in stages of destruction similar to those defined by Raul Hilberg for the Holocaust: registration of victims, organized indoctrination of killing squads, systematic use of media, mobilization of armed groups, and escalation of violence. Moreover, the genocide of Tutsis in Rwanda not only resembles that of the Jews in Nazi Germany but is thought by some to have been influenced directly by it. Philip Gourevitch, whose book *We Wish to Inform You That Tomorrow We Will Be Killed with Our Families* puts a very human face on the Rwandan genocide, notes that trophy seekers after the genocide found a movie version of Adolf Hitler's *Mein Kampf* in the wreckage of the home of the assassinated Hutu president of Rwanda, Juvenal Habyarimana. Similarly, Human Rights Watch, in the publication *Leave None to Tell the Story*, concludes from the discovery of films about Nazism at President Habyarimana's residence that he and his circle likely were admirers of Hitler.

As in every other case of genocide in the modern world, the Rwandan whole is a prism with many sides, a study in which the faces of resistance, of international attitudes, of the complicity of bystanders, and of the ultimate denials or rationales reflect coldly on one another but do not let us penetrate deep inside. An effort to penetrate the prism, to comprehend the idea of the evil thinking that leads to extermination of a people, is at the heart of this study.

Tutsis and Hutus

Preexisting prejudice seems to be a necessary if not sufficient condition for genocide in the modern world. In Rwanda, as in other genocide sites, one group and its supporters became the focus of such prejudice. For some students and teachers in the West, a convenient explanation of the 1994 genocide in Rwanda is "ancient tribal hatred" between the Hutus and the Tutsis. But the reality turns out to be far more complex, because ruling groups actively encouraged, manipulated, and exploited very modern forms of prejudice as a strategy to control the people of Rwanda (Document 12.1). At its worst, this strategy involved a racial logic that led Hutus to kill women and children so that they could not carry on family lines within the Tutsi group. With "Hutu power" as the predominant theme, the government persistently encouraged interclass struggle and ethnic division. What happened in Rwanda was not therefore a result of age-old tribal conflicts. Rather, it was an antagonism recast in modern forms and reshaped as a violent encounter.

In contrast to the situation in Hitler's Germany, in Rwanda the minority, the Tutsis, had been in control under an earlier monarchy and had at times been singled out for preferential treatment under the Belgian colonial government. With the coming of Rwandan independence in 1962, however, Belgium shifted policy and supported the "Hutu revolution," which established the first Rwandan republic. Although there have been numerous attempts since the late nineteenth century to stratify Hutus and Tutsis more rigidly in Rwanda, these attempts continued to break down. These attempts also suggest that, far from being a natural antagonism, the conflict between Hutus and Tutsis had its deepest roots in the imperialist policies of Belgian rule. Animated by late nineteenth-century ideas of race, Belgian scientists introduced a "nasal index" of measurement to quantify what they considered the classical long nose of "typical" Tutsis. Although spurious, this kind of modern racist thinking led to the registration of Hutus and Tutsis according to identity cards. In 1933 and 1934, the Belgians conducted a census and divided the country according to their racial calculations: Hutu (85 percent), Tutsi (14 percent), Twa (1 percent). Although Hutus and Tutsis continued to mix and intermarry, the lines of ethnicity had hardened and become codified. Belgium now ruled a country based on apartheid, with most privileges going to the Tutsi minority.

Ideology and Propaganda

Prejudice in Rwanda was carefully nurtured by the memory of this earlier imbalance so that Tutsis became the hated "other," considered "cockroaches" to be exterminated. In March 1993 the Hutu newspaper *Kangura* published an article entitled, "A Cockroach Cannot Give Birth to a Butterfly." In graphic terms, *Kangura* underlined the insectlike qualities it attributed to the enemy and underscored the ideology that a "cockroach," whatever one might think of him as an individual, is part of a group he can never leave.

The governmental power structure was well aware of the use of language as a tool for nurturing and refocusing prejudice. A document found in Butare prefecture quotes from the Communist leader V. I. Lenin and the Nazi propaganda minister Joseph Goebbels in explaining how to use lies and innuendo to best advantage. While bestial and degrading epithets were used for the Tutsis in song and slogan, the language for exterminating them was sanitized to sanction the killing. For example, Hutus were exhorted to "work" (exterminate) with "tools" (machetes and clubs) to help the Public Safety Committees (local killing squads) carry out the "Final Solution."

The media that used such language, particularly *Kangura* and the radio station RTLM, had tremendous influence. The people of Rwanda, 66 percent literate, could read or find someone to read to them. Free radios were also distributed by the government so that the messages of hate in music and slogan could be heard by everyone. Hutu power was a compelling ideal. At a rally in Kilgali in 1993 a leading Hutu politician concluded with this chant:

> Hutu Power! MRND Power! CDR Power! MDR Power!
> Interahamwe Power! JDR Power! All Hutu are One Power!

After each shout, the crowd roared its response: "Power! Power! Power!" Perhaps the most repugnant of the articles published in *Kangura* appeared in December 1990 under the title "The Hutu Ten Commandments" (Document 12.2). This text offers a revealing illustration of the effort to create a new apartheid in Rwanda more rigid than ever. Hutu President Habyarimana eagerly supported these "commandments," which were read in public meetings throughout the country. The Hutus employed additional techniques to bolster the radio message of music and slogans and the print message of tribal purity. Sophisticated in conception, these techniques both manipulated and caused events. At weekly propaganda meetings, teams of singers and dancers competed with one another in honoring Habyarimana and his party, the MRND. The president's image appeared on political buttons, and his picture was often posted in homes and businesses as well. The Hutus also employed a technique called "accusations in a mirror," the attribution to your enemy of your own plans for the future. The broadcast of a false news report that a Tutsi businessman's home had been burned, for example, gave a Hutu militia group address information and other details that led to the actual burning of the home.

The Killing Begins

The killing phase of the genocide was touched off by the assassination of President Habyarimana on April 6, 1994. The attack remains largely uninvestigated and its authors unidentified. By midday on April 7, Rwanda's moderate Hutu prime minister was killed, as were leading members of opposition parties and ten Belgian peace-keepers. Initiated by the military, these killings were carried out by the Hutu Interahamwe, a civilian militia, and aided by local officials and others at the grass-roots level (Document 12.3). In the streets of Kilgali this little song was being sung:

> Our enemy is one
> We know him
> It is the Tutsi.

Habyarimana's government had required communal public labor for tasks such as repairing roads, digging anti-erosion ditches, and clearing brush. Now these labor forces were turned into killing squads and the genocide defined as *umuganda* (public work). As the genocide progressed the "work" became a euphemism for extermination of the Tutsis and their Hutu sympathizers (Document 12.4).

The Rwandan government had organized various actions for community welfare in the past, including campaigns to end illiteracy and to improve public health. The hierarchy now used these organizations to coordinate the killing. Not only the military but also civilians became more and more deeply involved in the mobilization necessary for an effective extermination campaign. Indeed, what is remarkable about the genocide in Rwanda is the sheer number of people involved directly and indirectly in the process of killing.

There was also an economic dimension spurring some to participate in the killing. Hutus who had attacked Tutsis in the 1960 revolution had received the fields that had belonged to their victims. Now, in 1994, some were enticed by cash payments, food, drink, and even marijuana. Local officials encouraged the looting of Tutsi property after "the work" was finished. Among the victims were politicians, clergymen, Hutus, Hutu supporters, and many women and children who had survived the first wave of attacks on Tutsi in early April. Human Rights Watch points out that in the past Rwandans had not usually killed women in conflicts and even at the beginning of the genocide had often spared them. By mid-May, however, some killers urged eliminating Tutsi women who would produce Tutsi children. Some Tutsi women were killed by their own husbands.

Perpetrators, Bystanders, Rescuers

The line between perpetrators and bystanders is very thin. Even many of those who did not directly participate in mass murder may bear moral responsibility through their failure to assist its victims. Particularly in the case of Rwanda, organized religious groups have come under criticism for their indifference to genocide. In a country whose population was overwhelmingly Christian (65 percent Roman Catholic and 15 percent Protestant) the record of the churches is certainly mixed. Four days after the crash of the president's plane, when many Tutsis had already died, the Catholic bishops issued a statement of support for the interim government that was carrying out the killings. The statement came by way of the Vatican and it also included a denunciation of "troublemakers." One Protestant pastor fled to the United States, only to be extradited in March 2000 to face charges of the International Criminal Tribunal for Rwanda. At the same time, however, there are also stories of courageous members of the clergy who attempted to help. Rwanda's Muslim community has also been recognized for its efforts to protect Tutsi Muslims.

In the wake of the 1993 assassination of the president of nearby Burundi, Hutu refugees had returned to Rwanda, reinforcing the Hutu Power movement in numbers as well as propaganda. In 1994, as the predominantly Tutsi Rwanda Patriotic Front (RPF) advanced into Rwanda and the genocide slowed by early summer, Hutu refugees streamed out again to the camps at Goma and other sites near the border on the Zaire side of Rwanda. This area, informally called "Hutuland," became a staging ground for the reorganization of Hutu militia and continued attacks on Tutsi.

In Zaire, however, the government was also undergoing change. As President Mobutu lost power, the Hutus again returned to Rwanda from exile. In four days, six hundred thousand Hutus crossed the frontier. Those who had earlier regrouped in the refugee camps were now being pushed back into the waiting arms of the RPF. Despite the fact that international attention had at last been called to the Rwandan problems, the violence continued.

Among the bystanders who must take some share of the blame are the representatives of the international community. Although a military agreement of 1975 expressly forbade the involvement of French troops in Rwandan combat or police operations, the French funneled armaments to the Rwandan Hutu government throughout the early 1990s and supported the continued use of identity cards.

There was resistance, just as there had been in the ghettoes during the Nazi regime, and in just the same way the resistance seemed doomed from the start. In Rwanda the major location of resistance effort was at Bisesero in Kibuye, which had also been an important site for defense in the 1959 revolution. Eight busloads of soldiers were required to wipe out the survivors who had fled to Bisesero, where thousands of Tutsi died.

International Response

After the torture and killing of ten Belgian peace-keepers in the first days of the genocide, Belgium withdrew from UNAMIR, the United Nations peacekeeping force that had been slashed 90 percent by the Security Council. At this time Rwanda, represented by the Hutu interim government, held one of the rotating Security Council seats. The United States did little to hasten aid to Rwanda through their Security Council position, although President Bill Clinton would later apologize for not calling the genocide by its real name. Especially with respect to U.S. policy, the lack of clarity and willingness to label the situation in Rwanda a genocide came both from a desire to escape responsibility for sending reinforcements and from a feeling that intervention in internal affairs posed a difficult political issue (Document 12.5).

Aftermath

Throughout May 1994, the genocide dissipated slowly as the RPF advanced into Rwanda, although in some areas killers hurried to finish their killing. Several military leaders of the interim government who had tried and failed to register dissent to the killing through May and June signed a statement on July 6 denouncing and condemning genocide and urging cease-fire and negotiations with the RPF. The international community was at last openly aware of the government's lack of legitimacy. By July 15, the United States had ordered the Rwandan embassy closed and assets in the United States frozen.

Meanwhile, the RPF saved thousands of lives, although it bears responsibility for executions in summer 1994. These executions, summarily done, were under military rather than civilian auspices. The ideology of the victors was one of national unity. The newly formed government emphasized precolonial racial harmony and prided itself on the inclusion of Hutus in government positions. Still, the problem of reconciliation remains extraordinarily difficult and complex.

Although an International Criminal Tribunal was established to prosecute those who participated in the genocide, trials have progressed slowly. Thousands of prisoners await verdicts, many of them juveniles who will be held until they reach adulthood. In late April 1998, the Rwandan government carried out the public executions of twenty-two people condemned for leadership or participation in genocide. The huge numbers of defendants, the small number of lawyers, and difficulties of proving participation remain problems for which there are no easy solutions. Local, grass-roots courts are the next step. In Rwanda this is called "justice in the grass" and represents a return to traditional village justice. Although this approach is admittedly risky, officials in Rwanda are willing to try whatever is necessary to put the genocide behind them and to promote national unity. In the meantime, the wider moral responsibility of the international community remains problematic. The UN secretary-general, the U.S. president, and leaders of the Belgian Senate have rightly recognized their responsibility for failing to avert and halt the genocide, but such recognition of past mistakes seems unlikely to halt future problems (Document 12.6).

Document 12.1. Excerpt from *Leave None to Tell the Story: Genocide in Rwanda* by Alison Des Forges

Rwandan institutions were shaped by both pastoralists and cultivators. Although the power of the ruler derived from control over the military and over cattle, his authority was buttressed also by rituals firmly rooted in agricultural practices. By the end of the nineteenth century, the ruler governed the central regions closely through multiple hierarchies of competing officials who administered men, cattle, pasturage, and agricultural land. He exercised a looser kind of suzerainty over other areas, particularly on the periphery, which were dominated by powerful lineage groups, some of them pastoralists, some cultivators. In addition, he tolerated the existence of several small states within the boundaries of Rwanda, usually because their rulers were thought to control rainfall, crop pests, or some other aspect of agricultural productivity important for Rwanda as a whole. The late President Habyarimana and his circle counted themselves as the proud contemporary representatives of Bushiru, the largest such state within Rwanda at the beginning of the colonial era.

As the Rwandan state grew in strength and sophistication, the governing elite became more clearly defined and its members, like powerful people in most societies, began to think of themselves as superior to ordinary people. The word Tutsi, which apparently first described the status of an individual a person rich in cattle, became the term that referred to the elite group as a whole, and the word Hutu, meaning originally a subordinate or follower of a more powerful person, came to refer to the mass of the ordinary people. The identification of Tutsi pastoralists as power-holders and of Hutu cultivators as subjects was becoming general when Europeans first arrived in Rwanda at the turn of the century, but it was not yet completely fixed throughout the country. Rulers of small states embedded in the larger nation, important lineage heads and some power-holders within the central state hierarchy exercised authority even though they were people who would today be called Hutu.

Most people married within the occupational group in which they had been raised. This practice created a shared gene pool within each group, which meant that over generations pastoralists came to look more like other pastoralists, tall, thin and narrow-featured, and cultivators like other cultivators, shorter, stronger and with broader features. Within each group there were also sub-groups, the result of some distant common ancestry or of more recent patterns of marriage. Thus among pastoralists, some whose ancestors had arrived centuries ago were distinctly shorter, plumper, and redder-skinned than the taller and blacker-skinned descendants of nineteenth-century immigrants. Cultivators, who were relatively sedentary and chose mates from areas close to home, often exhibited traits characteristic of their places of origins: those from the south, for example, were generally shorter and slighter than those from the north central region

Although it was not usual, Hutu and Tutsi sometimes intermarried. The practice declined in the late nineteenth and early twentieth centuries as the gap widened between Tutsi elite and Hutu commoners, but rose again after Tutsi lost power in the 1959 revolution. With the increase in mixed marriages in recent decades, it has become more difficult to know a person's group affiliation simply by looking at him or her. Some people look both "Hutu" and "Tutsi" at the same time. In addition, some people who exhibit the traits characteristic of one group might in fact belong to the other because children of mixed marriages took the category of their fathers, but might actually look like their mothers. During the genocide some persons who were legally Hutu were killed as Tutsi because they looked Tutsi.

Source: Alison Des Forges, *Leave None to Tell the Story: Genocide in Rwanda* (New York: Human Rights Watch, 1999), 32–33.

Document 12.2. The Hutu Ten Commandments, 1990

1. Every Muhutu [singular of Hutu] should know that a Mututsi woman, wherever she is, works for the interest of her Tutsi ethnic group. As a result, we shall consider a traitor any Muhutu who:
   • marries a Tutsi woman;
   • befriends a Tutsi woman;
   • employs a Tutsi woman as a secretary or a concubine
2. Every Muhutu should know that our Hutu daughters are more suitable and conscientious in their role as woman, wife and mother of the family. Are they not beautiful, good secretaries and more honest?
3. Bahutu [plural of Hutu] women, be vigilant and try to bring your husbands, brothers and sons back to reason.
4. Every Muhutu should know that every Mutusi is dishonest in business. His only aim is the supremacy of his ethnic group. As a result, any Muhutu who does the following is a traitor:
   • makes a partnership with Batutsi in business;
   • invests his money or the government's money in a Tutsi enterprise;
   • lends or borrows money from a Mutusi;
   • gives favours to a Batutsi in business (obtaining import licenses, bank loans, construction sites, public markets . . .).
5. All strategic positions, political, administrative, economic, military and security should be entrusted to Bahutu.
6. The education sector (school pupils, students, teachers) must be majority Hutu.
7. The Rwandese Armed Forces should be exclusively Hutu. The experience of the October [1990] war has taught us a lesson. No member of the military shall marry a Tutsi.
8. The Bahutu should stop having mercy on the Batutsi.
9. The Bahutu, wherever they are, must have unity and solidarity, and be concerned with the fate of their Hutu brothers.
   • The Bahutu inside and outside Rwanda must constantly look for friends and allies for the Hutu cause, starting with their Bantu brothers;
   • They must constantly counteract the Tutsi propaganda;
   • The Bahutu must be firm and vigilant against their common Tutsi enemy.
10. The Social Revolution of 1959, the Referendum of 1961, and the Hutu ideology, must be taught to every Muhutu at every level. Every Hutu must spread this ideology widely. Any Muhutu who persecutes his brother Muhutu for having read, spread and taught this ideology, is a traitor.

Source: African Rights, *Rwanda: Death, Despair, and Defiance* (London: African Rights, 1995), 42–43.

Document 12.3. The Interahamwe: Excerpt from an Interview with Gloriose Mukakanimba, May 21, 1994

After the President's death, the Presidential Guard began to kill Tutsis. They began what they call their "work" on Thursday morning. At first, the target was prominent and rich people. But on Saturday, soldiers and interahamwe began to attack ordinary people. They shot you just because you were Tutsi. When they started using machetes, they didn't even bother to ask for ID cards. It was as if they had carried out a census; they knew you were a Tutsi. On Sunday, they started house to house killings in our area. It was systematic; soldiers told the interahamwe to ensure that there were no survivors. As our fear intensified, people abandoned their homes to hide in bushes and wherever they could.

Around 11:00 A.M. on Sunday a large group of interahamwe came to our house. They tried to break the gate. They had difficulties with the gate so they cut through the hedge. They came in and started searching the house. They accused us of keeping guns and grenades and asked us to produce them. We told them we had neither guns nor grenades. As they were about to leave, the leader of the interahamwe in our area, Pierre, who was the driver of the Archbishop, talked to those who had come to search the house. He had a gun in his hand. He signalled to them to go back in and kill. They called us outside, including one of the children, and told us to sit down. I sensed that sitting down meant death. So I refused; I did not see any reason why I should prepare myself to be slaughtered.

Suddenly, both my husband, Deo Rutayisire, and my brother, Maurice Niyoyita, who was visiting us, were given massive machete blows on the shoulders. I started running with my two-year-old who was in my arms. She fell and I saw them cutting her up. I ran with all the strength I had. Everywhere neighbors were screaming: "Here she is, here she is!" I jumped over fences and the neighbors who had been screaming were yelling instructions to the interahamwe, to point them in my direction. These were neighbors I had always considered friends, people I felt I had been kind to.

Source: African Rights, *Rwanda: Death, Despair, and Defiance* (London: African Rights, 1995), 591–93.

Document 12.4. The Corruption of Language: Common Euphemisms of the Holocaust and the Genocide in Rwanda

Terms Used by the Nazis

Liquidated

Evacuation

Resettlement

Made free of Jews

Special actions

Treated appropriately

The Final Solution to the Jewish question

Vermin (Jews)

Terms Used by the Hutus

Do your work (murder)

Tools (machetes and clubs)

Public safety committees (local killing squads)

The Final Solution

Cockroaches (Tutsis)

Document 12.5. Initial Response of the U.S. Government: Excerpt from a PBS *Frontline* Interview with Tony Marley, a Former Official of the U.S. State Department

Interviewer: What kind of discussion was there about whether this was or wasn't genocide?

TM: This was a long-running discussion over the course of several teleconferences, several days, perhaps even a couple of weeks. There were different views being trotted out. Some people were concerned that if we acknowledged it was genocide, that that mandated legally in international law that the U.S. had to do something. Others were concerned that if we acknowledged that it was genocide and didn't do anything, they were concerned about what the impact on U.S. foreign policy relations with the rest of the world would be following inaction after admitting it's genocide. . . .

There were those, and I was among them, that took a much more pragmatic view: "Let's look at the dictionary definition of genocide and it either is or isn't genocide." And to separate the definition from the political decision of whether or not something was to be done. Those that wanted nothing done didn't want to even acknowledge the fact that it could be genocide because that would weaken their argument that nothing should be done. They didn't want to say it was genocide. When they knew it was, they first moved through this charade of referring to it as acts of genocide. People were aware it was genocide and then approached the issue more either in institutional interest, institutional bureaucratic interest terms or in U.S. national interest. But at least we did advance the argument, the crucial credible question of whether or not to do something.

Int.: What other objections were there to calling it genocide?

TM: One administration official asked the question at a teleconference as to what possible impact there might be on the Congressional elections scheduled for later that year were the government to acknowledge that genocide was taking place in Rwanda, and yet the administration be seen as doing nothing about it. The concern seemed to be that this might cost the President's political party votes in the election and therefore should be factored into the consideration as to whether or not "genocide" could be used as a term.

Int.: How did you react to that?

TM: I was stunned and, I think, judging by the looks on the faces of the others in the State Department teleconference room, the amazement on their faces, they were too, because the outcome of the elections had no bearing on whether or not genocide was, in fact, taking place in Rwanda.

Int.: What did it tell you about the political leadership?

TM: It indicated to me that the calculation was based on whether or not there was popular pressure to take action rather than taking action because it was the right thing to do.

Int.: What kind of things were you saying in State Department conferences about genocide?

TM: Separate from the inter-agency conferences, we would have in-house discussions with the agencies and the State Department, and my personal position was: "Let's at least be honest among ourselves. Let's acknowledge what is real and then make the political decisions as to whether or not we can do something about it. But let's at least not pretend that genocide is not taking place. Let's not try to find some word to camouflage reality." That position was never taken into the inter-agency process, however.

Int.: Amongst yourselves, were you talking about any kind of intervention in Rwanda to stop the genocide?

TM: There were discussions about the military feasibility of creating safe havens in those parts of Rwanda that the combat operations had not yet reached in the war, where the genocide had not swept through. And these safe havens would have created buffer areas along the frontier to which people could flee that would keep them safe from the war and safe from the genocide.

Int.: Did that ever go beyond being discussions?

TM: Not by the United States. It was strictly feasibility discussions. Those discussions, frankly, never went anywhere.

Int.: But this was at a time when many people were dying.

TM: That's correct.

Int.: Did that make you frustrated at the time?

TM: For those that wanted to do something it caused frustration, yes. For those that were opposed to doing anything, it did not cause frustration.

Int.: For you?

TM: I was frustrated. I had advocated that there were a number of things we could do short of involving U.S. troops on the ground.

Int.: And the reaction?

TM: Well, again, these discussions never proceeded beyond being feasibility discussions.

Int.: When you saw the bodies coming into the lakes, did that make you think we have to do something now?

TM: There was a great deal of concern when the river was choked with bodies and they were floating into Lake Victoria and the refugee camps were along the shores of the lake, and villages along the shores of the lake, about water contamination and water-borne disease problems that could stem from this. This was a case where I felt the U.S. could have helped water purification efforts as well as providing equipment to help local forces recover the bodies from the lake and get them out of the water to prevent ongoing contamination.

Int.: Couldn't stop the killing, but could clear up the bodies.

TM: If we weren't going to stop the killing inside Rwanda, we could, at least, minimize the disease risk to those who had successfully escaped Rwanda or to those citizens of the neighboring countries that were now in danger potentially by disease, that had no involvement the Rwandan conflict one way or the other.

Int.: How did the military react upon it?

TM: It was not acted upon. It was deemed as being a non-starter essentially. It didn't go anywhere.

Int.: But why would anybody not want to do something as simple as that?

TM: Again, there was great reluctance on the part of many defense officials to have any U.S. involvement of defense resources.

Int.: What other concrete proposals did you come up with?

TM: At one point I had recommended that in response to the hate propaganda radio . . . that the U.S. could use military radio jamming equipment to block those radio transmissions, to take them off the air effectively.

Another possible step would have been using regional specialists and broadcast facilities to broadcast a counter message calling on people in the name of the international community to stop the killing. . . .

Int.: How did that go down?

TM: It was not favorably reacted upon. In fact, one lawyer from the Pentagon made the argument that that would be contrary to the U.S. constitutional protection of freedom of the press, freedom of speech, which of course was a completely specious argument because the U.S. constitution doesn't apply to Rwanda. I would have greater respect for the lawyer had he at least stated that that would be seen as an act of war and therefore had legal problems. But to try to prevent it on U.S. constitutional grounds was completely without merit as far as I was concerned.

Source: Tony Marley interview, *Frontline: The Triumph of Evil*, January 26, 1999, electronic files, Public Broadcasting System, www.pbs.org/wgbh/pages/frontline/shows/evil (retrieved November 2001).

Document 12.6. Excerpt from President Bill Clinton's Address to the People of Rwanda, March 25, 1998

I have come today to pay the respects of my nation to all who suffered and all who perished in the Rwandan genocide. It is my hope that through this trip, in every corner of the world today and tomorrow, their story will be told; that four years ago in this beautiful, green, lovely land, a clear and conscious decision was made by those then in power that the peoples of this country would not live side by side in peace. During the 90 days that began on April 6 in 1994, Rwanda experienced the most intensive slaughter in this blood-filled century we are about to leave. Families murdered in their home, people hunted down as they fled by soldiers and militia, through farmland and woods as if they were animals.

From Kibuye in the west to Kibungo in the east, people gathered seeking refuge in churches by the thousands, in hospitals, in schools. And when they were found, the old and the sick, women and children alike, they were killed—killed because their identity card said they were Tutsi or because they had a Tutsi parent, or because someone thought they looked like a Tutsi, or slain like thousands of Hutus because they protected Tutsis or would not countenance a policy that sought to wipe out people who just the day before, and for years before, had been their friends and neighbors.

The government-led effort to exterminate Rwanda's Tutsi and moderate Hutus, as you know better than me, took at least a million lives. Scholars of these sorts of events say that the killers, armed mostly with machetes and clubs, nonetheless did their work five times as fast as the mechanized gas chambers used by the Nazis.

It is important that the world know that these killings were not spontaneous or accidental. It is important that the world hear what your president just said—they were most certainly not the result of ancient tribal struggles. Indeed, these people had lived together for centuries before the events the president described began to unfold.

These events grew from a policy aimed at the systematic destruction of a people. The ground for violence was carefully prepared, the airwaves poisoned with hate, casting the Tutsis as scapegoats for the problems of Rwanda, denying their humanity. All of this was done, clearly, to make it easy for otherwise reluctant people to participate in wholesale slaughter. Lists of victims, name by name, were actually drawn up in advance. Today the images that haunt us all: the dead choking the Kigara River, floating to Lake Victoria. In their fate we are reminded of the capacity in people everywhere—not just in Rwanda, and certainly not just in Africa—but the capacity for people everywhere to slip into pure evil. We cannot abolish that capacity, but we must never accept it. And we know it can be overcome.

The international community, together with nations in Africa, must bear its share of responsibility for this tragedy, as well. We did not act quickly enough after the killing began. We should not have allowed the refugee camps to become safe haven for the killers. We did not immediately call these crimes by their rightful name: genocide. We cannot change the past. But we can and must do everything in our power to help you build a future without fear, and full of hope.

We owe to those who died and to those who survived who loved them, our every effort to increase our vigilance and strengthen our stand against those who would commit such atrocities in the future—here or elsewhere. Indeed, we owe to all the peoples of the world who are at risk—because each bloodletting hastens the next as the value of human life is degraded and violence becomes tolerated, the unimaginable becomes more conceivable—we owe to all the people in the world our best efforts to organize ourselves so that we can maximize the chances of preventing these events. And where they cannot be prevented, we can move more quickly to minimize the horror.

So let us challenge ourselves to build a world in which no branch of humanity, because of national, racial, ethnic or religious origin, is again threatened with destruction because of those characteristics, of which people should rightly be proud. Let us work together as a community of civilized nations to strengthen our ability to prevent and, if necessary, to stop genocide.

To that end, I am directing my administration to improve, with the international community, our system for identifying and spotlighting nations in danger of genocidal violence, so that we can assure worldwide awareness of impending threats. It may seem strange to you here, especially the many of you who lost members of your family, but all over the world there were people like me sitting in offices, day after day after day, who did not fully appreciate the depth and the speed with which you were being engulfed by this unimaginable terror.

We have seen, too—and I want to say again—that genocide can occur anywhere. It is not an African phenomenon and must never be viewed as such. We have seen it in industrialized Europe; we have seen it in Asia. We must have global vigilance. And never again must we be shy in the face of the evidence.

Source: Transcript: Clinton Meets the Rwandan Genocide Survivors, U.S. Information Service Washington File, March 25, 1998, www.usinfo.state.gov/reginal/af/prestrip/w980325a.html (retrieved November 2001).

Questions

_____

Document 12.1. Excerpt from *Leave None to Tell the Story: Genocide in Rwanda* by Alison Des Forges

1. What determines a race or tribe? What went into determining these categories in Rwanda? Why would a government be interested in solidifying identities and deepening divisions?
2. If you carried an "identity card," as the people of Rwanda were forced to do, what would it say?
3. How can we say that ethnic divisions are encouraged or discouraged? Do we have such divisions in the United States? Who attempts to encourage, or discourage, such divisions?
4. Based on Des Forges's description of Rwandan social institutions, how, and in what terms, would you describe the relation between Hutus and Tutsi?

LINKS

_____

Document 12.2. The Hutu Ten Commandments, 1990

1. What characteristics of extreme nationalism does this document exemplify?
2. The author of a study on the genocide in Rwanda, Philip Gourevitch, has written: "Genocide, after all, is an exercise in community building." In what ways is his statement true?
3. What parallels exist between the "Hutu Ten Commandments" and the Nuremberg laws?
4. Why should the (Ba)hutu "stop having mercy" on the (Ba)tutsi?

LINKS

Document 12.3. The Interahamwe: Excerpt from an Interview with Gloriose Mukakanimba, May 21, 1994

1. Why did the neighbors not help Gloriose Mukakanimba?
2. Why did some neighbors scream, "Here she is, here she is!"?

LINK

Document 12.4. The Corruption of Language: Common Euphemisms of the Holocaust and the Genocide in Rwanda

1. Why did the Nazis and the Hutus use these terms to describe the act of killing other human beings?
2. How does the following quotation from Joseph Goebbels relate to these euphemisms: "A lie, repeated often enough, eventually gains acceptance."
3. Consider the phenomenon of "sanitary language." How does such language still camouflage injustice today?

LINKS

Document 12.5. Initial Response of the U.S. Government: Excerpt from a PBS *Frontline* Interview with Tony Marley, a Former Official of the U.S. State Department

1. Consider the response of U.S. officials to the situation in Rwanda. How would you characterize these responses? Are they the responses of rescuers or of bystanders? Does the U.S. have an obligation to be more than a bystander? On what principle would this obligation be based?
2. Where does one draw the line between interference in the internal affairs of a nation and the need to intervene to save lives?
3. Construct an argument for intervention in 1994. What are the arguments against it?

LINKS

Document 12.6. Excerpt from President Bill Clinton's Address to the People of Rwanda, March 25, 1998

1. Do you agree or disagree with the position put forward in this speech?
2. From your study of the genocides in various places and times during the twentieth century are there common elements in how genocide is encouraged and carried out? Does analysis of these elements show early warning signs? Are there ways in which bystanders can help to ensure that genocides are avoided in the future?

LINKS

Timeline

1885:	Rwanda is assigned to Germany in the division of Africa at the Congress of Berlin.
1926:	Following Germany's defeat World War I, Rwanda comes under the control of Belgium as part of a mandate system within the League of Nations. The Belgian government recognizes the Tutsis as the dominant ethnic group within Rwanda and establishes indirect rule through a Tutsi monarch.
1933:	The Belgian administration introduces identity cards classifying the Rwandan population according to ethnic categories.
1959:	A revolution overturns Tutsi rule in Rwanda.
1961:	Elections held under the auspices of the UN establish Hutu leadership in Rwanda.
1962:	Rwanda becomes an independent republic under Hutu leadership. Many Tutsis are forced to leave the country.
1990:	The Tutsi-led RPF invades Rwanda but is driven back by the Rwandan government with the support of French and Belgian forces. Fighting continues through 1992.
1993:	The Arusha Peace Accords call for a new Rwandan government that will include the RPF and other opposition groups.
Apr. 6, 1994:	Rwanda's Hutu president is assassinated. The genocide against the Tutsis begins.
Apr. 21, 1994:	The UN Security Council votes to reduce the number of UN troops and observers from 2,500 to 270.
July 1994:	The RPF defeats the forces of the Hutu government and establishes its own control over Rwanda.
Nov. 1994:	The UN Security Council adopts a resolution establishing an International Criminal Tribunal for the prosecution of war crimes committed in Rwanda.
Dec. 1996:	National trials for the prosecution of participants in the genocide begin in Rwanda.
Mar. 1998:	U.S. President Bill Clinton visits Rwanda and apologizes for the failure of the United States and the international community to prevent the genocide.

Glossary

CDR. (Coalition for the Defense of the Republic) Extreme anti-Tutsi party that was one of the main organizers of the genocide in 1994.

Interahamwe. ("those who work together") Civilian militia attached to the MRND and centrally involved in the genocide.

Inyenzi. ("cockroaches") Spiteful term for the RPF.

MRND. (National Revolutionary Movement for Development and Democracy) The party of Juvenal Habyarimana, Hutu president.

MDR. (Democratic Republican Movement) Main opposition party in Rwanda. It led the revolution of 1959, which overturned Tutsi rule.

RPF. (Rwandan Patriotic Front) Political party and guerrilla group representing anti-Habyarimana forces, mainly in exile until 1994, when they successfully defeated the Hutu forces.

RTLM. Radio station close to Habyarimana that became a voice of genocide.

Umuganda. Obligatory labor demanded of Rwandan peasants for the public good.

UNAMIR. (United Nations Assistance Mission for Rwanda) UN peacekeeping force in Rwanda.

Further Reading

Children at War. Produced and directed by Alan Raymond and Susan Raymond. HBO, January 2000.

Des Forges, Alison. *Leave None to Tell the Story: Genocide in Rwanda.* New York: Human Rights Watch, 1999.

Gourevitch, Philip. *We Wish to Inform You That Tomorrow We Will Be Killed with Our Families.* New York: Picador, 1998.

Hilsum, Lindsey. "Where Is Kilgali?" *Granta*, October 1995, 147–79.

Neuffer, Elizabeth. "It Takes a Village." *New Republic*, April 10, 2000, 18–19.

Prunier, Gérard. *The Rwanda Crisis.* New York: Columbia University Press, 1995.

The Triumph of Evil. Frontline: PBS. 1999.

Part IV
Ethics

The Holocaust and other twentieth-century genocides leave us with profound questions about our world, about what is good and decent in human life, and about common moral purpose. Twentieth-century genocide is also a sober reminder of the potential for human beings to do unimaginable harm to one another. Six million murdered Jews and 21 million dead Europeans altogether are monuments to Nazism never to be forgotten. And the other 148 million dead from the past century we must also never forget. These inconceivable numbers dwarf our capacity to explain adequately and threaten to numb our effort to pose ethical questions. It seems too much to remember, let alone interrogate. Yet because of the enormity of suffering, we have a moral responsibility to question and to understand. Indeed, the effort to reflect critically upon ethical questions is itself a moral act: it is a collective expression of moral outrage, a critical response to the ethical affront of genocide itself.

As scholars we approach this task of understanding and explanation and the raising of moral questions with different critical tools and from different places. Our differences in discipline, training, religious background, and cultural experience mirror the range of ways to explain genocide and the disturbing moral questions it poses. In short, there are many ways to think about ethics and genocide. Some do so with secular, cultural categories. From such a perspective, genocide might signal the excesses of modern technological culture and the ends to which human beings will go to impose their will. Genocide is thus a grotesque act of political or ideological hubris. Others find philosophical and religious paradigms helpful. From these perspectives, the Holocaust may point to the failure of religion—we can never forget that the Holocaust took root in the heartland of Christian Europe—prompting the question Elie Wiesel's character Berish asks, "Where is God in all of this?" Genocide is evidence of idolatry, profound evil, and human sinfulness. For still others the genocides of the past century underscore the failure to understand human history, particularly modernity, adequately and reveal the disappointed promise of enlightened reason. After Auschwitz,

Bosnia, and Rwanda how can we possibly speak of a shared sense of moral purpose, human responsibility, and destiny? A century of genocide has shaken hope in a common historical experience and confidence that we really do understand who we are as human beings or what moral purpose we live by. Whether one turns for explanatory help to categories of political hubris, religious sin, or historical naïveté, or indeed in some other direction, we can all agree that twentieth-century genocide is an affront to ethics and morality and to any coherent understanding of the good.

13
Ethical Questioning

In *Night* Elie Wiesel's character Moshe the Beadle speaks of the power of the question: "Man raises himself toward God by the questions he asks Him." Critical understanding, whether in the religious or secular life, requires a questioning mind; ethical awareness demands it. In fact ethical awareness is nurtured and sustained through interrogation and inquiry. Because genocide and the Holocaust in particular invite the most profound questions, they are soil rich for the teaching of ethical values. One of the aims of this is to encourage readers to formulate critical questions about the historical, literary, and aesthetic record and the moral dimension of genocide. What is important to know? Why is it important to know it? Why is it important to question? Formulating a question is itself an exercise in moral consciousness; conversely, not to question or to want to know is a sign of moral irresponsibility.

Take the example of the Holocaust. One of the most disturbing ethical questions that the Holocaust raises is why so many people did not question the Nazi program of genocide but were willing to go along with, or at least not protest, against it. After all, Nazi anti-Jewish policies were not secret. From the very beginning people could see, if they wanted to, what was happening. The vast majority of Germans, and later other Europeans, only had to look out their windows to see the boycotts, the street demonstrations, the roughing up of Jews, and eventually the arrest and disappearance of their Jewish neighbors and friends. Moreover, some of the most notorious German concentration camps were built right in, or nearby, major cities. Even today, for example, the local municipal bus line of the city of Weimar serves the site of the Buchenwald concentration camp. So anybody with eyes and ears could know about what was going on if he or she wanted to know. Why did the public not see? Did people ever question? Did they want to know? Why did they not act to stop it?

The Nazi policy and program of genocide evolved slowly and incrementally as the Nazis, beginning soon after they came into elected office and continuing for nearly ten years, imposed one policy after another designed first to discriminate and marginalize, then to ostracize, and eventually to eliminate Jews. One of the disquieting facts is that this "purification" process, ethically reprehensible, was legally implemented. There were many, many steps along the way when people, good people—scholars, teachers, students, doctors, policemen, nurses, tradespersons, artists—could have resisted by questioning the authorities and the process. We know that early on in the few instances where there was protest, such as against the euthanasia program, the Nazi government responded. Often the Nazis seemed ready to try out new programs and to test the limits of public reaction and acceptance. When the public did not take notice and respond, the Nazi authorities proceeded to the next step.

Why was there so little moral outcry, why so little interrogation? The picture is complex. Against the backdrop of centuries-old irrational prejudice nurtured by Christian anti-Semitism, one reason for people's willingness to look the other way had to do with the Nazi regime's use of terror. The first persons sent to concentration camps were not Jews but German citizens who spoke out against the Nazis and their policies. It proves very difficult indeed to speak out against terror and illegality if by that very legal protest you bring on illegal arrest and torture of yourself and your family. Many Germans and later other Europeans in Nazi-occupied countries did not like what was happening but were at risk to speak out. A "righteous" few did put themselves and their family at risk. But why so few? The Nazi strategy was to co-opt legal processes and to reinforce them with brutal acts of terror and intimidation systemically applied. Still the vast majority did not help or hinder the Nazi effort.

Another reason is that it is much easier to go along with a group than to protest and be seen as an outsider. To ask why is often to disturb. How many of us have had the experience of being part of a group that has decided to do something that we disliked, perhaps even something extreme, but we went along anyway or came up with some lame excuse for not participating? Sometimes it is easier to tolerate immoral acts directed against others if we do not ask or think or acknowledge our shared humanity. In Germany few people dared to protest for a mixture of reasons—because of irrational sentiments, because of terror, because it was easier not to, because to question was to invite punitive consequences, and because many people did not see Jews as human in the same measure. The consequence was a Nazi program that grew and expanded until it became impossible for individuals to stop it.

First they came for the Communists,
but I was not a Communist—so I said nothing.
Then they came for the Social Democrats,
but I was not a Social Democrat—so I did nothing.
Then came the trade unionists,
but I was not a trade unionist.
And then they came for the Jews,
but I was not a Jew—so I did little.
Then when they came for me,
there was no one left who could stand up for me.

These famous words of the German pastor Martin Niemöller can be recast as a powerful statement about the consequences of not raising our voice, not asking questions. If we remain silent and do not raise our individual and collective voices in protest against discrimination, irrationality, and other immoral acts, we invite evil to grow. When we fail to ask about our common humanity, we risk losing our humanity. However, after a century marred by a multitude of genocides, our humanity in question, how do we face, and live with, our collective history? Or, to put it in the words of the great Russian writer Leo Tolstoy, "How then shall we live?"

The events of the Holocaust, indeed all acts of genocide, compel us to raise moral questions about perpetrators, bystanders, and victims and about ourselves as teachers and students of these human events, seeking as we must to understand and to question. Genocide turns the critical spotlight uncomfortably back upon those of us who cannot fathom our condoning, much less anyone's doing, such horrendous things to other human beings. Questions interrupt. How are we like or different from the perpetrators, the bystanders, the victims? Niemöller's words tell us that ethical response is as much a civic as a religious duty. Moral duty is as much about the interrogatory as the imperative. Critical understanding implies a heightened degree of moral self-awareness. But critical, historical understanding, no matter how thorough or rigorous, is not enough, however, if we are not prepared to ask: Is this woman my sister? This man my brother? This policy fair? This act legal? This judgment responsible? If the Nazi world teaches us anything, it is that the cost of not questioning can be disastrous to our fellow human beings.

In this chapter we pose seven ethical issues for critical reflection, or critical issues for ethical reflection. We deliberately pose these topics as questions in the hope of encouraging engagement and response. Other questions could be asked and should. These topics are not intended to be exhaustive but suggestive; they follow from the imperatives of good citizenship and moral conscience, ethics and remembering, and knowing what is good and doing the good.

LINKS

13.1. Is Prejudice a Prelude to Annihilation?

In the first act of Elie Wiesel's *The Trial of God* one of the play's central characters, a Russian Orthodox priest, vents age-old Christian prejudice against Jews. God has rejected the Jews, the priest argues, because the Jews have rejected Jesus, God's Son, the Messiah. The priest's accusation that the Jews have cast murderous spells (the infamous "evil eye") upon Christian children recalls the fabrications that circulated in Medieval Europe about the Jews: that they cannibalized Christian children, for example, or that they poisoned the wells and desecrated the Eucharist. Altogether these stories contributed to centuries of Christian resentment, often vicious, of Jews. Encouraged in Christian theology and art, this resentment paved the way for acts of extreme violence. Thus, Luther's prejudice against Jews expressed in his call to destroy Jewish synagogues prefigured Crystal Night in November 1938, when Nazi Brownshirts desecrated and burned Jewish houses of worship.

In Wiesel's drama we soon learn that the priest's anti-Semitic prejudice has enflamed a pogrom against the Jews of Shamgorod that has brought about the death of the innkeeper Berish's family and the gang rape of his daughter Hannah, who is left permanently damaged. In a play upon, and a reversal of, the suffering of Job, the innkeeper decides he will put God on trial. While railing against the Jews, the priest tries unsuccessfully to reason with Berish and his fellow Jews, to persuade them that they must leave town immediately because another devastating pogrom is on the horizon. The effort to get the Jews to save their own lives fails. Throughout it all, the priest's prejudice against Jews, unmistakable and onerous, is presented as irrational and ambivalent: yet the priest still expresses concern for the well-being of Berish, his daughter, and the visiting Jewish minstrels. How is it possible that the priest can be both prejudiced and caring?

Wiesel's play raises a central question: how are we to understand the moral connection between personal prejudice toward others and the ultimate consequences of this prejudice? Did Christian prejudice against Jews pave the way for the Holocaust? To what extent does Wiesel's intolerant priest bear responsibility for the horror done to Berish and his family, notwithstanding his efforts to save them at the end? How much responsibility does he have? How direct is his responsibility? The larger question that Wiesel's drama invites us to probe is the connection between prejudice and annihilation. In other words, is prejudice a prelude to annihilation? Was discrimination against Jews, fueled by centuries of Christian prejudice, resentment, and hatred, a necessary and sufficient condition for the Holocaust? Is there a straight, uninterrupted path from discrimination to destruction, from anti-Semitism to annihilation?

Prejudice may be defined as an unreasoning preference, a preconceived idea that prepares the way for a future course of action. In Wiesel's story and in historical Christian anti-Semitism, that future is one of discrimination, personal injury, and even death. Yet, as Martin Luther King Jr. understood of racial prejudice, it is damaging to both victim and perpetrator. When prejudice makes the transition to annihilation, however, the damage is overwhelmingly one-sided. The perpetrators of the Holocaust lived another day to discriminate and to hate—as millions of Jewish victims, and much of their religion and culture, perished.

Perpetrating annihilation involves more than hot-headed prejudice directed against a person of a particular group. In the Holocaust, for example, the target of annihilation was not just the person but the personhood of Jews, including their history, their culture, their past and future, their religion, and most especially their God. It is important therefore to distinguish between pogroms, periodic outbreaks of violence against European Jews, and genocide, whose systematic and thoroughgoing program of annihilation sets it apart.

The difference between a prejudicial and a genocidal attitude has to do with reason, calculation, and planning. In 1919, Adolf Hitler wrote: "Purely emotional anti-Semitism finds its final expression in the form of pogroms. Rational anti-Semitism, by contrast, must lead to a systematic and legal struggle against, and eradication of what privileges the Jews enjoy over other foreigners. . . . Its final objective, however, must be the total removal of all Jews from our midst." The key expression here is "total removal." Unlike the 'hot' forms of hatred expressed in pogroms, the annihilation of the Jews and Judaism was systematic, state-sponsored, and comprehensive. It expressed cool hatred. As the killing squad leaders discovered, a team was far more efficient if the killer did not look on the victim as a person. Prejudice, as Wiesel's priest shows, may inspire violence against individuals or groups of Jews. Genocide, however, involves erasing the humanity of the victim and annihilating the "idea," for example, of the Jew.

What makes annihilation different from personalized violence is the degree to which the victim is rendered systematically and comprehensively inhuman or nonhuman. The concentration camp world, as Primo Levi so powerfully describes it in *Survival in Auschwitz*, was a world systematically structured by violence in which the humanity of the victim was defined out of existence. This is why it was so important for camp inmates to be forced to adopt a different language, different dress, and different forms of address. The aim was to expunge the Jew of everything familiar and everything Jewish about the Jew from the world. This was what the Nuremberg Laws of 1935 set out to do in the promulgation of the Law for the Defense of German Blood and German Honor. This law defined who was a citizen and who was not, who had an acceptable level and type of German blood and who did not. But as the historian Saul Friedländer suggests in *Nazi Germany and the Jews*, more was required than the legal strictures of the Nuremberg Laws to eradicate Jews; a reasoned-through, comprehensive machinery was needed to deliver and sustain violence and reinforce redefinitions. Prejudice, even hatred, may be a sufficient condition for annihilation; but annihilation's necessary and sufficient prior condition is a universe of meaning, structured and enforced by the state and its laws, where the victim is in no way a person to the perpetrator. Annihilation is powered by cool hatred.

13.2. Is Genocide More Than Mass Murder?

When a disturbed person goes on a shooting spree or when a platoon wipes out a village, we call it mass murder. The culprits generally stand trial or face court martial, relatives are notified, and the dead are buried. After genocide, however, the dead are often lost, there are often no surviving relatives to be informed, and, while the leaders behind such a crime can be identified, the issue of who counts as the culprits can be blurred. Mass murder may or may not have bystanders; genocide always has bystanders. Mass murder may or may not be systematic; genocide is always systematic. Mass murder may or may not involve the promotion of an ideology; genocide always involves the promotion of an ideology. Indeed, it is born of an ideology that is genocidal.

Genocide is the murder of a people, a history and a memory, a teaching and a tradition, a culture and a community. It is the systematic process of extinguishing a language and a way of life, a consciousness and a conception of the world, along with all the wisdom that a people might have offered the world. It is murder of a future that might have belonged to a people and to the world. Hence, genocide has serious implications not only for its victims but also for its perpetrators, for the future it destroys belongs to both. And the children and the societies of both are affected for generations.

What does all this mean with respect to the genocide of the Jews of Europe? What is lost in the annihilation of their history, their teaching, and their community?

While one can argue whether the Jews are in fact the Chosen People (however that term may be understood), it is an unarguable fact that historically, in the texts and traditions of millions, the Jews have been deemed the Chosen People. What, then, are the Jews chosen for? According to Jewish tradition, they are chosen to attest to the chosenness of every human being. They are chosen to bear witness to an infinite responsibility to and for this human being who now stands before us. In short, they are chosen to signify a certain ethical teaching. In the genocide of the Jews of Europe that teaching was slated for annihilation.

Positing an accountability before the other human being in the light of a relation to a higher being is an ethical teaching that rests on a testimony to a definitive, familial connection to the other person and to a divine authority who makes one responsible for the plight of the other person. In the tale of creation transmitted by the Jews and thus signified by the presence of the Jews in the world, every human being derives from one human being. Therefore, according to that view, all are connected as a family is connected. If every human being has a familial tie to every other—if all people are one people—then genocide implies the destruction not only of a people but of what imparts value to all people. The value of humanity itself is implicated in genocide, a value affirmed in the act of giving.

Tadeusz Borowski illustrates how this value is undermined in the Holocaust in a brief passage from *This Way for the Gas, Ladies and Gentlemen.* "It is the camp law," Borowski writes, "[that] people going to their death must be deceived to the very end. It is the only permissible form of charity" (348). In the "concentrationary universe," where world has been perverted into antiworld, the act of charity does not enhance life but instead masks imminent death. Unlike forms of giving in the world, which create deeper bonds between people, this act of giving in the antiworld—"the only permissible form of charity"—is a deception that accentuates the chasm that separates one individual from another. It is not so much unethical as it is anti-ethical.

As an erasure of their teaching and tradition, the murder of the Jews is the murder of a teaching that affirms a divine authority that imparts sanctity to each individual. The passage from Borowski illustrates one way in which the testimony to our definitive relation to one another is targeted for obliteration in the genocide of the Jews. Eliminating all authority outside the camp authority, the genocide of the Jews, as understood from the standpoint of a Jewish ethical tradition, is the murder of the infinite, absolute dearness of the human being as a child of the Holy One.

One will note how radically the Judaic view of a person contrasts with the Nazi definition of the Jew in the Nuremberg Laws. Paragraph 5, Section 2 of the First Regulation to the Reich Citizenship Law states that a Jew is anyone who is descended from two full Jewish grandparents and is (1) an adherent of Judaism or a convert to Judaism, (2) married to a Jew, (3) born from a marriage with a Jew, or (4) was born as the result of extramarital intercourse with a Jew. Thus, the Nazis define a Jew either on the basis of natural accident or on the basis of individual will. That is why the Nazis could will that their actions conform to an ideological and judicial "good." A second document, the Protocol of the Wannsee Conference, states that the Nazis' task was to "cleanse the German living space of Jews in a legal manner." What would make the murder of the Jews legal or lawful? The will of the master race. In radical contrast to the Jewish teaching that the Nazis set out to eliminate, Nazi ideology is void of any notion that would invoke anything that transcends natural accident, historical circumstance, or human will in order to determine what is lawful.

Hence, unlike the traditional Judaic ground for the ethical good, in Nazi ideology there is no transcendent or higher dimension of human value or human goodness from which an ethical demand could derive. The question whether the Jewish testimony is true is irrelevant to the existence of the testimony itself. For the Nazis, the existence of such a testimony was itself antithetical to their worldview and their agenda for the domination of all other peoples.

One ideology often opposes another not because it is true or false but because it is a threat to an agenda. Because it is inherently antiracist, Jewish ethical teaching threatens the ascension of a "master race"—indeed, it threatens all thinking that equates race with value and that thus would open the door to genocide.

According to the ethical teaching arising from Jewish tradition, the prohibition against murder rests upon the infinite value of the other human being. Once the Jewish testimony to the dearness of the other and to the subsequent prohibition against murder is wiped out in the genocide of the Jews, the law against murder is reduced to a matter of political legality, social custom, cultural convention, rational deduction, and other such contingencies. The genocide of the Jews, then, is more than mass murder; in addition to destroying a people, a culture, and a tradition, it is the murder of the absolute prohibition against murder, as transmitted by the teaching and tradition of the Jews. That is why, in the words of Borowski, "the name of God sounds strangely pointless" in the antiworld of the murder camp, where "the women and the infants will go on the trucks [to be murdered], every one of them, without exception" (349–50). In direct contrast to the fundamental law of ethical relation that comes from the Jewish tradition, in the antiworld the fundamental law is "Thou shalt murder." Once the absolute value of the other human being is undermined, the door to making murder lawful is thrown open.

Any case of genocide entails the murder of a people's efforts to articulate the dearness of people, through the murder of their tales, teachings, and traditions. More than mass murder, genocide is a diminishing of the presence of truth in the world, a diminishing of the ethical good—and, from a Jewish standpoint, of the divine commandment—that would prohibit murder. Genocide also diminishes the human ability to refrain from murder. Indeed, the evidence of history is that as mass murder and genocide happen, they become more likely to happen again.

Remembering the history of genocide will not prevent genocide—unless that memory includes a mindfulness of the absolute prohibition against murder. Once that prohibition is relativized into cultural or historical contexts and contingencies, human ingenuity is quick to justify murder.

13.3. What Is a Choiceless Choice and the Extent of Moral Blame?

In William Styron's 1979 novel *Sophie's Choice* we are introduced to Sophie Zawistowaska, a survivor of Auschwitz, who has fled her past to start life over again in the United States. A non-Jew who was employed in the camp and assisted the Nazis, Sophie eventually becomes an inmate herself. She experiences first-hand the trauma of the extermination camp through the direct loss of family and friends, a loss in which she plays a direct role. But what role? Sophie makes all kinds of choices. At times she chooses to act in ways that are self-promoting and harmful to the camp's Jewish inmates. At other times her choices seem taken out of her hands and are not her own. Does it make sense to distinguish between kinds of choice? This is what Styron's novel tries to portray. In a memorable scene that gives the novel its title, the camp doctor, Jemand von Niemand, matter-of-factly presents Sophie with the option of saving one of her children at the expense of sending the other to its death. Citing the Bible, the doctor says: "Suffer the little children to come unto me." "You may keep one of your children. . . . The other one will have to go. Which one will you keep?" It is a nightmare "choice" that haunts Sophie for the remainder of her life. It is a choice that confounds students of the Holocaust after the fact. Does Sophie not choose her future? Is she not responsible for the decisions she makes?

This fictional account poses a real question: to what extent were Jews complicitous in the events that befell them before and during the period when the Final Solution was being enacted? Sophie's "choice" also raises the question about non-Jews and their responsibility for Jews and for themselves and brings to mind Pastor Niemöller's famous statement about who is responsible for speaking out for the other person (see above) and underscores the fact that the Nazi genocide included many more persons than Jews. What makes certain choices "choiceless"? From one point of view Sophie is complicitous in her own suffering: she makes the decision to let one of her children live and the other die. It is a decision she must live with, one that marks her as a tragic figure. From another perspective, the inescapability of her decision—she is "damned if she does, damned if she doesn't"—invites us to think of her choice in different, more nuanced, terms. The Holocaust leaves us with a persistent ethical question, which in principle is true of other genocides as well: in situations of profound violence could victims have done more to save themselves? Could they have chosen differently, more wisely perhaps than they did, to avoid or mitigate their own suffering and that of others? Looking from the outside we might wonder whether Jews should have taken more responsibility for their suffering and salvation. When we look back on such events from a different moment in history, we are presented with the task of distinguishing between different types and degrees of responsibility—not only on the part of perpetrators but of the victims themselves. This raises the larger question: is responsibility always the same thing for everyone? Is it always possible to be responsible? What social and real-world conditions must be in place for there to be responsibility and choice? Determining the nature and possibility of responsibility is a complex matter in part because the situations of suffering are unimaginable in our experience and because we tend to project our own experience on the victims of genocidal violence.

Making a choice like Sophie's to let one of her children live and the other one die was a regular, horrible occurrence among Jews who were forcibly confined to the ghettos. It is documented that Jews who held administrative roles in Jewish Councils made choices or "selections" of fellow Jews to be removed from the ghettos. Under Nazi orders Jews culled from their own communities intellectuals, the aged, the infirm, and even children for deportation. Jewish leaders, like Lodz's Chaim Rumkowski (Document 3.4), were compelled by threat of violence to the entire Jewish community to do violence to a select few Jews. From one point of view it makes sense to say that Rumkowski and other Jewish Council leaders were responsible for these decisions that resulted in the deaths of other Jews. Today, outside of the world of the ghetto, we could imagine their saying no as a virtuous and moral choice. From another perspective, however, the world in which they were forced to make such choices was so profoundly distorted that morality as we come to think about it did not exist. And if it did not, then the very concepts of moral complicity and blame must be carefully weighed before we pronounce judgment. What we now realize about the outcome of the ghetto liquidations is that the end was preordained and the leaders were not "choosing" at all. The decision to act ruthlessly in service of some larger purpose, to save a remnant of their community, was disconnected from the decision for the Final Solution, which had already been cast by Hitler. Still the question is asked, Why did not more Jews resist by force? Why did not more "Righteous Gentiles" step forward to save those who could not save themselves? Sorting out on what basis and by what standards we weigh blame and assign responsibility is daunting in part because we are comparing actions and decisions that belong to different "moral universes." The Holocaust stretches to the breaking point the notion of a universal, moral standard encompassing all human beings at all times, just as the Holocaust strains the notion of a Christian Europe, committed to Enlightenment and religious principles of human dignity and freedom. The Holocaust in particular and genocide in general test our basic assumptions about moral decision-making and what is necessary for choices to be choices.

These choiceless choices strain the notion of responsibility and complicity. In *Survival in Auschwitz* Primo Levi describes in matter-of-fact detail the inner workings of the world of the concentration camp, where the choice to assist another inmate, whether it be in the form of providing food or offering a helping hand, could lead to one's own death. From one point of view, more Jews should have laid down their lives for other Jews. Inmates who withheld care from their fellow Jews invite us to hold them morally accountable at least to some degree. But from another perspective, in a world where survival was never really possible, where death was the purpose of this form of "living," can we talk in the same way about "choice," "values," "morality," "responsibility," and "blame"? To judge the uncharitable behavior of victims according to the standards of a normal moral universe, where different behaviors are not only expected but possible is to miss the nature of the morality that was possible in the camps. Sophie's "choiceless choice" forces us to ask about the possibilities of choices in an inhuman, impossible world, a world where not only men and women but morality too was murdered.

Primo Levi describes the impossible moral or ethical situation of camps as the impossibility of morality itself. As a prisoner of Auschwitz, Levi once suffered from terrible thirst and reached out a barrack's window for an icicle only to have a guard take it from him. "Why?" Levi asked. The guard responded: "There is no 'Why' here." Imagine a world where questioning, thinking, living is not possible. Such was the world of the Jewish prisoner. In this way the world of the student today who asks about the Holocaust stands in stark contrast to the inhuman world of the extermination camp where Jews lived "as if" they were human. It is helpful to understand the worlds inhabited by Jews of the ghetto and the camps as lacking not only why but choice and blame in any ordinary sense. Social worlds where moral judgments make sense are worlds that must themselves make sense. Worlds where value and choice make a difference are worlds where meaning is possible. A camp environment that by its very design leads to certain death inevitably destroys all meaning by taking away all choices for life; it is a world where moral decision-making is also eliminated. Thus, the standards for judging responsible or irresponsible action in genocidal settings must account for the crucial differences between the ordinary and the extraordinary worlds. Accountability for choices presupposes a world where why is a possible question and where being accountable has meaning.

Think of the way we might regard children and their moral responsibility. Adults typically do not hold children accountable either legally or morally for their actions until they reach the age of majority, an age that varies from culture to culture, community to community. Today in the United States we are not inclined to hold a six-year-old child responsible for killing an elementary school classmate, although we may well hold his parent or guardian responsible for allowing the child to get hold of a gun or to be left unsupervised. As terrible as a child killing another child is in our world, we have a way to make sense and to assign moral blame, or at least to distinguish between types of responsibility on the part of children. But imagine a world of the camps where moral purpose is not permitted, where the structure of life makes choices for doing good or ill effectively nonchoices. In the camp world human beings have been robbed of their morality and their moral decision-making possibilities. If we are looking for the humanly possible the human must be possible.

In the struggle to make sense of culpability and blame, therefore, the challenge is to distinguish not only between victimizer and victim as individuals but between competing "worlds" of meaning and action wherein it makes sense to speak of moral agency and good intention, freedom and responsibility, love and hope. What was morally possible for victimizer was not morally possible for the victim. Such incongruities challenge the very notions of responsibility and complicity, even of morality itself, which seems universal to us. But worlds designed exclusively for death and dehumanization, like the ghetto and the camp, invite us to reflect not only upon the nature of human agency in religious or philosophical terms but also upon the historical and structural differences between societies and communities constrained by radical violence. Such worlds where choices like Sophie's are routine are foreign and shocking to our sensibilities perhaps in part because we come face-to-face with the horrible things one human being can do to another. Eliminating the possibility of making moral decisions was part of the horror of the Nazi regime.

13.4. How Does Good Happen?

In Jewish tradition there is a category that is perhaps unique to the Jewish tradition: the Righteous Gentile. It is alien to Greek thinking, for example, to suppose that one could be a non-Greek and still be as noble as a Greek; it is alien to traditional Christian thinking to suppose that one could be a non-Christian and still have a place in the "next world" or be "saved." Judaism, however, does not maintain that a person must be a Jew in order to be good, noble, or righteous. According to Jewish teaching, righteousness lies neither in the nobility of the blood nor in the content of a belief; it lies, rather, in the deeds of the hands. In short, it is an ethical matter, a matter of doing good.

While the category of the Righteous Gentile is much older than the Holocaust, the Holocaust made the notion familiar to the world. Who were the Righteous Gentiles? They were not individuals who belonged to a certain ethnic or political group or who adhered to a certain creed. Rather, they were people who saved lives. With the Righteous Gentiles, the good is not a belief or a feeling; it is a deed performed, an event made to happen.

Ever since Stephen Spielberg filmed *Schindler's List*, Oskar Schindler has become perhaps the most famous of the Righteous Gentiles. Raul Wallenberg is also well-known for his rescue of hundreds of Hungarian Jews. There are, however, others. Otto Busse was a director of a German factory in Bialystok, where, at great risk to himself, he came to the aid of people in the Bialystok ghetto and partisan fighters in the forests. Paul Grüninger, a police officer in charge of the Swiss border police, helped dozens of Austrian Jews to cross the border illegally into Switzerland. Sempo Sugihara, the Japanese consul in Kovno, Lithuania, saved Jewish lives by issuing transit visas enabling them to go to Curacao. And there is André Trocme, the pastor of the French village of Le Chambon-sur-le-Ligne, who organized the entire village of five thousand to save many Jewish lives.

As difficult to understand as the evil of the Holocaust may be, there is also something baffling about the goodness of the Righteous Gentiles. There is no particular pattern of culture, religion, education, or upbringing that would explain how this good happened. Indeed, it appears that the good was not conditioned but enacted, even, or especially, when the Righteous Gentiles had every rational reason to decide otherwise, when acting as they did cost many of the Righteous their lives, as well as the lives of their families and communities.

The thin line separating those whose courage enabled them to care from those whose fear caused them to look away is illustrated in a scene from Art Spiegelman's *Maus*. Anja and Vladek disguise themselves as pigs (Poles) and wander through the streets seeking shelter from the Nazis. They go to the home of a Polish woman named Janina, who "always offered she would help" them. When the moment comes to help the Jews at her door, however, Janina cries out, "My God! It's the Spiegelmans! You'll bring trouble! Go away! Quickly!" Janina could make an offer when she did not have to decide anything; when the moment came for decisive action, she did nothing.

The examples of the Righteous Gentiles tell us that good is not caused—it is decided. The suffering of another human being implicates us and summons us to respond. Those who risked their lives to save Jews in the Holocaust engaged in a testimony to the value of the other human being that was antithetical to Nazi ideology. They affirmed and sustained precisely what the Nazis had targeted for annihilation—not only in the body of Israel but also in Israel's ancient teachings concerning our infinite responsibility to and for the other human being. The infinite scope of that responsibility cannot be conceptualized in a moment of contemplation. But it can be acted upon. The question put to Cain is not "What have you contemplated?" but "What have you done?"

Recall in this connection the powerful scene near the end of *Schindler's List*, when, surrounded by the hundreds of Jews he has saved, Schindler gazes upon his car and cries, "The car! Why did I keep the car? It would have bought ten more lives!" Through eyes informed by his own actions, Schindler sees what is signified by the two color scenes of Sabbath observance that frame the film. He sees that when he saw the child in red, in *adom* (the Hebrew word for red), he saw Adam (Hebrew for the human being—the two words are spelled with the same four letters). Thus when Schindler sees the girl in red, he sees the human being. And to see the human being is to be summoned to an ethical action.

Like Schindler, as we offer help, we see what is at stake in helping. And seeing what is at stake, we see that we have not yet offered enough. Helping one person opens our eyes to the suffering of another and instills in us a sense of urgency. In the same way, addressing one genocide impels us to address another—not to be "fair" but because engaging one opens our eyes to a certain responsibility for the other.

The character of Schindler from Spielberg's film once more provides an illustration. The measures that he takes to save lives do not arise from personal inclination or self-satisfaction. Instead, something takes hold of him and he is summoned to help in such a way that he cannot do otherwise. What is it? It is life itself, which some ethical thinkers as far back as Plato regard as the life of the Good: and so Schindler comes alive by doing good.

13.5. What are the Limits of Forgiveness and Reconciliation?

Forgiveness is a central theme in Christianity. According to the teachings of Christianity, as material creatures bound to the earth, we human beings are always being drawn away from the divine and into sin and evil. There is no way we can avoid doing evil. But acts of forgiveness at least offer us a way to bridge the gap that sin and evil opens up and to reconnect us with those we have wronged or those who have wronged us. This is one of the reasons that God sent Jesus, his son, into the world. His appearance among us is interpreted by Christians as a sign not only of God's love but also for God's readiness to forgive. In fact, God's reaching out to us should be a model for our own reaching out to those who have sinned against us, and even of the blessedness of reaching out first. Such reaching out of course also requires, finally, a response from the evil-doer. True reconciliation requires a willingness to take responsibility for what one has done and to accept forgiveness in humility and contrition.

What does this mean in terms of the Holocaust? For many Christians, and speaking from within that tradition, the Holocaust only shows on a large scale that we are all sinners and all in need of forgiveness. The expectation is that acts of contrition and repentance by Germans (and others) should be met, or even anticipated, with gestures of forgiveness and reconciliation by victims.

From the Jewish perspective, however, this kind of forgiveness presents a problem. Forgiveness in Judaism is seen as a concrete act that happens between the victim and the perpetrator. If one person hurts another, this very person must sincerely repent and ask the victim for forgiveness. Only then can the victim respond with forgiveness. In fact, the Jewish tradition holds that if the victim refuses to offer forgiveness to someone who is truly sorry, then the victim himself or herself is committing a sin. The assumption is that the first act of forgiveness is for the perpetrator to directly approach the victim and to make the victim's loss good as far as possible. Clearly this mechanism of forgiveness cannot work if the perpetrator does not ask for forgiveness or if the victim is dead and so unable to be recompensed. And there is certainly in the Jewish understanding no way for one person to forgive a second person for pain or harm inflicted on a third person. In this instance, forgiveness can only be a matter between the perpetrator and God.

Because of these two very different understandings of forgiveness, Christians sometimes see the Jewish refusal to offer forgiveness to the Nazis, or to Germans more generally, as mean-spirited, while Jews often see the Christian insistence on forgiving the perpetrators as dismissing Jewish suffering and of siding with the perpetrators.

A good example of how the logic of forgiveness plays out is found in the book *The Sunflower*, in which Simon Wiesenthal tells of a strange encounter he had while a slave laborer under the Nazis. One day, at a hospital to which his labor unit had been sent, he was called to the bedside of a badly wounded German soldier. The soldier confessed to Wiesenthal that he had volunteered to join the SS, the elite unit of the Nazi Party, and that he had participated in the mass slaughter of Jews. Now, on his deathbed, the wounded soldier was begging the only Jew available to him for forgiveness. Wiesenthal refused, feeling that it was not up to him to offer forgiveness to this soldier on behalf of those he had tortured and killed. The book, and the essays accompanying it, explores Wiesenthal's reaction and its philosophical and theological implications. Should Wiesenthal have granted this dying youngster, who was clearly repentant, a measure of forgiveness? Would such a gesture really have relieved the soldier from the responsibility for the atrocities in which he willingly participated?

The story touches on a much larger issue, the limits (if any) of responsibility and guilt. Whom do we hold accountable for the atrocities of the Holocaust? The leaders who issued orders but never actually pulled a trigger or dropped a gas canister into a roomful of prisoners? The soldiers who were trained to follow orders and then did so when ordered to shoot captured civilian men, women and children? The townspeople who watched their Jewish friends and neighbors being harassed, arrested, and deported but then never spoke out? The other countries of the world who knew what was happening but refused to accept refugees, thereby lending support to Hitler's claim that no one cared about the mass slaughter of Jews? The circles of responsibility stretch out further and further, but do all these people bear the same measure of guilt? And what about the young idealistic man who joins an elite military unit like the SS out of patriotism but then comes to regret and abhor what he did? These are the questions that Wiesenthal's book opens up.

From the Holocaust itself, hundreds of stories have emerged about people deeply implicated in the Nazi bureaucracy who nonetheless helped Jews on the sly. These are people who kept the system going and yet subtly subverted it as well. Oskar Schindler is one example. He saved hundreds of lives by, in part, playing along with the system and acting out of selfish motives (the desire for cheap workers for his factory). Was he a hero? Or was he a scoundrel who happened to do some good along the way? Or was there something else?

Another angle on this is the story of a German bureaucratic functionary in the German Foreign Office, a man named Martin Luther. His story is investigated in detail in a book by Christopher Browning, *The Final Solution and the German Foreign Office*. Luther saw that siding with the SS and its anti-Jewish policy against the more moderate Foreign Office was a way to promote his career. He did not hate Jews, but he was ambitious and was willing to work within the system as he found it. Does this make him a perpetrator of genocide with an equal measure of guilt with those who consciously planned the genocide? A similar question arises in connection with Chaim Rumkowski, the leader of the Lodz ghetto in Poland. Rumkowski decided that the best chance of saving the Jews in his ghetto (some 160,000–200,000 people) was to make the ghetto indispensable to his Nazi overlords. So he willfully turned his ghetto into a brutal labor camp. Eventually the entire ghetto's population was shipped to death camps, where most, but not all, were killed. Moreover, Rumkowski's gamble almost paid off. The ghetto was liquidated a few short months before a rapidly advancing Russian army reached Lodz in summer 1944. Was he a collaborator? Or was he trying to use the system to save his people? These, and many other such stories, show us that people rarely work out of pure motives and thus that the allocation of blame and praise is a complex undertaking.

What confounds the situation even more is the reality of the Nazi regime as a terror state. It was made abundantly clear from the very beginning of the Nazi rule that helping Jews was a grave crime, an act of treason even, and would be treated harshly. And in fact thousands of common German civilians were arrested for resistance to Nazi edicts, sent to concentration camps like Dachau, and often shot or tortured to death along with their families. By the end of the war, for example, the concentration camp at Dachau was full of members of the clergy who had dared to speak out. What would you have done in a similar situation? What did people in this country do, for example, to help African Americans during the heyday of the Ku Klux Klan? Can we really expect people to be heroes in the face of such real and horrible threats? On one hand, is it really fair to condemn people if they act "unheroically" to save their own lives and the lives of their families? On the other hand, it was the silence of so many people— Germans, other Europeans, the churches, the United States—that made it possible for the Nazi regime to implement its policy and continue it year after year.

13.6. How Have Christians Responded to the Holocaust?

In the early twentieth century, Germany considered itself, with some justifi-
cation, to be the center of the intellectual life of modern, especially Protestant, Christianity. Martin Luther had begun the Protestant Reformation in
the middle of Germany in the sixteenth century and ever since had been
regarded by many as both a Christian and a German hero. In the eighteenth
and nineteenth centuries, German universities led the way in the academic
study of Christianity, producing world-famous theologians as well as scholars in biblical studies, early church history, the history of Christian art, and
ethics. Even American scholars felt that it was impossible to gain an international reputation in Christian studies without having studied at a German
university. Given this background, one would have expected Christian leaders, whether Protestant or Catholic, to have offered principled opposition to
the racist and right-wing nationalist ideology of Adolf Hitler and the Nazi
Party. Instead, the official organs of the Christian community capitulated to
the Nazi state from the start. In summer 1932, for example, even before
Hitler became chancellor, Protestant pastors laid the groundwork for the
German Christians, the main association through which German Protestants
supported the Third Reich. The Catholic Church also made its peace with
the Nazi Party early on, in the form of a concordat signed between Pope
Pius XI and Hitler on July 20, 1933. For Protestants and Catholics, part of the
impetus to seek accommodation with the Nazis was to shield church property from confiscation and to protect church personnel. Yet, despite all the
historical, political, and social considerations, the simple fact remains that
vast numbers of Germans (and other Europeans) who were Christian readily
became accomplices with Nazi genocide. Moreover, German Protestant theologians, such as Gerhard Kittel, Paul Althaus, and Emmanuel Hirsch even
argued that Nazi ideology completely accorded with Christianity.

   To be sure, there was some principled opposition from within the Christian community. Groups such as the Pastors' Emergency League and the
Confessing Church actively resisted attempts by the state to co-opt religious
institutions, but these were minority voices. The one single systematic religious pronouncement against the Nazis was the papal encyclical *Mit Brennen-
der Sorge* (With burning anxiety). Smuggled into Germany and read from
Catholic pulpits across Germany on March 21, 1937, the encyclical protested
not racism and discrimination but Nazi attacks on Catholic institutions.
Sadly, from this time until the end of the war, there was virtually no organized public resistance by European Christian institutions. The one major
exception was the Bulgarian Orthodox Church, whose leader, Metropolitan

Stefan of Sofia, succeeded in forcing King Boris to halt the deportation of Bulgarian Jews. Otherwise, most religious protest came only from individual clergymen who exposed themselves to enormous risk to speak out.

The most well-known of the German protesters included Father Bernard Lichtenberg, the provost of Saint Hedwig's Church in Berlin; Dietrich von Bonhoeffer, a Lutheran pastor; and Pastor Martin Niemöller. Along with Archbishop Clemens August Graf von Galen, Lichtenberg publicly protested against the Nazi euthanasia program. He was subsequently arrested and imprisoned and upon his release from prison sent to Dachau. Bonhoeffer and Niemoeller were instrumental in laying the foundations for the Confessing Church. Later imprisoned for trying to help smuggle Jews out of Germany to a safe haven in Switzerland, Bonhoeffer spent the rest of the war in Flossenburg concentration camp and was executed on April 19, 1945, just two weeks before the arrival of U.S. troops. Niemöller had been arrested as early as 1937 for "abuse of the pulpit." He spent most of the time until the end of the war in Sachsenhausen concentration camp and then Dachau.

These religious leaders were the exceptions. Complicitous silence and active participation more accurately describes the role of Christian churches in the Holocaust. After the war, their involvement became a major issue of discussion between Jews and Christians, as well as within the Christian community itself. Not all the victims of the Holocaust were Jews, Elie Wiesel has said, but all of the perpetrators were Christians. An overstatement, this claim nevertheless points to a central problem for Christian thinkers and theologians. How could the Holocaust happen in the most advanced and "Christian" country in Europe? One particular focus of attention has been the long history within Christianity of negative teaching concerning Jews and Judaism. In the wake of the Holocaust, many Christian thinkers wondered whether such church teachings had helped pave the way for Christians to tolerate, and even participate in, discrimination against Jews. The process of coming to terms with Christian silence during the Holocaust and what that silence means began only slowly. While a few statements were issued in the first decades after the war, the first major break with traditional Christian-Jewish relations came with the Vatican II Council in Rome in 1962–65 and the subsequent publication of the revolutionary papal encyclical *Nostra Aetate*. This encyclical calls for respect by Christians for all other religions. Of Judaism in particular, it states, in part, "What happened in His passion cannot be charged against all the Jews, without distinction, then alive, nor against the Jews of today. Although the Church is the new people of God, the Jews should not be presented as rejected or accursed by God, as if this followed from the Holy Scriptures." It goes on to call for a change in all Catholic catechisms to reflect this new view of Judaism. The Catholic confrontation with the Holocaust advanced even further under the leadership of Pope John Paul II, a Polish native who had witnessed the Holocaust at first hand. On April 7, 1994, the Vatican hosted a major "Papal concert" to commemorate the Holocaust. Among the events was a papal meeting with survivors and a joint Catholic-Jewish worship service, the first in history. These public events raised expectations that a fuller Catholic confession of complicity would follow. Such a statement was published in March 1998, entitled "We Remember: A Reflection on the Shoah." In this declaration, the Holy See's Commission for Religious Relations with the Jews noted that Christian conduct during the Nazi period was "not that which might have been expected from Christ's followers" and that for Christians today, the actions "of their brothers and sisters during the World War II must be a call to penitence." Whether this statement is an adequate response to what happened is still a matter of heated discussion between Catholics and Jews.

It should be pointed out that several other statements were issued by local bishops, especially in anticipation of the fiftieth anniversary of the collapse of Nazism. Among these is a statement by German Roman Catholic bishops calling their Church "a sinful Church and in need of conversion."

In 1994 the Hungarian Roman Catholic Bishops issued a proclamation during Advent, the weeks before the celebration of Christmas, acknowledging that many people claiming to be Christians "did not raise their voices in protest against the mass humiliations, deportation, and murder of their fellow Jewish citizens." The following year, the Declaration of the Polish Episcopal Commission for Dialogue with Judaism was published, as was a statement by the bishops of the Netherlands. In 1997, at the former Nazi transit camp at Drancy, leaders of the Italian, Swiss, and French Catholic Churches noted in their Declaration of Repentance that the history of the Church required renewed scrutiny and that it was necessary to beg forgiveness for the sins committed by Church members.

The reaction of Protestant churches to the Holocaust has been much more varied. The first significant statement addressing Christian culpability in the Holocaust was issued in 1980 by the Synod of the Protestant Church in the Rhineland. It recognized "Christian co-responsibility and guilt for the Holocaust" and called for "a new relationship of the Church to the Jewish people." A similar statement, denouncing the teaching that the Jewish people were rejected by God and acknowledging Christian responsibility for the Holocaust, was issued by the Evangelical (that is, Lutheran) Synod of Baden in 1984. In addition, the German Council of Protestant Churches issued a joint statement with the Catholic bishops in 1995 pledging both groups to work for the preservation of all human life. In North America, many Protestant groups have come to grips with the Holocaust. In 1987, the Presbyterian Church (USA) led the way by producing a study paper acknowledging the long history of anti-Judaic teachings in Christianity and affirming that the Jewish covenant with God had never been broken. In that same year, the General Synod of the United Church of Christ issued its own statement calling for a new relationship with Judaism. This flurry of activity was followed in 1993 by the Statement of Relations Between Christians and Jews of the Disciples of Christ, which calls for a reexamination of how Christian teachings had portrayed Jews and Judaism. This was followed in 1994 by the acceptance of The Declaration of the Evangelical Lutheran Church in America to the Jewish Community and in 1995 by a declaration of the Alliance of Baptists echoing the teachings of *Nostra Aetate*.

13.7. What Is the Relationship Between Ethics and Remembrance?

One powerful and recurrent theme in literature on the Holocaust is that of the moral duty to remember. This duty extends to other genocides as well. Imperatives of this kind are inscribed on monuments and in books. Indeed the teaching of the Holocaust and other genocides answers to this ethics of remembrance. Why do we feel the need to remember the victims and the events? What is the ethical content of remembrance? And why do we think that forgetting would be to do a further wrong to these victims? Like all ethical questions raised by the Holocaust and other genocides, these admit of many answers. Here we sketch a few answers, as avenues for continuing discussion.

- Remembering is morally important because it awakens us to the danger of genocide, making us more vigilant. It might be argued, for example, that the memory of the Holocaust made the West more attentive to the outrages being committed in Bosnia and Kosovo. Here memory is a tool (the "lessons of history") in the service of an essentially future-oriented concern.
- The imperative to remember can emerge from a thirst for justice. Sometimes seeking justice entails that the criminals be brought to trial in an international venue (the Nuremberg Trials or the war crimes trials arising out of the strife in the former Yugoslavia). More generally, it means not allowing these injustices and their agents to find a final absolution in forgetfulness and the passing of time.
- Remembrance can also be something we owe to the victims. Here the impetus is neither a future-oriented concern nor a desire for justice and retribution. Rather, it is as if we have a debt to the victims of genocide that we repay through memorialization at the sites of their deaths, with museums, through days of remembrance, and in teaching and study.
- Finally, the imperative to remember is an act that in and of itself says no to genocide by its refusal to forget. Forgetting would complete the work of the genocidal perpetrators by effacing from the world the last traces of the victims. To remember, then, is something that we must do to protect and affirm our shared humanity. Forgetting would cause us to lower our guard against future repetitions of these crimes. Indeed, forgetting would be to do an injustice to the victims, violating our unspoken commitment to keep the memory of them alive and, in the same moment, tacitly allowing an amnesty to the perpetrators.

Questions

_____

13.1. Is Prejudice a Prelude to Annihilation?

1. Is prejudice rooted in our interactions with one another? Is there a difference between being "biased," that is, to have a leaning toward, and being prejudiced? Give an example.

2. What is the cost of living with prejudice? What does it take to change prejudice? Is it more than adopting a different set of attitudes? Or does it mean changing one's whole "world of meaning"? Wiesel's priest was able to live in a world shaped in part by Christian anti-Semitism, yet nonetheless he still expressed genuine concern for Berish and his friends, but at what cost? Do we move back and forth between different worlds and their different value systems? In contemporary terms can we be "racist" or "homophobic" in one setting and the opposite in another and still be ethically coherent?

3. Martin Luther King Jr. often spoke of the human cost of racial bigotry to the bigot. What happens to the humanity of the annihilator? From a different angle, can one ever forgive genocide?

4. In instances of genocide such as the Holocaust, where the humanity of the victim is targeted for destruction, how difficult is it for survivors to live anything like a "normal" life afterward? In the aftermath of the Bosnia genocide, the Dayton Accords have put in place social structures that seem to enable the warring ethnic communities to coexist. Can former enemies really become countrymen after such violence? What role can international awareness play in enabling enemies to address long histories of oppression and to provide meaningful and moral closure to past injustices?

13.2. Is Genocide More Than Mass Murder?

1. In what ways does the perpetrator suffer through his or her assault on the humanity of the other human being?
2. What are some examples that illustrate the point that a community is greater than the sum of its parts?
3. To what extent did Hitler succeed in ridding Europe of Jewish life and Jewish history? Why does it matter?

13.3. What Is a Choiceless Choice and the Extent of Moral Blame?

1. In reflecting upon Sophie's choice to save the life of one child by sending the other to certain death, what real choice did she have? Does it make sense to describe this as a "choiceless choice"? Can she in any sense be held accountable?
2. Can you think of another morally challenging situation where your whole world is threatened to its very core? For example, killing someone to defend another life? Is this like "Sophie's choice"? How is it different? What is it about the concentration camp that is so dehumanizing?
3. Should the victims of extreme violence, like Sophie, be held accountable for their actions? Should the perpetrators of extreme violence be held accountable for their actions? Should the same standards apply to both? If not, why not?
4. What responsibilities do we as students and teachers have to the victims (and perpetrators) of genocide to fully understand the social and historical settings of genocide when making judgments about whether or not they acted morally? Can we ever be in a position to judge them?

13.4. How Does Good Happen?

1. Is responsibility for the welfare of other people something we choose, or is it something that lays claim to us?
2. What is at stake in making good happen?
3. Can we ever do enough good? Why or why not?
4. Who exactly is our "neighbor," the one who implicates us in our responsibility for him or her?

LINKS

13.5. What Are the Limits of Forgiveness and Reconciliation?

1. How do we decide who is responsible for something like the Holocaust? Do we blame only the planners and the leader? Do we include the tens of thousands of soldiers, policemen, and other government workers who carried out the "dirty work" of the Holocaust? What about the millions of good men and women who saw what was going on and stood by silently? What about countries such as the United States and Canada who accepted only a small number of refugees fleeing the Nazi regime?
2. If you were Wiesenthal, would you have offered "forgiveness" to the soldier? Do you think his repentance was sparked by true regret or only by the fact that he was dying and Germany was losing the war? Would knowing the reason for his regret have made a difference in your decision?
3. Many countries that were implicated in the Holocaust are paying reparations or making public statements of apology. But these gestures are being made sixty years after the events by people who were not the perpetrators and to people who are largely not the victims. Do you find these actions a helpful way toward reconciliation and forgiveness?

LINKS

13.6. How Have Christians Responded to the Holocaust?

1. One argument made by the Catholic Church is that in signing the Concordat in 1933, the Pope was simply trying to save the Church, which was under severe attack from all sides. But others have argued that had the Catholic Church spoken out forcefully and openly from the beginning, it would have given moral and spiritual encouragement to opposition groups. The Church's silence in effect strengthened the Nazis' hands and robbed resisters of powerful backing, especially in Catholic areas of Europe. Which position makes more sense to you and why? Does a religious institution have an obligation to speak out against inhumane policies even if by speaking out it may harm its own clergy and its own members? Would the obligations of the Church be different in a totalitarian state, like that of Nazi Germany, that does not hesitate to engage in mass arrest, torture, and murder?

2. A second controversy has been the relationship of Christian communities to Jews. Christianity has a long history of teaching that Jews stand outside of God's plan of salvation (Christian "contempt for Jews") because of their refusal to accept Jesus as the Messiah. Early Christianity even argued that the old covenant with Israel was broken because of the sins of the Jews and that the Church was the new covenant that was replacing the old. This teaching of "supercessionism" made it easy for many Christians to have sympathy for the suffering of their Jewish neighbors but to feel at the same time that their suffering was part of the divine scheme of things. After the Holocaust, the Catholic Church and many Protestant denominations decided that these teachings were not only dangerous but wrong and have begun to teach that Jews and Christians are equally under God's covenant. Other Protestant groups argue that to treat Judaism as still in a full covenantal relationship to God is to destroy the very reason for Christianity's existence. It also destroys the idea that Christianity should have a special "mission" for the Jews. How should Christian attitudes toward Jews change in the light of the Holocaust?

LINKS

13.7. What Is the Relationship Between Ethics and Remembrance?

1. Why is it important to remember the Holocaust, an event that occurred more than fifty years ago?
2. What would happen if we decided to forget the past?

LINKS

Further Reading

13.1. Is Prejudice a Prelude to Annihilation?

Friedländer, Saul. *Nazi Germany and the Jews*. Vol. 1, *The Years of Persecution, 1933–39*. New York: HarperCollins, 1997.

Levi, Primo. *Survival in Auschwitz*. Translated by Stuart Woolf. New York: Macmillan, 1993.

Rubenstein, Richard, and John Roth. *Approaches to Auschwitz: The Holocaust and Its Legacy*. Atlanta: John Knox, 1985.

Wiesel, Elie. *Night*. Translated by Stella Rodway. New York: Bantam, 1982.

———. *The Trial of God*. Translated by Marion Wiesel. New York: Schocken, 1995.

13.2. Is Genocide More Than Mass Murder?

Dawidowicz, Lucy. *The Golden Tradition*. New York: Syracuse University Press, 1996.

Dobroszycki, Lucjan. *Image Before My Eyes*. New York: Schocken, 1977.

Rummel, R. J. *Death by Government*. New Brunswick, N.J.: Transaction, 1994.

Vishniac, Roman. *A Vanished World*. New York: Noonday, 1997.

13.3. What Is a Choiceless Choice and the Extent of Moral Blame?

Langer, Lawrence L. *Preempting the Holocaust*. New Haven: Yale University Press, 1998.

Styron, William. *Sophie's Choice*. New York: Random House, 1979.

13.4. How Does Good Happen?

Fogelman, Eva. *Conscience and Courage*. New York: Doubleday, 1995.

Geier, Arnold, and Abraham Foxman. *Heroes of the Holocaust*. New York: Berkeley Publishing Group, 1998.

Paldiel, Mordecai. *Sheltering the Jews*. Minneapolis: Fortress, 1997.

Sherrow, Victoria. *The Righteous Gentiles*. San Diego: Lucent Books, 1998.

13.5. What are the Limits of Forgiveness and Reconciliation?

Browning, Christopher. *The Final Solution and the German Foreign Office*. New York: Holmes & Meier, 1978.

Keneally, Thomas. *Schindler's List*. New York: Simon and Schuster, 1982.

Minow, Martha. *Between Vengeance and Forgiveness: Facing History After Genocide and Mass Violence*. Boston: Beacon, 1998.

Neier, Aryeh. *War Crimes : Brutality, Genocide, Terror, and the Struggle for Justice.* New York: Times Books, 1998.

Wiesenthal, Simon. *The Sunflower: On the Possibilities and Limits of Forgiveness.* New York: Schocken, 1997.

Wyman, David S. *The Abandonment of the Jews: America and the Holocaust.* New York: Pantheon, 1984.

———. *Paper Walls: America and the Refugee Crisis, 1938–1941.* Amherst: University of Massachusetts Press, 1968.

13.6. How Have Christians Responded to the Holocaust?

Ericksen, Robert P., and Susannah Heschel, eds. *Betrayal: German Churches and the Holocaust.* Minneapolis: Fortress Press, 1999.

Falk, Randall M., and Walter J. Harrelson. *Jews and Christians: A Troubled Family.* Nashville: Abingdon Press, 1990.

Flannery, Edward H. *The Anguish of the Jews: Twenty-three Centuries of Anti-Semitism.* New York: Macmillan, 1965.

Hochhuth, Rolf. *The Deputy.* Baltimore: Johns Hopkins University Press, 1997.

Peck, Abraham, ed. *Jews and Christians After the Holocaust.* Philadelphia: Fortress, 1982.

Rittner, Carol, Stephen Smith, and Irena Steinfeldt. *The Holocaust and the Christian World.* London: Kuperard, 2000.

13.7. What Is the Relationship Between Ethics and Remembrance?

Wiesel, Elie. "Why I Write." In *Confronting the Holocaust: The Impact of Elie Wiesel.* Edited by Alvin Rosenfield and Irving Greenberg. Bloomington: Indiana University Press, 1987.

Index